Inside the Stealth Bomber

The B-2 Story

Inside the
Stealth Bomber
The B-2 Story

Bill Scott

with an Introduction by
Col. Richard S. Couch, USAF

TAB AERO

Blue Ridge Summit, PA

FIRST EDITION
SECOND PRINTING

Library of Congress Cataloging-in-Publication Data

Scott, Bill. 1946 –
    Inside the stealth bomber : the B-2 story / by Bill Scott.
      p.   cm.
    Includes index.
    ISBN 0-8306-3822-9
    1. B-2 bomber. I. Title.
UG1242.B6S36 1991
358.4'282—dc20   91-10362
                                 CIP

For information about other McGraw-Hill materials, call 1-800-2-MCGRAW in the
U.S. In other countries call your nearest McGraw-Hill office.

Acquisitions Editor: Jeff Worsinger
Book Editor: Norval G. Kennedy
Production: Katherine G. Brown
Book Design: Jaclyn J. Boone   TPR4

To the men and women who ARE
the United States' aerospace defense industry.

Contents

Acknowledgments

IT TAKES A LONG LIST OF PEOPLE to bring a behind-the-scenes book about a new military aircraft into print, especially when that aircraft program is classified and ultrasensitive to political pressures. My sincere thanks to all of those who made it possible to write such a book at this stage of the B-2's development.

Very special thanks go to Col. Rick Couch, USAF, who was the driving force behind *The B-2 Story*. Without his great memory, strong loyalty to and faith in his colleagues, professional credibility, and excellent salesmanship within the Air Force community, the first page could never have been written. This is truly Rick's book.

A salute to the courageous Air Force officers who dared to trust that *The B-2 Story* would be accurate, and allowed the project to go forward: Gen. Mike Loh; Maj. Gen. Dick Scofield; Maj. Gen. John Schoeppner; Col. Ray Crockett; and Lt. Col. Jan Dalby.

Many thanks to Northrop's Chief B-2 Test Pilot Bruce Hinds; public relations experts Tony Contafio, Terry Clawson, and Ed Smith; and several other key players (who shall remain unnamed) for their unselfish assistance.

A heartfelt thank you to Linda, Erik, and Kevin Scott, as well as Ann and Mary Couch, who put up with this project and provided invaluable encouragement. You are owed a lot of make up weekends.

BILL SCOTT

Introduction

TOO OFTEN, THE AMERICAN PEOPLE ONLY HEAR about defense procurement in terms of $300 hammers, $800 toilet seats, and multimillion dollar bombers. There is a good reason for that. No one ever exposes the American public to anything else. Only stories about apparent excesses within the Department of Defense ever make the six-o'clock news. Success in the constant battle to develop, manufacture, field, maintain, and support well-built, effective defense systems rarely seems worthy of mention.

Even though negative issues about defense procurement seem to get the most media attention, American citizens want to know about the successes; they like to hear the other side, too. Taxpayers want a more complete picture of what is really being done with all their dollars, but isn't being reported. They want to also hear the positive stories, not just the negative.

Bill Scott does this in his story about the B-2 Advanced Technology Bomber. By focusing on one high-visibility program, he has taken a fresh look into the complex U.S. weapons acquisition process, highlighting not just newsmaking problems, but also elements that make the system work.

I was fortunate to have a supporting role in the B-2 program's early days, then had an opportunity to describe for Bill what working on a project like the B-2 was like. As a seasoned editor for the aerospace magazine *Aviation Week & Space Technology*, and an experienced flight test engineer, he is in a unique position to tell *The B-2 Story*.

This book provides an in-depth perspective of what was happening behind the scenes during the development process as the advanced technology bomber transitioned from a "black world," tightly classified, program to a highly visible target for the world media and the American Congress.

There also is a human side to the story, and it is told here in a way that adds warmth to what tends to be a cold and impersonal process. This humanization, by shedding some light on one aspect of the B-2's development, lets the reader share the heady successes achieved in bringing this unique aircraft from a dream to it's maiden flight. It is a story of dedicated Americans who work hard to give U.S. military aviators the best aircraft in the world.

The B-2 Story provides an enlightening look into the way this nation buys its weaponry. The Department of Defense, for a variety of reasons, uses a very complex, lengthy method of purchasing new weapon systems. The entire procurement cycle can take 10 to 15 years or longer. During this time, political winds can blow an aircraft program in several directions, causing major changes in the overall scope and the final product. Plans laid out at the start of a program sometimes bear little resemblance to the end item.

These changes don't necessarily have a thing to do with the weapon system itself. They often are adjustments forced by revised national priorities. Major revisions of a program might be responses to shifting, fluid threats that the weapon system must counter, or new technologies that change the original requirements. Any or all of these environmental factors can have a huge impact on the overall cost and schedule of a major acquisition effort like the B-2.

Teamwork is a vital element of today's defense procurement cycle. The Air Force, its contractors, subcontractors, and thousands of others involved in the acquisition of a weapons system must work together throughout the entire process. We can no longer afford an adversarial relationship between customer and supplier.

Although it must start at the top, teamwork at all levels of the process ultimately depends on the lowest common denominator: the individual. Each person involved in the acquisition of new U.S. weapon systems is a vital element that can affect whether the system works in the field or not. It is the dedication of the engineer, contracting officer, manufacturing technician, test pilot, and their thousands of colleagues that makes the whole team function effectively. This is especially true when the team is trying to take a giant step forward in aerospace technology.

In this book, Bill conveys the importance of the program teamwork by focusing primarily on B-2 development test activities and the people who perform them. The reader must understand, however, that the ground and flight test community is only a small part of this massive acquisition effort. The story might just as well have been told from many other perspectives.

Government and contractor experts in the fields of contracts, manufacturing, design engineering, systems safety, software development, integrated logistics support, and other program areas also were extremely important players in bringing the B-2 to the point where it could even be tested. As a result, the interpretations presented in this book were shaped by the author viewing the B-2 program from primarily the test perspective.

This is not a kiss-and-tell book, either. Much of the B-2 program is still classified, and that limits what can be said about the airplane and the program at this stage. But the *The B-2 Story* still serves the reader well:

- For American citizens, the book should renew confidence in the institutions that spend your hard-earned tax money. Despite its complexities, the weapons acquisition system works because the tireless efforts and creativity of defense contractor and Air Force teams make it work. Many devote long hours and make personal sacrifices well above and beyond the call of duty.

- For elected representatives, this book should restore confidence in the people who implement the programs you have authorized. Despite funding turmoil and shifting priorities, these programs are being carried forward by people who can find ways to get the job done, even in the face of great adversity. *The B-2 Story* will not provide ammunition for those looking to derail defense programs in favor of their own private agendas and priorities. This is simply a positive account, showing how creative people in industry and government, when given the chance, are able to successfully work their way through any issue.

- For the news media, *The B-2 Story* is a reminder that the essence of this country lies in what its people can accomplish through ingenuity, knowledge, leadership, dedication, and persistence. The defense industry has many of these stories, and they should be told. In an easy to understand way, Bill Scott has told one of them.

COLONEL RICHARD S. COUCH, USAF

1

Out of the dark

"ABORT! ABORT! ABORT!"

Those three words can mean only one thing to a test pilot: Stop immediately; something serious is happening.

But to the horror of a test director and 67 engineers staring at video monitors in stunned silence, the world's newest and most expensive strategic bomber continued to accelerate down the runway, headed for liftoff on its maiden flight. The director scanned a communications panel in front of him, making sure he was transmitting on the right radio. He was. He keyed his microphone again and, trying to remain calm, repeated, "Abort! Abort! Abort!"

Still, the aircraft continued to accelerate down Palmdale's Runway 04, approaching speeds never reached during taxi tests a few days earlier. What was going on? Why didn't the pilots answer?

Data flickered across screens in the control room, and strip charts inched forward as computer-driven ink pens raced across the paper's surface. Those squiggles and blips of light instantly revealed the aircraft's health to the engineers who watched them intently. Everybody in the room essentially stopped breathing, locked onto their screens.

Telemetry reception was still solid; millions of data bits were still being transmitted from the aircraft to the control room 25 miles away. Why didn't the pilots respond to voice communications?

* * *

COL. RICK COUCH:

In the cockpit, we were busy monitoring speed, engine parameters, and a dozen other vital numbers. In a few seconds, the B-2 Stealth bomber would be airborne.

We never heard the TD's abort command.

I called, "One-oh-three," alerting Bruce Hinds, Northrop's chief B-2 test pilot, that we had reached a predetermined check speed."

* * *

He didn't answer, just as the pilots had briefed. More important things were occupying him at that moment. Right hand firmly holding the bat-winged bomber's control stick, left hand cradling four engine throttles, Hinds' full attention was locked on the wide concrete strip racing toward him.

"Rotate!" Couch called.

Hinds added a touch of back pressure to the stick; the nose lifted slightly. He was looking for a pitch attitude of 7 degrees, but never reached it. At about 6.5 degrees of pitch, the huge aircraft rose from the runway and climbed into a brilliant blue desert sky. The B-2 bomber was airborne.

When the B-2 lifted off the Palmdale, Calif., runway at 6:37 a.m. on July 17, 1989, about 1,000 people actually witnessed the historical moment. Northrop and Air Force employees cheered from inside the airfield fence. About 100 reporters lined the runway, many tracking the aircraft with long-lensed still and television cameras. Several hundred "unofficial" aviation enthusiasts watched from jammed roadsides outside the airport perimeter, defying attempts by local authorities to keep them away. This was aviation history, and people were determined to share the moment.

That night and in the following days, millions around the world saw and read about the B-2 flight via television news clips, newspapers, and magazines. The bat-winged bomber, shrouded in the mystery of heavy classification for years, had finally emerged from the "dark" and was visible to all.

The public had waited a long time to see this airplane. True, it had been rolled out of a Palmdale Site 4 hangar on November 22, 1988, but that event was tightly controlled. Only a select group of reporters and invited guests were on hand that day to witness the radically different bomber's brief emergence into the sunlight.

The B-2 "Stealth" bomber had evoked tremendous interest since the first hint of its existence was revealed in the late 1970s. A secret, advanced bomber was officially acknowledged at a Washington press conference on August 22, 1980, when Secretary of Defense Harold Brown discussed stealth technology as "an instrument of peace." While defense officials noted that the new technology would greatly reduce the ability of enemy radars to detect or "see" stealth weapon systems, they made it clear that work in the area would remain classified. Specific design features of stealth aircraft or missiles would be protected, preventing the Soviets from building effective countermeasures.

Defense officials alluded to programs that used stealth technologies, but would not get into specifics. After all, the press conference was supposedly held to stop information leaks that had been showing up in the press for months. Of course, at the time, there also was considerable debate in Congress over the need for a new strategic bomber.

The same issue had arisen in the presidential campaign underway at the time. Then-President Jimmy Carter had been accused of being "soft on defense" by candidate Ronald Reagan, who repeatedly criticized Carter's earlier decision to kill the Rockwell International B-1 bomber program.

It has been suggested that Brown's reference to the secret stealth bomber program was a political move designed to show American voters that the Carter administration had an alternative to the B-1, and was not undercutting the U.S. strategic defense forces. Whether this was true or not is still a subject of debate.

Regardless of its political roots, the Advanced Technology Bomber concept was given life—and an official go-ahead—during the Carter years. That decision unleashed a secret technology development effort unlike any since the heady days of the Manhattan Project during World War II.

2

The early years

THE B-2 PROGRAM WAS SHROUDED IN SECRECY from the moment it came to life in the late 1970s. At that time, the United States' defense posture was at a critical juncture, and a number of factors combined to make this an ideal time to introduce the concept of a stealth bomber that could penetrate the Soviet Union.

The Carter Administration had finally conceded that U.S. defense capabilities had eroded to the point that military units were at a serious disadvantage when compared to the Soviets'. It had been difficult to convince some key officials, but indisputable intelligence reports confirmed that the Soviets were building a powerful military machine at an unprecedented rate. They were outspending the U.S. in every critical area of defense, and becoming increasingly aggressive in projecting communist influence outside Soviet borders.

Jolted into action, government officials began assessing the future needs of U.S. military forces to counter a growing and more capable Soviet threat. An important catalyst for launching the B-2 program was a general recognition that the manned bomber leg of the nation's strategic triad—comprising land-based intercontinental missiles, long-range bombers, and submarine-launched missiles—would be obsolete by the mid-1990s. Aging B-52s would no longer be able to penetrate upgraded Soviet defenses and hold critical targets at risk.

Unless its bomber force was modernized, the U.S. would have to rely only on submarine and land-based ICBMs to maintain a viable nuclear deterrence posture into the next century. That significantly weakened the nation's nuclear response flexibility, and effectively abandoned the three-pronged strategic plan that had maintained a balance between the world powers since World War II.

Any new bomber, however, would have to be technologically advanced enough to slip through an ever-tightening net of Soviet radar defenses well into the next century. Overlapping radar coverage would continue to be the most effective means of detecting an intruding aircraft, most experts concluded. A penetrating bomber would, in essence, need to have a radar signature measured in inches to survive. If the aircraft could not be detected easily, it had the effect of reducing a ground-based defense radar's range to something much smaller.

For example, if a radar site had an effective range of 100 miles against a B-52-sized bomber, it might only have a 20-mile range against an aircraft having a much smaller radar cross section. The Soviet radar net, in effect, would have been "shrunk" by a stealth bomber fleet. Critical, high-value targets such as Soviet command and control centers would immediately be held at risk by the new aircraft, which could penetrate into the Soviet heartland by simply flying through gaps in defense radar coverage.

To counter that possibility, the Soviets would have to build hundreds of new radar sites in order to plug those gaps. That, in turn, would be tremendously expensive, straining an already stressed Soviet economy. Some estimates, made by the Air Force B-2 community, put the cost of upgrading Soviet radars to the necessary density at about $800 billion.

STEALTH

Stealth technologies being investigated at the time under several superclassified Pentagon programs, if incorporated into a bomber design from the start, offered the potential of reducing the radar signature of an airplane having a 200-foot wingspan to a few hundredths of a meter.

Intercontinental bombers would look like insect-sized objects to enemy radar. In other words, bomber-sized stealth aircraft would appear to be no bigger than a moth or big bee.

A series of B-2-related articles printed by the *Washington Post* in the fall of 1989—a few months after the aircraft made its first flight—named William J. Perry, President Carter's under secretary of defense for research and engineering at the time, the "godfather of stealth technology." When he assumed the defense post, Perry was quick to see the national security benefits stealth techniques offered for any number of weapon systems.

Perry also knew about Lockheed's experimental stealth aircraft being tested in the Nevada desert under a program sponsored by the Defense Advanced Research Project Agency (DARPA), and was aware of their potential. Built under the Have Blue project, the two fighter-type jets had proved that an airworthy aircraft could be designed with significantly reduced acoustic, infrared and—most importantly—radar signatures. Those aircraft evolved into the Lockheed F-117A stealth fighter.

Perry focused Defense Department attention on the potentials of stealth technology, and, by 1978, both the Air Force and Navy had plans to incorporate stealth methods into weapon systems. At the time, most detailed knowledge of the new technology was limited to a small circle. National security officials saw the need to protect the information as the group's size expanded. Projects that had been handled as unclassified or at the secret level soon disappeared into the "black world" known as SAR (Special Access Required). To learn anything about these highly classified projects, a person had to demonstrate a definite "need to know."

A manned, long-range bomber using stealth technology was one of three main projects created under the *low observables* or *L.O. Office*. The term low observables generally refers to characteristics that make the aircraft difficult to detect with conventional radar, infrared, or acoustic sensors. Eventually, that office and the Air Force contracted with Lockheed, which had already demonstrated knowledge of stealth technology, and Northrop Corp. to develop a bomber concept. Top government officials gave Northrop little hope of winning a follow-on Advanced Technology Bomber (ATB) contract, but the Pentagon wanted to broaden U.S. expertise in the new all-important stealth techniques.

Most key officials, though, recognized very early that a "stealth bomber" was years away. A tremendous amount of materials development, manufacturing techniques and detailed design were required first. Meanwhile, Air Force generals pointed to the growing Soviet threat and asked, "What do we use for a penetrating bomber between now and when the ATB is ready for service?"

An interim solution was developed that called for resurrecting Rockwell's B-1 bomber, which President Carter had cancelled, but incorporating several stealth technologies to make it more survivable than the original B-1 model. By building 100 of the new B-1Bs, the Pentagon could provide a manned penetration capability into the 21st century while the higher-risk ATB was being developed.

Although quite similar to its B-1A predecessor, the B-1B would not be quite as simple to develop, test and produce as planners thought. Many in the flight test community warned that a high degree of concurrency—performing flight tests on the first bombers while production models were being built for delivery to the Strategic Air Command—could be expensive. Despite these and other cautions about the difficulties a B-1B version would encounter, a simplistic view prevailed in Washington. In the end, a 100-aircraft B-1B fleet was built and delivered on time and within budget, but not without significant problems that created additional post-test program costs.

FIRST CONTRACTS

An Air Force decision to acquire any new aircraft follows an intense period of study that assesses potential enemy threats over the next 20 or more years, and a definition of the capabilities that will be needed to counter those threats. If upgrades to existing fleet aircraft cannot meet a projected threat, a new design is considered. Planners look at the available and future aircraft technologies, trying to balance potential benefits against risk of development.

In the B-2's case, the drastic change in technologies from earlier aircraft involved a number of risks. One of the most important questions was: Can we actually build and maintain a fleet of bombers that incorporates complex curvatures, exotic materials, and other new stealth methods? Both competing contractors assured the government that it could be done, but the resulting aircraft could be costly.

In 1981, the Air Force completed its evaluation of the concepts and proposals developed by Lockheed and Northrop, and elected to take another step on the road to acquiring a stealth bomber fleet. Northrop Corporation was selected to develop the Advanced Technology Bomber (ATB), as the B-2 was first called, under a $200 million initial contract, according to the *Washington Post* articles.

It was a major coup for Northrop, which had been known as primarily a fighter manufacturer in recent years. After the failure of its F-20 Tigershark venture, aerospace industry analysts gave the firm little chance of winning a competition for an exotic aircraft like the ATB, especially versus Lockheed. Against all odds, though, Northrop won. And, eventually, the ATB could be worth billions to the company.

The program was still highly classified, but had grown to the point that a multimillion dollar contract award to any company was hard to hide. Financial analysts quickly spotted the huge figure and focused public attention on Northrop as the bomber contractor. On April 8, 1982, Northrop bought a massive unused Ford manufacturing facility in Pico Rivera, Calif., and converted it to a top-secret plant housing about 10,000 workers. Still, Northrop employees could not reveal, even to their families, anything about the project.

EARLY STAGES

Well before contract award, during the early concept development phases, Northrop had assembled an impressive team of designers. Two men, in particular, would be credited with "fathering" the flying wing concept that would evolve into the B-2 seen today: John Cashen and Irv Waaland.

Cashen was the low observables designer and Waaland the aerodynamic chief. The two disciplines often were at odds during the aircraft's development process, but, in the early days, both camps were in surprising agreement.

* * *

JOHN CASHEN:

The B-2 did not evolve from the old [Northrop] flying wings. Our designers came up with this design because it was the right answer to meet the defined mission requirements for the next strategic bomber. In fact, the idea for a flying wing came almost simultaneously to both Irv and me.

We had done about a six-week requirements study, not talking about what the aircraft would look like, but focusing on the job it had to do—[what we call] *mission analysis trade studies* and a *functional requirements analysis*.

Both Irv and I had been working on ideas for the right design, when the master designer came out of [a new secure room], looking for Irv and me.

He wanted to know what had to be done next ... the designers were set up and ready to go to work.

I went in and sketched on the blackboard pretty much what is today's B-2. The dimensions would come later, but I knew it would be a flying wing, with this [wing] sweep, this planform, this rough shape. I said, "Start on this and see how it comes out."

About two hours later, I bumped into Irv [Waaland], who had been in a meeting during that time. He walked up and said, "You know that bomber we're going to do? Let's do a flying wing." I told him I had the same idea, and we had started working on it two hours earlier. I told him to go look at my sketch and let me know what he thought.

We both came up with the same idea, because the requirements drove it that way. It was the right answer.

* * *

Much of the public fascination with the B-2 cannot be attributed entirely to the secrecy surrounding its development or its stealthy designs. A good bit of the interest is because the new bomber revived the flying wing that Jack Northrop, the founder of Northrop Corporation, conceived and built some 50 years ago. When Northrop and the Air Force admitted publicly that the new bomber would be a large wing, many people naturally assumed the B-2 could trace its roots to the YB-49 flying wing of that earlier era.

In fact, none of the Northrop team that worked on the B-2 had ever been associated with the original YB-49. Managers on the B-2 even had a hard time finding a company employee who had any experience with the old flying wings. After all, that effort ended about 35 years before the B-2 concept surfaced.

Even more frustrating, though, was the lack of data; engineers looked through company archives for basic flying wing information, but with no luck. They found that Jack Northrop, in a fit of despair, had destroyed most of the data after his beloved YB-49 flying wing project was cancelled by the U.S. government years ago. Some YB-49 data finally were found in the archives of Northrop University, but none existed within the company.

Jack Northrop, at age 86 and ailing, was not consulted as a design resource for the B-2, but corporate leaders felt the company patriarch should know his dream had been reborn. Thomas V. Jones, then Northrop's chief executive officer, approached the Air Force about obtaining a special security clearance for Jack. In 1980, service officials agreed and arranged for the elderly Northrop to see the B-2 design.

* * *

JOHN CASHEN:

We were allowed to show [Jack Northrop] what the B-2 would look like, but couldn't tell him it had special stealth characteristics. He was brought to the front area of the Hawthorne [California] complex where all our work was done at that time—the advanced projects area, Northrop's version of the Skunk Works.

Jack had been invited for a luncheon meeting in the conference room there. It was attended by only about six people, including Irv [Waaland] and me. After lunch, Irv reached under the table and pulled out a small box, about the size of a cigar box, and asked Jack to open it.

Jack had Parkinson's disease, so his hand shook quite a bit. He carefully pulled the lid off, took the airplane model out and started to cry. After awhile, he said, "Now I know why God has kept me alive for the last 25 years."

* * *

When he composed himself, the famous designer slowly turned the B-2 model—which looked very much like the aircraft does today, 10 years later—around in his hands, looking at it from every angle. Finally, Northrop said, "You know, the next design change I had planned to make to the YB-49 was to get rid of the aft verticals."

He then started firing technical questions at the engineers, asking about span, aspect ratio, and loading. After each answer, he responded with the YB-49's exact equivalent number. The figures were still embedded in his memory.

One year later, Jack Northrop passed away. He had made a tremendous impact on the aviation industry, introducing such concepts as monocoque fuselage construction and flush rivets. He had left the industry at the age of 57, an embittered and broken man after his YB-49 bomber had been cancelled by the Air Force. He never again worked as an aviation designer, largely because his enthusiasm and dreams died with the flying wing program. In his final days, though, he had seen that dream rekindled in the B-2.

NIGHT WATCH

In designing the B-2's stealth features, Cashen and his compatriots developed, built, and tested hundreds of components and models of the bomber to evaluate their low observable characteristics. Some tests could be done in the laboratory, but most required special radar test ranges and new facilities. Many were conducted on a special government range at White Sands Missile Range (WSMR) in New Mexico, typically at night.

At one point, the team identified a need for a large *sting*, a slender, slanted post that supported a model or piece of material being tested on a radar range. It had to be big enough to hold husky test items several feet in the air, but portable enough to move quickly. Although most work was done at night to avoid being seen by curious passersby, test time was still structured around the overflight patterns of Soviet satellites, which could spot ground activity either in the day or night.

Working around a satellite schedule, engineers would race out and mount their test item on a sting, blast it with radar signals, and record the required data. Periodically, they would either cover or completely remove the item and put it inside a building or vehicle, depending on its size, and wait until a spy satellite passed overhead.

A lot of time and effort was being wasted shuttling test items and equipment to and from the sting, but maintaining a high level of security was an absolute necessity, too. The answer was to build an underground facility equipped with a sting that could be raised or lowered at will. Rather than design a unique, expensive facility for what would be a relatively short project, program officials decided to use plans for an already existing structure. The Minuteman 3 ballistic missile silo was an ideal candidate.

The hole was dug and the silo built to Minuteman specifications, except that a test sting was placed in "the hole" in place of a nuclear-tipped missile. The whole facility was big enough to allow raising or lowering the sting without removing the test article. It clearly improved test time efficiency.

Ironically, Soviet satellites recorded the new silo construction and lodged a complaint with the U.S. government. Russian analysts believed the U.S. had built a new missile site, possibly in violation of existing treaties. Although U.S. officials could deny that a missile was in the new silo, they could not reveal the actual purpose of it, other than to call it a test facility. Evidently, that worked, although it would be reasonable to guess that the Soviets made sure their satellites kept a close watch on the new White Sands silo.

* * *

JOHN CASHEN:
We took about 120,000 radar cross sections [tests] on this program. They were done by engineers spending many, many nights in the desert, freezing their fannies off and seeing a lot of December sunrises. And there are some southwestern desert locations where this is not a real pleasant experience!

We were away from home far more than any of us liked . . . at the plant 16–17 hours a day, or clear off-site for weeks. We missed a lot of our kids' [growing up] during this development period. The bomber became our life's work. And it wasn't for just a short period. It was 10 years, almost to the day, from the start of design to the first flight.

Just having to work like this was bad enough, but the whole situation was exacerbated by security. We could never tell our families where we were going or how long we'd be gone. Our wives nicknamed the B-2 "Lady-M" because many of them were absolutely convinced we husbands had mistresses—that's why we were never at home. It wasn't until the first flight that we could show our families what we had been working on.

We could only talk about the program in special access [SA] facilities, too . . . some of the world's largest SA facilities, I might add. Believe me, there's been nothing on the scale of [the B-2 program] since the Manhattan Project. And there were a lot of parallels to that program, too.

* * *

TEST PILOTS BROUGHT ABOARD

Although the stealth bomber would not fly for another eight years, Northrop started looking for a chief test pilot. The company's leaders knew the value of having pilot inputs to early designs, a tactic that should avoid expensive changes later, after the aircraft started flying.

Bruce Hinds, an experienced test pilot with thousands of flight hours behind him, had just retired from the Air Force and was looking for a second career. He applied to several aerospace firms, attended interviews, and waited. One of his choices was Northrop, which, he knew, had recently won the ATB contract.

Northrop needed a top-notch test pilot for the massive program, but classification was so strict, the company could not tell Bruce, or anybody else, what they would be doing if hired!

* * *

BRUCE HINDS:

I first got involved with the B-2 in 1982, shortly after contract award. Nobody steered me to Northrop, and they never wooed me at all. I knew they had won the ATB contract, and assumed that's where I would be working. Security checks took about three or four months, so I kept interviewing with different companies.

Northrop [eventually] hired me as the chief test pilot. Or, at least I thought I was! Security was really tight in those days. Nobody could tell me what I was going to be doing when I interviewed. They liked the resume, and said I would fit into the job they had, but couldn't tell me anything. Only after I had hired on and was inside did I find out what I would be doing. I knew it would be a long time before we'd fly, so I worked a lot with the labs.

* * *

When Hinds joined the Northrop B-2 team, it consisted of about 800 people, most working in a separate building somewhere in the Los Angeles area. It was called "A-Y," which meant "away from Hawthorne," the main plant where much of the company's aircraft work has been performed for decades. The facility was a leased office building, but, even today, employees will not divulge its location. Northrop had purchased the huge Ford plant in Pico Rivera and was refurbishing it during this time, but all ATB work was being done at the remote A-Y building and at Hawthorne.

The group was part of Northrop's Advanced Systems Division, which encompassed early B-2 functions and a host of other, mostly stealth-related projects at the time. In essence, it was the Northrop "Stealth Division." Eventually, these other programs "went away," according to company executives, and the unit was renamed the B-2 Division. The name change occurred in 1988, shortly after the Air Force officially designated the ATB as the B-2 bomber.

Hinds was immediately brought into the B-2's design process, and was involved in many early decisions and studies. Although the basic design had been established as part of the precontract proposal to the Air Force, detailed work and refinements occupied much of the pilots' and engineers' time in the early program stages.

As chief test pilot, Hinds started working with a fixed-base (nonmoving) simulator of the aircraft, which had been isolated to a secure area at the Hawthorne plant. When a large-amplitude, moving-base simulator was needed, a classified cockpit was set up in another simulator in the same area and tied to its own computers, separated from the Hawthorne Aircraft Division's computers.

Hinds and other pilots operated this way for about three years, as the Pico Rivera simulator evolved. Initially, the Pico unit was a fixed-base simulator, but, by 1985, was a full motion-base tool that included a wide-field-of-view visual system. This upgrade significantly improved the simulator's realism and was a tremendous engineering tool for working out pilot-related design issues.

AIR FORCE PREPARATIONS

On the Air Force side, plans were made to construct a large new test complex in the old South Base area at Edwards AFB, Calif. Eventually, that facility would shelter several B-2 test aircraft, hundreds of civilian and military personnel comprising the test force, and some of the most advanced technical equipment ever made available to the flight test community. In a 1990 speech, Maj. Gen. John Schoeppner, Jr., commander of the Air Force Flight Test Center at Edwards, said almost $200 million had been invested in B-2-related support facilities there.

* * *

COL. RICK COUCH, Air Force test pilot and third CTF director:
I first became involved in the ATB project shortly after source selection—when Northrop was named the prime contractor—helping define manpower and funding needs of the projected flight test program. These estimates were included with the Air Force's *program memorandum objective* (POM) submission, a key element of the budgeting and funding process. During this period, I attended all general officer-level briefings presented by the ATB program manager at Air Force Systems Command's headquarters [in Washington, D.C.], becoming familiar with the full range of challenges facing the bomber program.

Most of our efforts at that time were devoted to reducing development risks, and defining program costs and schedules. Specific areas were identified, and all activities and risks related to them were monitored closely to ensure technical, cost, and schedule impacts were minimized. One of these was composite materials manufacturing techniques. It offered the potential for significant spin-off benefits that could be applied to military and commercial programs far removed from the ATB.

A major resource issue we tried to resolve in this period was the question of what aircraft to use as an *avionics flying testbed*. Based on my past experience flying avionics development tests on Lockheed C-141s, I suggested using that aircraft as an ATB testbed. Key managers from the ATB System Program Office (SPO) and the Air Force Flight Test Center

(AFFTC) at Edwards favored a Boeing C-135 that had been modified with a large nose radome and high-capacity generators capable of carrying excess electrical loads.

At the time, SAC had an aircraft that required only minor modifications to meet our testbed needs, but command officials were reluctant to turn it over for test work. That particular C-135 crashed about a month after we gave up trying to get it.

An early-model KC-135A assigned to Wright-Patterson AFB, Ohio, test duties was finally designated for our use. This old *water wagon,* so named because it used engine water injection to improve takeoff performance, was sent to a company near Dallas for ATB project modifications. Although we tried to convince the program office that replacing the standard engines with newer fuel-efficient turbofans was warranted, the projected $2 million cost was considered excessive.

* * *

In 1983, the Air Force decided the ATB's mission would have to be modified to improve the bomber's survivability, necessitating a major aircraft redesign. Early mission planning had envisioned the bomber as a high-altitude penetrator, operating at 30,000- to 50,000-foot altitudes, and Northrop was designing to this requirement. As capabilities of the Soviet Integrated Air Defense System improved, though, Air Force officials decided the new bomber would have to be capable of flying either high or low to successfully complete its nuclear mission.

Higher wing loading would be encountered during low-level flight at 200–300 feet above the ground, where turbulence can be much worse than at higher altitudes. As a result, the ATB's wing and a number of internal structural elements had to be strengthened to tolerate the more severe low-altitude environment without shortening the aircraft's fatigue life. A major change in the entire aircraft design was adopted as the only feasible course, although that decision would delay the program at least a year.

Some reports indicate the resulting redesign effort first introduced the flying wing bomber's unique trailing edge—the sawtooth configuration seen today. The new wing was lighter, stronger, and even more "stealthy," and Northrop was commended by the Air Force chief of staff for a "brilliant job," according to the *Washington Post.* Under the revised schedule, first flight was targeted for December 1987. Original plans to have a unit of advanced bombers in operation by 1987 obviously were abandoned. Now, the first operational SAC units would not receive production ATBs until the early-to-mid-1990s.

* * *

COL. RICK COUCH:
My place in the bomber program was determined in 1983 when the ATB program manager stopped at my desk and asked if I would be interested in taking the job as the first uniformed ATB test force director. I thought carefully about it for roughly two seconds and responded with a definite "Yes!" I didn't know it at the time, but that answer put me in line to be a pilot on the aircraft's first flight. When I finally recognized that little

bonus, needless to say, I was honored and excited. For any test pilot, a first flight is about as good as it gets. Few people are given that opportunity even once in their flight test career.

Over the next two years, I cleared a number of obstacles, such as an Air Force senior service school, and moved my family from Washington, D.C., to Edwards AFB, Calif. In July 1985, we were back in the Mojave Desert, assigned to the Air Force Flight Test Center.

Four years of hard work by a lot of very dedicated, capable people would pass before the crowning moment of that first flight.

* * *

3

Making it happen

ONCE THE U.S. GOVERNMENT ADMITTED that stealth technologies were to be used in the country's next generation of combat aircraft, the "white world"—those who did not have access to this classified information—naturally wanted to know more about it.

What is this "stealth" business? Why use it? What makes an airplane "stealthy," and how do you build it that way?

Scientists, engineers, reporters, and self-acclaimed experts asked these questions. While general concepts were aired publicly, only the small military/industrial community working on these new aircraft were privy to the answers.

In the final analysis, stealth technology is one more attempt to do what pilots have been striving for since the airplane was first introduced to combat: Avoid detection, then deny the enemy gunner a target for as long as possible; ideally, disappear into the sky.

In modern air warfare, the ultimate mission of a "friendly" fighter or bomber is to slip past enemy defenses and deliver conventional or nuclear armament on a target. That target might be heavily defended airfields, factories or equipment concentrations, nuclear missile sites, or maybe another airborne fighter. In each case, the friendly aircraft must "hide in the sky" long enough to seek out the target, hit it, and escape to safe airspace.

The enemy defenders, of course, are simultaneously trying to detect the intruder aircraft, intercept it, lock-on their weapons, and fire before the "friendly" can drop his bombs or launch a missile. The defenders' first task, detection, typically is accomplished through radar, infrared (IR), visual sighting, acoustic, or electronic emission methods.

Radar systems send out short pulses of electromagnetic energy that hit a target and bounce back to the transmitter. Thanks to sophisticated electronic techniques at the receiver, those returned pulses provide information about a target aircraft's presence, speed, direction, and size. Radar is the primary aircraft detection method used by military forces, although there are ways to evade detection through a variety of countermeasures.

Infrared detectors sense subtle heat differences between objects. For example, an aircraft has a certain heat "signature" that looks different than the air around it or ground below it. However, weather, particularly heavy rain, drastically cuts the range at which infrared (IR) sensors are effective. Still, modern infrared devices are sophisticated enough that designers expend considerable effort reducing a new aircraft's IR signature.

Acoustic sensors, even the human ear, can detect noise that an aircraft makes. And other types of electronic sensors will detect radar or other electromagnetic emissions radiated by an invading aircraft.

The pilot flying a new bomber or fighter against any of these detection sensors hopes the design engineers of his aircraft recognized a very important fact: As the probability of detection goes up, the pilot's probability of survival goes down. The more "stealthy" an intruder aircraft is, the better its chances of completing the mission.

The ultimate in "low detectability" would be to make the aircraft invisible, quiet, and free of electronic emissions. The physics of our world preclude this happening anytime soon, but stealth techniques enable engineers to reduce the aircraft's various signatures considerably. For example, a bomber as big as the B-2 can be designed to have a head-on radar cross section no bigger than that of a large insect.

That would be analogous to making the family car look like a marble to a highway patrolman's radar. Such fuzz-buster stealth techniques would make that car essentially invisible to a radar trap.

Designing a stealthy aircraft—one that has a low probability of being detected by radar, infrared, acoustic, or other electronic sensors—while still ensuring it will fly well, boils down to an exercise in compromise. Air Force generals, experienced pilots, and intelligence experts explain what they would like to have in a stealthy airplane, then aerodynamic, materials, powerplant, and electronics engineers try to apply today's technology to meet those military needs.

Generally, what emerges from this process is a less-than-ideal design, but one that is a balance between *real* requirements and what can actually be built. Minimizing the chances of detection by radar was a very high priority for the B-2, so Northrop and its subcontractors devoted considerable effort to decreasing the bomber's radar cross section. That objective, blended with techniques for reducing the aircraft's infrared and other signatures, yet balanced with aerodynamic requirements, resulted in the unique all-wing, blended-surface shape of the B-2.

HISTORICAL PRECEDENTS

Back in the 1940s, pilots and engineers testing the Northrop YB-49 prototype bomber discovered that the flying wing shape was very difficult to detect with the human eye. Further, tests conducted along the California coast indicated that the large aircraft reflected radar signals poorly, complicating the task of radar operators trying to track the bomber during testing.

Without a conventional vertical tail, the low-profile, flat wing presented few reflective surfaces for light or radar pulses. Looking at the aircraft from almost any perspective revealed very few discontinuities that could bounce a radar signal back to its source. In fact, most of the YB-49's shape seemed to bounce radar pulses away from the source. As a result, the bomber either looked quite small on a radar screen, or it could not even be detected until it flew closer to the transmitter.

This 30-year-old information was not lost on the B-2's designers. As a result, the no-tail flying wing was considered an attractive candidate for a stealth bomber. Adding other low observable features, made possible by new materials and computer-based design techniques, provided a realistic, complete package that could meet Air Force needs—a bomber with a very low probability of detection, yet with long range and a significant weapons capacity.

The flying wing concept was not without its critics, however. There just weren't a lot of airplanes around without tails, and for good reason—they had a reputation for poor stability, making them difficult to fly safely.

Despite this apparent detraction, aeronautic historians can point to several flying wing or tailless aircraft designs. About the time the Wright brothers were experimenting at Kitty Hawk, John William Dunne, an Englishman, was experimenting with tailless gliders and flew a motor-powered hang glider in 1908. His concepts were forerunners to a whole series of aircraft that combined the inherent aerodynamic efficiencies of a no-tail design with simple structural considerations. Despite these attractive features, none of the tailless designs were ever mass produced.

During World War II, Germany was preparing to produce hundreds of the Horton Brothers XVIII flying wing design when the war ended. This plywood and carbon-sandwich aircraft also had six jet engines buried in the wings, much like the B-2 does today, and probably would have presented a minimal radar cross section.

Jack Northrop's family of tailless flying wings has remained a source of fascination and controversy for more than 40 years in the United States. Although Northrop's aircraft never went into production, they provided support for the B-2 development effort. Northrop designer John Cashen said, "The B-2 did not evolve from the old flying wing. However, the YB-49 did contribute to the B-2, by giving us confidence that a large flying wing could fly. We knew it had been done successfully once before."

From a pilot's perspective, the tailless flying wing can be reduced to a very simple question: How does it fly? If one pulls back on the stick and the nose goes up, then pushes and the nose goes down, the flying wing acts like any other airplane, at least in the pitch direction.

Typically, though, a tailless design has stability problems in the lateral (rolling) and directional (yawing, side-to-side) axes. A vertical tail fin on a traditional airplane acts a lot like the feathers on an arrow or the blade on the tail of a weathervane—it keeps the nose pointed into the wind. Without a tail or some other means of providing side-to-side stability, moving the rudder pedals or rolling sideways might cause an aircraft to wallow through the air. The nose might wander back and forth and the wings wag up and down, making the aircraft difficult to fly.

Pilots can compensate for some of this motion through skill and practice, but, if it is too pronounced, the aircraft can be easily upset, especially by turbulence. At best, the aircraft would be a poor bombing platform, and, at worst, it could be dangerously unstable.

Modern computer technology, however, has given us *fly-by-wire* flight control systems that compensate automatically for any inherent instabilities of tailless aircraft. In the B-2, sophisticated computerized flight controls make the big bomber fly like any other, more traditional, design.

* * *

COL. RICK COUCH:
    The fact that the B-2 has no vertical tail is only apparent when a pilot walks up to the aircraft. Once in the cockpit, it's not noticeable. The B-2 flies much like any other aircraft, even better than most of them.

* * *

THE PROCUREMENT MAZE

An equally challenging task necessary to transform the new bomber from an idea into a flying vehicle was negotiating the federal acquisition process.

Procuring a major weapon system like the B-2 can take 10–15 years going from the *statement of need* to putting a fleet of aircraft in the field. This tortuous route is transited by every weapon system that enters any military service inventory. A nightmare of bureaucracy and political wrangling, it is made even more cumbersome by a patchwork of regulations imposed over the years by Pentagon and Congressional officials to prevent abuses of the system.

Having a rough idea of how this system works, or doesn't, is necessary to appreciate many of the forces that have shaped the B-2 program so far, and which might ultimately determine its fate. Although the U.S. defense acquisition process was undergoing significant changes at the time of this writing, there were several basic elements of the system that, in the past, have had a direct impact on the B-2 program. Many of these elements will be retained, even if a revised system is put in place sometime in the future.

The following will explain some facets of the acquisition process, with a focus on how they affect the testing element of the system:

Acquisition of the B-2 began with a detailed requirements document, prepared in the 1970s, that addressed the threat faced by a manned bomber in the 1990s and beyond. The ultimate user, the Strategic Air Command, was responsible for analyzing future threats to the U.S., then proving that existing Air Force aircraft could not survive against that threat.

To put it bluntly, SAC determined that Soviet radar systems, antiaircraft missiles and fighter forces were advancing to the point where aging U.S. B-52s (*Buffs*) would be sitting ducks. A Northrop official once explained this threat by saying, "The Soviet Union is literally awash with [air defense] radars. It's amazing that anybody over there has any children, there's so much microwave radiation in the air!"

A briefing paper prepared in late 1989 summarized the Soviet air defense network this way:

- About 10,000 radars.
- Roughly 3,000 fighter interceptors.
- Approximately 8,000 surface-to-air missiles (SAMs) with more being added all the time.
- New airborne warning and control aircraft that direct the air battle, vectoring fighters and other defenders against intruders.

The chances of several nuclear-armed Buffs getting through these Soviet defenses and hitting their targets were getting smaller every year. If the U.S. could no longer hold those targets at risk of being destroyed, the nuclear bomber force would no longer be an effective deterrent against Soviet aggression.

The Air Force and Department of Defense then reviewed SAC's work, its statement of need, and certified that the need for an improved bomber force was valid. Once SAC's need had been officially validated, or certified, that triggered a multistep process aimed at finding ways to satisfy SAC's requirements for an improved bomber force.

First, various alternatives for satisfying the need were considered. Could existing bombers be modified and upgraded? Were there technologies or systems somewhere else that could be adapted to meet Air Force requirements? Or would a totally new weapon system have to be built?

At this stage, a decision to buy a new aircraft had not been made yet; only studies of any number of different concepts were being conducted. The Air Force was trying, at this point, to determine what was available that could meet SAC's stated need, and how it could be acquired within a reasonable time. These studies concluded that only a new bomber would satisfy SAC's requirements.

Normally, the second step is to develop prototypes or engineering models of an aircraft that could, potentially, meet those needs. Two competing systems typically are designed and reviewed as possible candidates. This phase might include actually building a couple of competing prototypes.

Whether proof-of-concept vehicles or prototypes were ever built for the B-2 program is unclear. *Aviation Week & Space Technology*, a highly respected U.S. aerospace publication, has periodically received reports of flying wing aircraft seen in remote desert regions of the western U.S. since the early 1980s. Those periodic reports persist even today, with repeated sightings of large, very quiet, triangle-shaped aircraft reported by residents in areas around Edwards AFB, central Nevada, and Arizona as recently as mid-1990.

Rumors continue to circulate to the effect that both Lockheed and Northrop built prototypes for a fly-off competition. When Lockheed lost, its aircraft supposedly were destroyed, possibly at the White Sands Missile Range in New Mexico. On the other hand, these might only have been large models used for low observables testing, which took place at White Sands. Until more of the B-2 program is declassified, only those with the proper clearances know for sure. The official Air Force position has consistently been that no flying prototypes of the B-2 were ever built.

Under a typical aircraft acquisition program that builds flying prototypes—such as the YF-16 and YF-17 lightweight fighters in the mid-1970s, or the more-recent advanced tactical fighters of the '90s—the primary objective of this phase is to demonstrate the feasibility of a particular design. Reams of data are reviewed, aimed at answering a key question: Can this aircraft perform the mission that the using command has defined?

If the answer is "Yes," formal proposals are solicited from aerospace contractors. The technical, management and cost aspects of the submitted proposals are reviewed and a contract awarded. All this assumes that Congress has approved funding for the program, which involves a whole different set of protracted procedures. While vitally important, the funding process is very complex and considered beyond the scope of this book.

Finally, the decision is made to proceed with *full scale development* (FSD) of the system, in this case, the B-2 bomber. The FSD phase includes building several aircraft and thoroughly testing them to make absolutely sure they will be able to perform the desired mission. Tests focus on assessing the engineering or technical features of the aircraft, and, most importantly, their operational capabilities. That means both *development* and *operational tests and evaluations* are performed: DT&E and OT&E.

In an ideal world, all testing would be completed and the Air Force assured everything works perfectly before a commitment was made to manufacture hundreds of the aircraft. In practice, this approach would extend the procurement process to 20 years or so, and is economically unacceptable. Contractors that hired thousands of people to design and build the full scale development aircraft, and all the hundreds of suppliers who provided parts and services to the program, can hardly afford to sit quietly on the sidelines until development and operational testing is completed. The cost of keeping this team intact for several years, doing essentially nothing, would be enormous.

These factors, keeping development cycles as short as possible and maintaining an economical manufacturing capability, naturally result in overlapping testing and production cycles. Production aircraft, those that will be sent to active Air Force units, are built before testing of the full scale development birds is completed.

That means two acquisition phases are underway at the same time: *production* and *testing*. Problems are inevitable, but the process is manageable, if done correctly. Every time the test program identifies a problem area that must be corrected, aircraft already on the production line either must be modified there, or tagged for updates after they are in service. As a result, production aircraft normally are identified in *blocks*, where maybe 10–20 vehicles all have the same configuration. Eventually, the first block of aircraft is modified to the latest configuration. Rarely, however, are all aircraft configured the same at any given time in their life.

Throughout the entire service lifetime of any weapon system, the Air Force continually reviews the basic need for that system, the threat it is supposed to counter, and methods for improving it through newer technologies. This aspect of the acquisition process often escapes many people; military aircraft are never finished; they are constantly being updated in order to remain effective in an ever-shifting, very complex defense environment. A new aircraft is affected for years by everything from a changing, more dangerous military threat, to the interests and preferences of Congress and the administration.

The defense acquisition process is characterized at every step by three all-important elements: cost, schedule, and performance. If any one of these varies significantly beyond preset limits, the program is in trouble. Consequently, each step of the process is monitored very closely, and managers are constantly making tradeoffs between these three elements to ensure the aircraft and its systems work correctly, and will be delivered on time at a reasonable cost.

Any military procurement program is carefully managed by a well-structured hierarchy. While the president of the United States and the Congress obviously have enormous clout over a program like the B-2, its actual management chain starts at the Department of Defense. The primary players there are the secretary, or SecDef, and his undersecretary, the defense acquisition executive. They have the final say on procurement issues within all the military services.

Continuing down the chain, the Air Force's senior acquisition manager is the USAF undersecretary for acquisition. Next is the program executive officer, who, on the B-2 program, also serves as the program director. For a large, highly visible program such as the B-2, this has evolved from a colonel's to a two-star general's slot.

The program director heads the System Program Office, or SPO, which is the focal point for everything that happens in converting the stealth concept into a fleet of B-2 bombers. The SPO comprises all the elements necessary to acquire a modern weapon system for the Air Force. It includes engineers, contract monitors, configuration control personnel, testing experts, program control monitors, software experts, representatives of the Strategic Air Command (the end user) and, normally, someone assigned to the General Accounting Office, the congressional watchdog agency.

The total SPO workforce will ebb and flow as the program goes through its various phases. The B-2 SPO started with only a handful of people, grew to more than 400, and eventually will decline to about 100 after the B-2 production run is completed.

Within the SPO, the test office is responsible for all B-2 ground and flight testing. This includes every imaginable test: wind tunnel, laboratory, simulator, component, flight, and logistics. The test office does a tremendous amount of planning and coordinates all the different phases of testing to make sure all are compatible and supportive of the others. It is the main interface between the Combined Test Force at Edwards AFB, where the aircraft actually is put through its testing paces, and the rest of the SPO for any test-related issues.

Outside the SPO, B-2-responsible offices are set up in the various Air Force commands that ultimately will have something to do with the aircraft. These include the Air Force Systems Command (which handles procurement and test); Strategic Air Command (the using organization); Logistics Command (the people who will provide long-term supplies and heavy maintenance throughout the aircraft's lifetime); and the Air Training Command (which trains flight crews and maintenance personnel).

Several people at the Pentagon are assigned to coordinate with and support any number of other interested parties. When a B-2 briefing is scheduled in Washington, these people provide all the legwork and day-to-day mechanics to make sure things go as planned and specific issues get resolved.

The necessary communication and coordination that occurs up and down these extended lines of authority present a staggering challenge. Different issues naturally flow through different routes, and it is easy for someone to inadvertently get left out. This not only can cause interpersonal or interoffice problems, but might also have a detrimental effect on getting an issue resolved. Often, it is the agency or person left out that might have an important input that should be considered. In fact, they might even be the key to a solution.

The one person expected to coordinate all these diverse elements, remaining cognizant of everything going on at each level, is the program director. He is the first to be blamed for a problem, and, possibly, the last to be credited for a solution. If the program is a disaster, the SPO director's career can be shattered. Even with a hand-picked, competent staff, he has one extremely difficult job.

The B-2 program, since its inception, has had a number of SPO directors and will surely have a few more as the aircraft wends its way through the development and fielding process. Insiders, though, around the time the first B-2 made its maiden flight, said the current director then would someday be credited with bringing the program to fruition. A former colleague of his said, "When the full story of this program can be told, people will see how well it's been managed. And [the two-star director] is the guy who made that happen."

WHERE TESTING FITS IN

Flight tests and logistics tests are an integral part of the aircraft full scale development phase of the acquisition process. This is where "the rubber meets the road." The test organization is tasked with evaluating the entire weapon system, plus finding and identifying engineering design problems so they can be fixed.

To some, the testers are almost obstructionists. Why can't they just try out the equipment and report what they see? Why are they always harping about problems they find, essentially holding up progress by insisting every little thing be changed or fixed?

Obviously, testing would be of little use if there were no feedback to the design process, where changes can be implemented and the entire aircraft improved. Consequently, in the Air Force today, testing is seen as an opportunity to perform engineering evaluations on hardware (the aircraft itself) and software (the computer programs that make everything work together). Finally, testing provides operational users the chance to try out the aircraft and its systems early in the development process, evaluating how well the final product will perform the intended mission.

Modern military aircraft are so incredibly complex that it is impossible to design and build a perfect system the first time. Through rigorous testing, any glitches in the B-2 can be found before they get to the field, where they could prevent SAC from performing its vital mission. By finding and eliminating as many problem areas as possible during the test phases, a good, functional, easily maintained aircraft can be delivered to SAC.

Flight testing and the people who do it have been the victims of misleading stereotypes for years. Overzealous authors and Hollywood directors have depicted flight test as a glamorous, silk-scarf operation living on the edge of danger every day. They show the square-jawed, steely-eyed test pilot showing up just in time for a flight, climbing into the new, unruly aircraft, and blasting off into the wild blue yonder. He fearlessly puts the wild beast through a series of demanding maneuvers, deftly handling the inevitable problems that arise, then lands without so much as squealing a tire. After turning over the all-important data he has collected to awed ground-bound engineers, the test pilot returns to the bar for a well-earned brew.

It's a nice fantasy, but the Hollywood scenario couldn't be farther from the truth. In fact, today's test pilots are highly trained and educated professionals who are an integral part of a larger team of equally capable pros. Most are engineers as well as skilled, experienced pilots. True, flight testing can be risky—there is no such thing as a "routine" test flight—but today's test teams strive to identify potential risks, then do everything they can to minimize them.

Pilots spend most of their time helping the team prepare for tests that will be conducted, both on the ground and in the air. After a flight, they participate in long, often tedious debriefings or discussions about the significance of something observed during a test. They also influence decisions about what should be done about a particular problem, and the need for follow-up tests on subsequent flights.

On the B-2 program, pilots were involved from the start, performing a number of tasks that the stereotype test pilot of Hollywood's big screen would probably never be caught doing.

* * *

BRUCE HINDS: Northrop test pilot:

Back in the early, build-up period, I did a lot of test planning. In fact, I was called the "manager of test planning" in those days. I had about 90 people, mostly flight test engineers, working with me. There were no other pilots working on the program [full time] until 1984, when Leroy Schroeder was brought in as the second pilot.

There was one other pilot [Dick Thomas] accessed to the program [early on], but he was working on another project essentially full time. For about three years, I was the only pilot, so it was pretty busy.

Amazingly, the detailed plans we are working to [in 1990] are essentially the same ones we developed back in the proposal stage . . . same number of hours and same time span [to complete the testing]. There's been a lot of juggling, but we still have the same number of [test] aircraft, and the breakdown of work for each aircraft is essentially unchanged.

That's worked out, I think, because the test planners had a lot of time to massage their work. But, even after all the massaging, they still came up with about the same answers; there was very little changed.

But that seven-year thinking process, the time from start of planning until the first flight, was very valuable. [That time] was [a fallout] of the change in requirements from a high-altitude-only aircraft to a low-altitude mission, too."

* * *

Pilots are trained to fly any test that needs to be done, but, on a large program that uses several aircraft to conduct different evaluations in parallel with each other, a pilot will tend to specialize somewhat. One pilot might evolve into being "a structural loads guy" and another "the avionics pilot."

Both Northrop and Air Force pilots contributed to the aircraft's design and now fly the B-2, which is characteristic of a combined or joint test force these days. In the past, contractor pilots always flew the first tests and military crews essentially only double-checked the contractor's findings. That required separate test phases and needlessly duplicated many tests, stretching out an already lengthy development phase. By jointly testing an aircraft, with contractor and military pilots alternately flying as aircraft commander, a consistent set of data can be acquired much more economically.

EARLY AIR FORCE PILOT INPUTS

The B-2 program is a good example of this joint military/contractor pilot involvement process, even in the early stages. Typical of most modern-day aircraft development efforts, the B-2 program was structured such that operational Air Force pilots were involved in the nitty-gritty of early design decisions.

The first project pilots assigned were experienced operational types sent directly from the Strategic Air Command. They even preceded test pilots from Edwards, which would get deeply involved in the program, but not until later. For the first three years, the SAC pilots had a major impact on a large number of Northrop's design decisions.

For example, some of the SAC officers had F-111 fighter-bomber experience, a factor that greatly influenced decisions leading to the B-2's two-man cockpit configuration. They also were well-acquainted with the rigors of very long combat missions. As a result, their input forced Northrop to concentrate on features that would reduce pilot workload.

Air Force pilot involvement, though, was a two-edged sword. Because military service assignments typically are relatively short, the F-111-dominated group of pilots was replaced about 1½ years later by a new contingent: B-52 guys. The B-52 pilots brought with them a completely different frame of reference than that of their predecessors.

Naturally, it took time to bring the new group up to a certain level of knowledge before they understood Northrop's design goals for the B-2. In the meantime, though, the new group thought the B-2 should have a lot of B-52-like features, essentially tending to undo what the F-111 group had wanted.

As one Edwards-trained pilot later said, "Everybody wants the new airplane to fly like their last one, at least until they get used to the new one. That's just human nature. There's a lot of truth in the saying that 'The best airplane I ever flew is the one I just left.' "

Fortunately for the contractor team, there was enough continuity maintained between overlapping Air Force pilot groups that few features actually had to be changed. But it wasn't easy. A senior contractor official said, "It took about a year to get the new guys to accept that 'this is what we're going to do.' Of course, by then, they were about ready to leave, and we'd get a new crop in and have to start over, educating them. Still, it gave us a good operational point of view early on. That paid off."

MILLIONS OF TESTS

Before the program ends, the total number of tests conducted on the B-2 will number in the millions, counting both flight and ground evaluations. That might seem excessive, but, in fact, these tests are considered the minimum required to perform a total engineering and operational assessment of the aircraft and to correct important deficiencies before the bomber is turned over to SAC.

About 40,000 hours of dedicated ground tests planned for the B-2 fall under a category known as *logistics testing*. Although they are not new to the full-scale development process, logistics tests are receiving more up-front emphasis in the B-2 program than has been the case on earlier aircraft acquisitions. Integrating these with the more-visible flight test program should ensure that the Air Force can maintain the B-2 sooner and at less cost when it enters active service.

Logistics tests were developed by bringing experienced maintenance personnel into the planning process very early in the program. These were people who had paid their dues in the trenches, doing everything from changing engines in subzero weather to trying to get a wrench on an inaccessible bolt or nut while lying under the aircraft in a pool of water after a torrential Southeast Asia rainstorm.

Although there is very little glamour in being covered with grease and smelling of JP-4 jet fuel, the maintenance man or woman is an essential member of any flying unit. Every pilot depends on his maintenance team to provide a safe, functional aircraft for each mission, whether it's a routine training sortie or a life-and-death combat flight. In order to do that, maintenance personnel must have detailed, accurate information about the entire vehicle.

Similarly, if the aircraft is designed, built and tested with the maintenance task in mind from the start, it will be cheaper to operate, taking fewer people and less time to repair and service. In a nutshell, making sure that happens is why logistics testing is vitally important. More will be said about this process later.

4

Security

ONE CHARACTERISTIC CLEARLY SETS THE B-2 PROGRAM APART FROM typical large Air Force weapons acquisitions efforts: The almost total security that surrounded early development phases.

From the program's inception until April, 1988, the Air Force did not publicly acknowledge a new bomber even existed. That approach started at the top. The secretary of the Air Force had designated the Advanced Technology Bomber program as a *Special Access Required* (SAR) effort, which triggered specific ways of handling information and clearing people for that data.

SAR meant that every individual who worked on the ATB or B-2 had to obtain a special security clearance and demonstrate a valid "need to know." Without this clearance, a person was prohibited from working on any classified aspect related to the B-2, or being briefed on what the program was even about.

Although the average American citizen understands the need to safeguard sensitive military information, it is often difficult to comprehend why so much money is spent on keeping a program like the B-2 secret for so long. Some of the reasons given make perfect sense from a national security standpoint and are easy to defend. But other reasons for classifying specific data or actions defy logic and baffle even those charged with not only adhering to them, but also enforcing them.

WHY CLASSIFY?

The primary reason for tight security, of course, is to prevent potential adversaries from determining exactly what is being developed. Denying them even basic knowledge of a weapon system precludes development of countermeasures or other systems that can defeat one's new weapons. That applies not only to complete systems, but also to the technologies involved in creating those systems.

The longer this information can be withheld, the longer that weapon system will remain a viable deterrent and, if it ever came to it, a wartime advantage. Often, strict security forces the adversary to spend critical research funds to understand basic technologies, such as a new material's response to radar energy.

Some defense experts point to the remarkable similarities between many U.S. military aircraft and their Soviet counterparts (the F-15 Eagle and MiG-29 Fulcrum fighters; the B-1 Lancer and Blackjack bombers), raising the question "Who copied whom?" If the U. S. spends billions of dollars developing new designs, why should they be revealed free of charge to a potential adversary? Protecting all aspects of that design, they say, forces the other guy to spend a similar amount.

The Soviets rarely expend any money devising countermeasures until they fully understand what Western forces have developed. And extending the lag time between a weapon's genesis and an adversary's understanding of its technology and design gives friendly forces a critical advantage.

Many defense professionals argue that, even in peacetime, an adversary's uncertainty about a weapon system tends to make him think twice about flexing his military muscles on the world scene. In other words, tight security can be a powerful tool in the psychological arsenal of deterrence.

To the flight crewmember, lag time is extremely important. His survival in a combat situation can depend directly upon an adversary's knowledge or ignorance of allied aircraft and systems. The security campaigns of World War II—"Loose Lips Sink Ships"—are just as valid today as they were 50 years ago. As a result, Air Force and defense contractor personnel take security very seriously.

On the B-2 program, security at times appeared to take top priority over everything else. This, in many ways, actually made life easier for those working at the program management level. In other ways, it complicated day-to-day tasks and one's personal life considerably.

* * *

COL. RICK COUCH:

For those of us working on the B-2 program every day for years, the high level of security caused problems most people can't even imagine. First of all, you couldn't tell anyone outside the program what you were doing. That in itself made every friend and relative, especially wives and husbands, want to know all the juicy details.

Everybody wanted to be taken into your confidence, at least a little bit, so responses to questions became very difficult. You don't want to simply lie to your wife, children, parents, and friends, so what do you do? My tactic was to just act deaf and dumb. For a Texas Aggie, that wasn't too difficult! But [because] I've been acting that way since 1981, I now have a lot of friends and relatives who are convinced I'm an absolute idiot. Other people simply lied about their jobs or just told partial truths.

Travelling to other locations as part of the job was especially difficult. We couldn't tell our spouses where we were going: "I'm going east," or "I'm going to Los Angeles" was about all we could say. This, of course, caused some serious doubts, especially for wives, that were hard to overcome.

We often had to carry classified materials while travelling, which created a whole new set of problems. The security rules also varied, depending on the destination. Carrying classified around Edwards AFB involved different procedures than when driving to Los Angeles or flying on commercial airlines to Dayton, Ohio, where the Systems Program Office was located.

To keep the amount of classified material being hand-carried to a minimum, we relied heavily on a secure facsimile, or fax, machine to shuttle information around. That worked most of the time, but, occasionally, charts and viewgraphs for face-to-face briefings had to be hand-carried. That's when the fun began.

You haven't lived until you've spent the night in a Los Angeles hotel with a double-wrapped package of classified materials in bed with you. On another occasion, while travelling to Washington, D.C., I was grounded in St. Louis by a snow storm that closed all the Washington-area airports. The storm disrupted air traffic on the East Coast so badly that I spent three days in a hotel near the St. Louis airport, trying to get a flight.

I was carrying a briefcase full of classified materials, which meant it never left my side. The thing was so big that it was very inconvenient to carry to and from a restaurant all the time. Consequently, I elected to have the hotel's room service bring most of my meals to the room. After several days of this, I started wondering if I might spend the rest of my life in St. Louis.

Eventually, I took a taxi to Scott AFB, just outside of St. Louis. I had hoped to catch a military flight into Andrews AFB, near Washington, but it, too, was closed by the bad weather. But at least the command post at Scott agreed to lock up my briefcase, giving me some respite from classified courier duties. Finally, after four and one-half days, the weather broke and I arrived in D.C., briefcase securely in hand.

Another strange requirement arising from a strong security orientation prevented us from wearing military uniforms when we visited certain facilities during the early days of the B-2 program. On the surface, that seemed logical . . . it avoided anyone making a connection between the military and contractors working on the program. Actually, though, most military people stand out like a sore thumb, even in civies . . . just ask any Middle Eastern terrorist. It was difficult, at best, to hide the fact that we were Air Force visitors, so the requirement was of dubious value.

The civilian clothes posed a few unique problems for the military people at these off-site locations, too. In uniform, a person's rank insignia lets you know immediately whether you are talking to a lieutenant or a colonel. Take away the blue uniform, though, and there is no sure way to distinguish the two. In a heated meeting, this created a few problems when you weren't sure what to tell the person pontificating on something. Do you say, "Sir, I have to disagree on that point," or would "Mister, you're full of sh– –!" be more appropriate?

Telephone conversations between two program-cleared people were always interesting when unsecured lines were used to conduct business. Of course, if the discussion was to involve classified information, we resorted to special telephones with secure lines.

But if none of the information was actually "classified," yet still possibly considered "sensitive," we normally resorted to cryptic comments and a string of bizarre acronyms designed to communicate a specific idea to the other person, while baffling any "spy" listening in. For example, "Did you know that 181 was testing the RDR and NSS using the RNTP in the FTB at 243 this week?"

It took awhile to learn this obtuse language, but once we did, we could talk some real dirt . . . nothing classified, you understand . . . over the telephone and never worry about who might be listening.

* * *

At the organizational level, the Special Access Required designation created some unusual situations. For example, at Edwards AFB, a contingent of military and civilian government personnel worked on the B-2 program from the early days of source selection. But, until 1988, they could never acknowledge that the bomber was slated for testing at Edwards. This constraint complicated dealings with other agencies on the base, as well as with visitors, and approached the ridiculous, at times.

A full colonel, while giving several visitors a flight line tour, was asked about the huge hangar complex being constructed for the B-2 at South Base. Without looking, he deadpanned, "What buildings?" Although everybody on base, and most regular visitors, knew exactly what they were, nobody in a position of authority could acknowledge the hangars were being built for the B-2.

During this period, before Edwards' role was declassified, several base personnel working in the plans and programs section included a new effort called "The Advanced Technology Bomber" in planning documents that forecast base workload in the late 1980s. When B-2 SPO officials first learned that this item was contained in unclassified planning guides, they panicked, fearing a serious breach of security had occurred.

Of course, what had really happened was a simple case of two-plus-two. The Air Force had already admitted an ATB existed. Without any further information, sharp planners assumed the aircraft would be tested at Edwards, then placed the program in exactly the right spot in their plans. That was only one of a series of incidents where uncleared people stumbled onto the B-2 project and had the often paranoid security officials thinking Communist spies had infiltrated the program.

CONTRACTOR SECURITY

If the Air Force seemed to impose stringent security requirements on the B-2 program, it paled when compared to the procedures and emphasis contractors placed on it. As one employee stated: "The Air Force had specific requirements, but Northrop always tried to go one better. Why? Just to make sure there was plenty of overkill. If we suffered a breach of Northrop security guidelines, there was a good chance it would probably still fall within Air Force rules."

At one time, Northrop reportedly interviewed 10–12 people for every one it hired. The ones not offered jobs might have been qualified, but might have presented some kind of perceived security risk. Or, they might have had something in their background that would take too much time or expense to investigate as part of the security clearance process. Usually, the job seeker turned away never knew exactly why he or she was not hired.

Bruce Hinds, who would be the first man to fly the B-2, initially was not told what job he would perform, then lived under some strange security rules after he was hired. For the first year of employment, the company mandated that Hinds could not tell anyone that he worked for Northrop, even his family. The Air Force didn't care, but Northrop still imposed the restriction. Their logic went something like this: If people knew Hinds worked on a classified program for Northrop, and also knew he was a "big airplane test pilot," they would put the two pieces of information together and "discover" the B-2 program!

The humorous part was that almost everybody in the Antelope Valley—an area that includes Palmdale, Lancaster, and Edwards, AFB, Calif.—who knew Bruce also knew he worked for Northrop on the super-secret advanced technology bomber program. It was simply a natural assumption, partly because he could not talk about his job! Regardless, he could not confirm or deny that fact.

Partly for security reasons, Hinds was paid to move to Los Angeles, putting him close to Northrop's B-2 facilities in the area. He bought a duplex in Whittier, staying there during the week and returning to his own home in Lancaster (approximately 80 miles away), where his family lived, on weekends. He lived this way for six years. Although he would get home during the week for an occasional special function, the lifestyle was still very tough on the Hinds family.

* * *

BRUCE HINDS:
I missed a lot of my kids' growing-up years. I'd leave home and be gone for two weeks, and could never tell the family or anybody else where I was going or how long I'd be gone. It caused a lot of family stress.

Normally, I'd jump on a corporate jet and land off in the boonies somewhere. I went to a lot of the ranges where we were doing RCS [radar cross section] work.

* * *

Hinds estimated that about 10–20 percent of his time was spent on the mechanics of security: checking safes, inventorying classified documents, and changing safe and door locks and combinations at regular intervals. Managers had even more to worry about. They found that much of their time, and budgets, could be absorbed by these and other security matters, such as documenting any potential security violations made by subordinates, writing reports, and a dozen other duties. Every bit of this security-related activity had a price, too. A significant percentage of B-2 program costs, especially in the black days of high classification, went to security.

Examples of security overkill proliferate; every employee has his or her personal anecdote about the onerous or sometimes-ridiculous logic of security. One example of mindless security overkill occurred in the summer of 1990, after the first B-2 had been flying around the Antelope Valley off and on for a year.

When AV-2, the second flight test aircraft, was ready for transfer from the final assembly building at Palmdale, Calif., to the B-2 paint hangar a few dozen yards away, security was part of the move. Regulations dictated that the freshly-built B-2 be covered if it was being moved outside during the day. Employees complied, covering the bomber's top surface with large plastic sheets they called "garbage bags," opened the hangar door and started towing the aircraft to the paint building.

Now, doing anything outdoors in the Antelope Valley requires taking the ever-present wind into consideration. The security regulations failed to do that, so the plastic sheets covering the B-2, naturally, blew off as soon as the aircraft was outside. Security officers went crazy, according to Northrop employees. They started screaming for observers to "get out of here" and demanded that the aircraft be towed back into the assembly building immediately.

Later, after dark, all the lights in the assembly building and on the concrete ramp were doused, and the aircraft was towed over to the paint hangar—without the garbage bag covers.

When asked to explain what the big problem was, a Northrop official could only shake his head and say, "It's just the [security] rules. They say the airplane had to be covered if it moved in the daytime. No, there wasn't really anything revealed because it was unpainted; just the rules, you know?"

As a footnote: During the nocturnal move, a company photographer documented the event as the aircraft was pushed back into the paint hangar. The resulting photo was routinely cleared through corporate and Air Force channels and, in spite of all the security-related excitement, was printed in the August 13, 1990, issue of *Aviation Week & Space Technology*. Within days, more than 150,000 readers around the world had seen the picture.

Whether complying with or enforcing such rules, most people on the B-2 adopted a philosophy that essentially said, "I didn't write the rule book, I just read it and go along with what it says to do." Whether events had passed by the rule book or not, blind adherence, with no room for sensible flexibility, is the way security typically gets handled on highly classified programs.

* * *

COL. RICK COUCH:

Sometimes we could use "security" as a good reason to get someone off our backs. For example, if a bureaucratic transportation officer insisted on knowing why I wanted a large shipment of material moved from Hill AFB, Utah, to Edwards, I had a simple response that implied that he really didn't want to know the real reasons. Loosely translated, it meant, "I can't tell you, but, believe me, it's damned important." Although overstated a bit, this approach usually made a strong impression and got results quickly.

Occasionally, we would run up against a well-meaning person who wanted to play hardball, demanding to be briefed into the program before he would provide some critical support we really needed. Now, that attitude was a bit hard to swallow, but we worked up a technique to take care of it. We would give the untrusting soul a completely unrelated indoctrination, briefing him into absolutely nothing, then ask him for whatever we really needed. It never failed to work.

It should be noted, though, that the Air Force is populated by good soldiers who normally understood that we were working on a classified program. When one of these people questioned one of our requests, we would simply explain that we couldn't give him a straight answer . . . and that was good enough. He just accepted our constraints and did his job without further proof of our legitimacy. I can honestly say that I never saw a single case where this trust was violated, either. There were a few close calls caused by overanxious hard-chargers, but no abuse of the system.

There were times when our own people, those cleared into and working on the B-2 program, tended to talk too much, particularly after a few drinks. This flagrant breach of security could not be tolerated, so it caused more than a few problems.

Generally, we would have our security officer sit down with the offender, who would be reminded that he could be "prosecuted for the willful disclosure of classified defense information." Needless to say, this usually made a rather powerful immediate impression . . . and had a lasting ripple effect through the organization. As a result, there were very few incidents that required this type of strong action.

There was a single case, though, where one of our guys just couldn't keep his mouth shut. The second time he was overheard in the club, bragging about the B-2 and his association with the program, I called him into my office and fired him. That unpleasantry stunned an Air Force professional with 18 years of service, but it also put the whole B-2 Combined Test Force on notice that we could not tolerate such behavior.

About a month later, while talking to a guy who had recently transferred into our organization from a technical school in Illinois, I learned that the firing of that man had been the talk of the school for awhile. Word like that travels fast.

* * *

PHYSICAL SECURITY AT EDWARDS

The Edwards Test Support Facility (TSF), which would be home for all B-2 aircraft during the flight test program, was built from the ground up with security as a high priority. It was located south of the main Edwards AFB complex, well removed from the base's flight line. The entire 120-acre B-2 compound was enclosed with a 12-foot security fence, which incorporated a number of protective devices, and bright lights illuminated the area every night.

The Air Force assumed responsibility for all security outside the fence, using the same security police units that patrol the entire, huge, test base.

Northrop, as the B-2 prime contractor, handled security inside the fence. Base security police and Northrop TSF plant protection guards drew up detailed joint plans that defined who would do what if the test facility was ever attacked.

For a base as remote as Edwards, surrounded by thousands of acres of hostile desert, such precautions might seem to be expensive overkill. However, the B-2 is considered a very important strategic weapon system, and a likely target for any radical or terrorist faction seeking global exposure. There were plenty of crazies out there who might try to blow up a bomber, just for the international notoriety.

A security complication the test force faced right away was the recurring need to bring certain people into the B-2 compound. These included furniture movers/installers and maintenance men who did not require a project briefing, yet were routinely in close proximity to those working with classified material.

Standard procedures appeared straightforward: anytime an uncleared person was in the area, all classified materials were to be put away and discussions terminated. But if an uncleared person was in the area over a long period, there was a tendency for people to forget the visitor was not privy to project specifics. Cleared workers would start discussing sensitive subjects and classified documents would eventually be pulled out of the safes. Keeping cleared personnel cognizant of an uncleared person's presence prompted an unusual solution.

* * *

COL. RICK COUCH:

To keep our folks aware that an uncleared person was in the area, we gave the visitor small red lights that resembled a coal miner's lamp, but which flashed continuously and made a God-awful pinging noise. A person could get a real complex walking around all day with that flashing, pinging light, and having everyone stop talking as the visitor passed by. It was a bit humbling, but it worked.

* * *

At Palmdale, similar but even more humbling procedures often defied logic. In May, 1990, the Air Force and Northrop made the ultimate security concession when they allowed invited reporters inside the B-2 factory. After a lengthy briefing covering all aspects of the bomber program, reporters were taken in small groups to a crow's nest, or balcony-like, overlook built into the east wall of the main final assembly area. From this position, roughly 20 feet above the floor, a person could see several of the big bombers in various stages of construction. The point to be made, though, is that virtually the entire manufacturing area was visible, including areas enclosed by 10- to 15-foot-high blue plastic fences that partitioned several zones from the main floor space.

Less than a week later, after showing the entire factory floor to about 50 or more reporters, an unsuspecting Northrop supplier ran smack into the illogic of mandated security rules. A vendor's technician had been brought in to the Palmdale Site 4 factory to work on the coating of an aircraft windshield. Typically, vendors' representatives are not cleared for the B-2 program, so special procedures apply.

These methods were developed early in the program to handle the periodic requirement to bring in a person, usually for only a brief time, to perform some specialized task. These experts usually worked inside the blue-fenced areas somewhere on the factory floor. The blue bullpens prevented uncleared experts from seeing the rest of the facility, especially the big aircraft being built a few feet away.

So, put yourself in this man's position: He has just driven maybe 70 miles from Los Angeles to Palmdale, has found his way to the Site 4 security gate and into the main building. Theoretically (according to security logic), he has no idea what is being built inside the massive multistory complex, even though aircraft pictures are posted here and there, and newsletters lying around refer to the Northrop B-2 Division.

His security escort arrives and takes him to Building 401, the manufacturing area. There, he is asked to put a paper sack over his head, effectively blindfolding him. He then is led by the hand for about 30 feet across the forbidden factory floor to the blue-fenced zone where he will work on the problematic windshield. Supposedly, the specialist doesn't even know for which aircraft the window is made!

And all this after any number of noncleared people had viewed the entire factory floor from the balcony: dignitaries, congressmen, and even the nation's press. Again, the only reason given to humbled vendors is "those are the rules," whether they make any sense or not.

THOSE EXASPERATING BADGES

The B-2 program, like many other classified efforts, used plastic security badges to identify people cleared for access to most project facilities. Unfortunately, every area used a different badge and code for access. For example, at the Edwards test facility, every cleared person was issued a badge having his or her picture and a four-digit code imprinted on it. When entering the secured buildings, one ran his badge through a reader and punched the four-digit code into a special keypad to open the door. The wrong badge/number combination would not unlock the door, preventing unauthorized entry.

A different badge was used for access to Northrop's Pico Rivera plant, and a third badge was required for the SPO offices at Wright-Patterson AFB, Ohio. Naturally, every subcontractor plant had its own badge and access procedures.

* * *

COL. RICK COUCH:
Keeping all the badges and codes straight was taxing for some of us mental midgets that travelled between these sites a lot, especially when the differences were subtle. For example, the same badge and number

code was used at Northrop's Site 4 production plant in Palmdale, Calif., as at its Pico Rivera facility, but with a slight twist. The badge reader at one plant required running your badge through face-left while the other demanded face-right.

All these badge/number variances drove me crazy. One day, I had an early-morning simulator session scheduled at Pico Rivera. Standing in front of the door, I realized I couldn't remember the right numbers. After a few false tries, the guard checked his list, found I was authorized, and let me into the plant. But to get into each of the compartmented work areas, like the simulator, I had to use that badge and string of numbers. I tried every combination of face-left, face-right, and number schemes I could think of, but nothing worked. I finally had to tag along with someone else, just to get into the right area so I could go to work.

Later, back at Edwards, I fished out my list of numbers and found that I was one digit off. Frustrating moments like that were not uncommon, just an accepted spinoff of high security.

* * *

Physical safeguards such as fences, 24-hour patrols and personnel badges constitute many of the more visible methods used to protect B-2 program materials, manufacturing techniques, and electronically transmitted information. But they still are not the complete security story.

Considerable effort also has gone into implementing recurring checks that become routine for people working on a program like the B-2. Every cleared person is exposed to intense, repetitive security indoctrination through classes, memos, and signs throughout the workplace. Briefcases and lunchboxes are subject to daily inspections. Work areas are checked and double-checked to make sure nothing classified is left unguarded. Common trash is segregated into unclassified and classified, then disposed of accordingly. Even typewriter and computer printer ribbons are protected.

THE HUMAN ELEMENT

Each person working on the program must have a security clearance. Whether it is Secret, Top Secret or SAR depends on his or her need for access to certain levels of sensitive information. Requirements for obtaining these clearances vary somewhat between contractors and the government, but typically involve a thorough scrutiny of a person's past history. Background investigations probe a person's financial status, his employment record, past residences, and lifestyle. Neighbors, relatives, friends, and creditors are questioned to ensure the potential employee is reliable and trustworthy.

Over the years, the U.S. government has developed profiles of people who might be considered a high security risk. For example, having lived in a Communist-controlled country, or having foreign relatives in certain areas of the world are reasons enough to have a clearance denied. A past history of drug

Artist's rendition released by the Air Force in April, 1988, was the first confirmation that the B-2 bomber was a flying wing.

Climbout on the second flight of the B-2 bomber shows the landing gear in the down and locked position minutes before it was retracted for the first time.

Got it made . . . everything is looking good and the long runway of Rogers Dry Lake is directly below. The B-2 CTF's new test support facility buildings are faintly visible just under the right main gear door.

The tanker refueling probe attaches well aft of the B-2's cockpit. Although wingspans are not significantly different, side profiles of the two aircraft dramatize how their sizes vary greatly.

The B-2 slowly closes on a KC-10 tanker during initial aerial refueling tests. This angle dramatizes two points of interest: the relative sizes of the two aircraft, as well as the B-2's radical design, which was dictated by mission requirements and made feasible by modern technology.

The B-2's minimal frontal area is apparent when viewed head-on. With few visible surfaces to reflect radar energy back to a source, this aspect illustrates the difficulty of detecting an attacking bomber.

USAF

The first of a breed, B-2 No. 1 skims over a cloud deck in the southern California desert. Despite serene skies and smooth progress through early phases of flight test, the stealth bomber program will face turbulent times in Congress for years.

Northrop

First public showing of the No. 1 B-2 was on November 22, 1988, at a closely controlled rollout ceremony in Palmdale, Calif. The sinister-looking gray aircraft marked a radical departure from previous manned strategic bombers.

B-2 test pilots say the bomber handles more like a fighter than a huge bomber. It has snappy roll rate and is capable of tight turns.

Top view reveals that B-2 No. 1 had not been coated with production radar-absorbent materials. Later, these were added, and surfaces smoothed prior to low observables testing. Different shades also highlight sections built by the three primary structures manufacturers. Note yarn tufts covering control surfaces on each side of the lower 90-degree break in the trailing edge. These tufts help engineers understand airflow patterns in that area.

Tail-on view shows the B-2's small engine exhaust ports, drooped trailing edge control surfaces and a triangular auxiliary power unit air inlet door outboard of the left engine nacelle. An orange trailing static cone, stowed on the spindly support framework near the center tail section, is extended in flight to provide an undisturbed source of static air pressure. The cone is unique to flight test aircraft. Note the slightly deflected beavertail, or Gust Load Alleviation System (GLAS), center tail surface.

B-2 No. 1 rolls out on the main Edwards runway, welcomed to its new home by Air Force tower controllers.

The bomber accelerates during initial taxi tests at Palmdale. Trailing edge surfaces have started to retract, indicating the aircraft is exceeding 65 knots.

Low-speed taxi tests completed, the B-2 taxis back to its Palmdale Site 4 hangar. Note how the outboard trailing edge surfaces open when a right turn is commanded by cockpit rudder pedal displacement. Auxiliary air doors on the aircraft's right engine nacelles are closed, indicating those engines have been shut down.

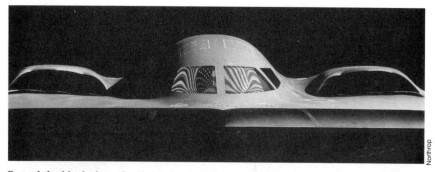

Out of the black; into the light. Sunlight struck the B-2 for the first time when it was unveiled at the 22 November 1988 rollout. Before that, the aircraft had been moved between hangars only at night.

use, a criminal record of anything more serious than a few traffic violations, and a reputation for fast living can prevent the issuance of a clearance.

Contractors occasionally had difficulty hiring people needed for the program, simply because many of those interviewed could not pass strict security criteria. Many excellent applicants were turned down for seemingly innocuous reasons. One lady had been born in Communist China, but was smuggled out with her family when she was three years old. Although she had lived most of her life in the U.S., had no living relatives in China, and was as American as they come, her birth origin was enough to prevent her from even being considered for employment on the B-2 program.

Ironically, there is no evidence that the government profiles of high-risk people or tight screening have ever unearthed a professional spy. Perhaps these procedures discourage any would-be turncoats from even applying for a clearance. More importantly, though, the security clearance process tends to weed out people who might be susceptible to bribes, blackmail, or other forms of pressure after they had been given access to classified data.

Even with these tight security measures, the B-2 program is still subject to the threat of human intelligence, or *humint*. The infamous Cavanagh case involved a Northrop engineer who tried to give the Soviets details about the B-2. Instead, he actually provided information to an FBI agent and wound up going to jail.

* * *

COL. RICK COUCH:

Humint is still the most valued intelligence any potential adversary can get, and is the hardest to protect ourselves against. To discourage information leaks, people on the B-2 program were taught to look for certain activities or characteristics that a spy might exhibit. At Edwards, we had several conscientious people come forward to report what they thought was suspicious behavior exhibited by other employees. We treated each incident very seriously, but it always turned out to be something innocuous.

Particularly troublesome aspects of security that plagued the B-2 program were the rules governing age and experience. All program-cleared individuals had to be at least 25 years old, be above the rank of lieutenant or sergeant, and have at least three years of government service.

This rule was initially imposed for two reasons: First, all classified Air Force programs were intentionally manned at levels below those of normal unclassified efforts, simply to minimize the number of people exposed to sensitive information. Consequently, new, untrained people without the necessary skills or experience could not be given access to these programs. Second, we wanted to force a level of maturity onto all aspects of the B-2 program.

The downside of this policy, however, was that we restricted our recruiting to a rather limited pool of available engineers and maintenance technicians. As a result, we always had trouble filling the manpower slots that had been allocated. Our military and civilian rank structure also was skewed . . . we had too many qualified people vying for too few high-ranking jobs.

* * *

A danger inherent to any large classified program in this country is that minor embarrassments or gross mismanagement can be hidden from the American Congress and taxpaying public. Covering up mistakes or excesses by classifying a program is not an accepted practice in open societies, and is not tolerated.

Although the B-2 program has been accused of hiding its dirty laundry behind the veil of classification, this view is not backed by available evidence. Officials acknowledge that almost total secrecy in the early stages of the program certainly helped those involved to focus their energies and expedite the project. However, that was never the reason for classifying this particular program so tightly.

* * *

BRUCE HINDS:

Tight security helped us control the application of our technical expertise, and control costs, for about six to eight years. [Groups] were small and could stay focused on technical problems without much outside influence.

Since '87, we've had a gradual release of information as the program has opened up some. Now [1990], we have the worst of both worlds: all the "white" world requirements to meet [reporting and oversight], but all the "black" world security requirements to deal with. It makes it pretty tough to operate for all concerned.

* * *

SECURITY AND THE NEWS MEDIA

The U.S. press corps constitutes one of the primary checks and balances against corruption and misuse of public funds in an open society. The B-2 program, despite its clear need for security protection through classification, was considered a prime target for probing reporters. The program attracted considerable interest for a number of reasons: it was a large effort, which implied a substantial commitment of public funds; it was a sophisticated weapon system that could affect the international nuclear balance; it employed the mysterious stealth technologies; and, its very secrecy was simply intriguing to many people. Public interest in the B-2, therefore, ran high.

Rumors abounded that the aircraft was a large flying wing design, yet practically invisible to radar. It supposedly used exotic materials and shapes, and had special engines that produced very little noise, heat signatures, or contrails. Reporters pounced on these tidbits of information about the aircraft, its cost, and the people who worked on the program.

Because rumors often were impossible to verify, responsible publications were relegated to building files of seemingly unrelated scraps of information until a pattern could be identified. Reporters resorted to unorthodox means of gleaning data, even to the point of stationing themselves outside the Palmdale Regional Airport perimeter at 2 a.m., hoping to glimpse the big aircraft as it was towed from one hangar to another. More than a few hours were consumed by these reporters, trying to decide where one crossed the fine line that separated the public's right to know from an act of out-and-out espionage.

Others printed anything they could find about the B-2, whether it was right or not. After all, if officials that knew the truth could neither confirm nor deny any story on television or in a newspaper, who could challenge it?

Periodically, the Air Force would release a few bits of data about the aircraft, and eventually designated it as the B-2 bomber. Finally, in April 1988, the service released a drawing of the aircraft, giving specific shape to all the rumors and speculation.

Along the way, however, the aircraft had been inadvertently branded with a high price tag, possibly through a shortsighted twist of the Air Force's effort to restrict information about the program. The total number of aircraft, 132, that was to be procured, and the total program cost, roughly $70 billion, had been released as separate pieces of data. Any reporter or congressional staffer with a calculator concluded that each aircraft would cost $530 million, a cool half- billion dollars.

Despite the Air Force's best efforts to publicize actual fly-away costs of the aircraft (more like $280 million at that time, which was in the same ballpark as the B-1 bomber's cost), that astronomical half-billion-per-aircraft figure has stuck like a burr—and continued to grow as the total number of bombers is decreased through administration and congressional budget cuts.

Astronomical costs and other myths about the aircraft were starting to plague the B-2 program, causing government officials and the American public to demand more information. Data were slow in coming, but Air Force leaders reluctantly started releasing selected information, knowing that the lack of specifics about the program posed an urgent threat to its political survival. Restricting knowledge about the aircraft might counter the long-term threat from a military adversary, but congressional critics could kill the program before the Soviets ever had to worry about a B-2.

From a more practical standpoint, it was clear that the B-2 would definitely become more visible when it started flying. It was economically infeasible to build the aircraft at a remote location, and moving it from Palmdale to Edwards or a secret test site was best done by flying it.

Earlier, some officials had suggested that the aircraft only be flight tested at night. That was possible, but was risky. The concept ran counter to good safety principles for testing, and would slow the program down considerably. It seemed more realistic to acknowledge that people were going to see the bomber sooner or later. Trying to keep it a complete secret would be atrociously expensive over the long term, and would probably be unsuccessful.

For whatever reason, the B-2 program was slowly brought out of the dark and into public view. That transition was both humorous and anxiety-provoking for those working on the program.

* * *

COL. RICK COUCH:

An interesting aspect associated with the B-2 coming out of the closet was watching how some people, especially the media, jumped at any and all information about the B-2. To us, it seemed like they thought we were finally bringing them into the family, making them part of the fairly small group that had been working on the program for years. For insiders, it was almost laughable, watching everybody clamor for what seemed to us like innocuous information.

The press liked to tout that the program was "coming out of the black world!" That was confusing to us, who never considered the B-2 as really "black." That term conjured up images of mysterious, covert doings in the shady world of a central intelligence agent. If the B-2 was really "covert" in that sense, the press would never know anything about the program. We did not meet that criteria for "covert"; therefore, the B-2 was never "black," just classified.

Our security guidance had to be modified as the Air Force released more information about the aircraft and program. Before April, 1988, we simply never confirmed or denied any of the speculation that had been going on for years. But once the Air Force said there really was a B-2, it was hard to know how to answer questions about the program.

Also, our people were proud of being associated with the B-2, and there was no way to stifle that. They were part of a handpicked elite, and they hadn't been able to enjoy that position. But it wasn't easy adjusting from being totally classified to only partially classified. After working so long and hard to protect every secret, no one was willing to say too much, fearing that the wrong thing would be said. At the same time, it was tough to find the right level of openness . . . a little like having one foot in hot water and the other in ice water, then trying to decide whether you were hot or cold.

* * *

5

Critical design review

THE ADVANCED TECHNOLOGY BOMBER PROGRAM was accelerating on several different fronts after the contract was awarded to Northrop. At Edwards AFB, about 100 miles northeast of the Los Angeles International Airport, the test team set up shop in a well-used building at North Base. Isolated from the main base, in a separate area at the north end of Rogers Dry Lake, North Base had its own runway and aircraft support complex. It had traditionally been home to classified programs, but was only temporary quarters for the ATB/B-2 team until their own new complex could be built.

Col. Rick Couch's office was located in a large classified vault that had been used years earlier during top-secret U-2 testing and, later, by the Air Force's Office of Special Investigations—for what purpose, nobody seemed to know. This office, and a desk inside it, should have alerted Couch to what lay ahead for him as commander of the B-2 Combined Test Force (CTF).

* * *

COL. RICK COUCH:

On my first day of work after reporting to Edwards, I was shown to that office in the vault. The desk left a lot to be desired . . . it listed toward one side, reminding me of the Titanic going down. Everything I put on the desk slid into my lap.

I pulled a quick inspection on the desk's legs and found the problem . . . someone had interchanged the front and back legs. Muttering a few things to myself, I went to work on them, and just about had everything sorted out when one of our enlisted supply guys sauntered in. He casually asked how I liked my new desk.

Finally, it sunk in . . . I'd been had on my first day as The Old Man. It was easy to see, then, what kind of problem kids made up this organization. Like any other Air Force outfit, this one would work hard and play hard . . . and nobody, regardless of rank, was exempt from the odd practical joke.

* * *

One of the immediate priorities for test team managers was attending the first ATB orientation class. Conducted by Northrop at its Pico Rivera facility in the Los Angeles basin, the class provided an overview of the bomber and its systems. As an initial effort, the presentation was excellent, providing a good introduction for those who would someday fly the complex beast. For the Edwards team, it was particularly motivating.

Armed with hard-core knowledge of the aircraft, the test experts could then launch into their primary tasks: Building an efficient test force, acquiring the technical equipment that would be used to support the aircraft at Edwards, and planning everything needed to flight test six of the bombers.

Even though the first B-2 would not fly for several years, the Combined Test Force at Edwards immediately started drawing up detailed plans, determining how it would be involved in each step of development and operational testing. These plans would be reviewed at the program's *Critical Design Review* (CDR) in late 1985, ensuring that everything needed for flight and ground testing would be in place when the first B-2 landed at Edwards.

The new bomber was not unlike many other large, complex aircraft that had been tested at the desert base, such as the C-5 Galaxy airlifter and the B-1B bomber. Consequently, the basic program would consist of classical performance, flying qualities, and avionics testing, using techniques that were well established at Edwards. In addition, there would be a series of specialized low observables (LO) evaluations to confirm the aircraft was as stealthy as it was supposed to be. If it wasn't, the aircraft's effectiveness as a penetrating strategic bomber would be severely limited.

TEST BIRDS

Each of the six aircraft that would fly as part of the flight test program would be devoted to specific, primary tasks. Each one also would serve as a backup or augmenter to one or more of the other test aircraft.

This early designation of roles was important for a number of reasons. Several of the first B-2s would be delivered to Edwards with certain capabilities and instrumentation tailored to their particular test role. For example, the performance test aircraft would not need a full complement of avionics, but would be heavily instrumented to accurately measure airspeed, altitude, fuel flow, engine parameters, etc.

The first flying B-2 would be essentially a hand-built aircraft, instrumented for basic airworthiness demonstrations—proving the bomber would fly right. Just as the early planning called for, almost a decade ago, Air Vehicle No. 1 (AV-1), as the first B-2 is called, is being used for flight envelope expansions, aircraft systems development, and initial low observables testing.

In simple terms, this aircraft has steadily increased speed and altitude on a series of flights, verifying that the B-2 could fly as fast, as slow, as high, and as low as it was designed to. This build-up technique is typical of today's flight testing process; basic facets of the aircraft are tested separately before moving on to more complex, integrated aspects.

In each step, carefully thought-out tests are performed in a precise, controlled manner, and the resulting data are reviewed thoroughly before moving on to the next, more aggressive step. The process is very methodical and scientific, involving pilots, engineers, managers, and maintenance experts working as a team. It might not be as exciting as the stereotyped flight testing that Hollywood persists in depicting, but it's safer and more productive. Today's flight test is truly a team process, designed to minimize the risk of an accident.

Aircraft No. 2 was designated the "loads" airplane. It would fly test profiles designed to stress the airframe and accurately determine how it would respond to turbulence and maneuvering loads encountered in combat. While ground tests would "bend" other B-2s (ones that would never fly) to make sure nothing would break when subjected to flight loads, actual airborne tests would verify the aircraft's structural integrity. In addition, aircraft No. 2 served as a backup for No. 1 and vice versa. If one of these B-2s was lost in an accident, the other would pick up its test workload.

Today's sophisticated military airplanes are practically flying black boxes, filled with exotic electronics gear that do everything from keeping the vehicle flying with the sharp end forward (*fly-by-wire* flight controls) to determining precisely where a weapon will hit the ground (*fire control system*). Lumped together, these aviation electronics are called *avionics* and typically constitute about half, or more, of an aircraft's total cost. Integrating, certifying, and testing these very complex, computerized systems is a massive task.

Consequently, two B-2s were dedicated to avionics testing. As the primary avionics test aircraft, No. 3 would be the first B-2 equipped with a full set of offensive avionics and mission equipment. It would perform the initial avionics development and integration testing, sharing the workload with aircraft No. 4.

Weapons delivery and certification testing also would be done on aircraft No. 3, 4, and 5. This type of testing, just as the others, requires an incremental, very methodical process. First, it must be proven that a bomb can be dropped from a weapons bay without hitting the aircraft or tumbling or performing some other wild gyration. Once weapon separation effects are known, then comes the real test, seeing whether that weapon will hit a target accurately.

Testing experience has shown that strange flow field effects, acoustics in an open bomb bay, and a thousand other unknowns can determine whether weapons tests are easy or very difficult. In the past, bombs on some aircraft have dropped cleanly from their supports, only to tip nose-up, do a back-flip, and rip a huge hole in the airplane's wing, underbelly, or tail surface. As a result, good planners will schedule weapons work as early as possible, hoping that any problems uncovered can be solved during the test program.

Aircraft No. 5 was designated the climatic test bird, meaning that it would spend very little time at Edwards AFB. No. 5 was to be flown to Eglin AFB, Fla., where it would spend months in the Air Force's Climatic Laboratory. There, the bomber would be subjected to hundreds of hours of blistering heat, freezing cold and driving rain, simulating every imaginable climate the aircraft could possibly experience in its lifetime.

As if that wasn't enough torture, the aircraft would then deploy with a test and support team to desert, tropical, and arctic locations. Each of these one-month deployments would again evaluate how the B-2 would operate in actual service.

Long ago, the Air Force proved that these climatic tests were invaluable, uncovering deficiencies that could cripple the entire bomber fleet if not fixed. Tests on B-2 No. 5 would prove that the aircraft's four engines would, indeed, start and run normally when it is −40°F. And that the environmental control system (ECS) would keep both pilots and the precious avionics gear cool and working correctly in the 130°F heat and blowing sand of the Sahara Desert.

Finally, No. 5 would be subjected to all-weather testing, including icing trials. Flown behind a modified air refueling tanker, the B-2 would be doused with a spray of water and air, the mixture controlled on the tanker end. This spray will collect and freeze on the bomber if the tests are conducted at an altitude where temperatures drop below freezing. Yellow dye in the water will highlight where ice builds up on the B-2's airframe, providing invaluable information when photographed from another aircraft immediately after the ice is formed.

If everything looks good, the bomber will be flown in heavy, wet storm clouds where snow and icing conditions are known to exist, making sure the aircraft will perform as advertised before it is ever flown into bad weather by an operational SAC pilot in the field.

Aircraft No. 6 was tagged to be the catch-up airplane, primarily for logistics testing. Although the other five B-2s in the program would be used for logistics or maintenance evaluations, No. 6 would ensure an aircraft was available specifically for this important function.

In addition, at least one B-2 was to be flown to Kirtland AFB, New Mexico, for *electromagnetic pulse* (EMP) testing. The bomber would be placed on a huge wooden platform, dubbed *The Trestle* because it resembles an old railroad bridge, and blasted with very high energy pulses. This simulates electromagnetic conditions that an aircraft would experience when exposed to a nuclear detonation, even many miles away. The resulting electromagnetic pulse contains tremendous energy that can burn out an aircraft's avionics unless they are shielded properly.

After the flight test program was underway, however, the plans for aircraft No. 5 and 6 were modified somewhat. Now, in addition to their original activities, they will pick up other tasks, because they are the first test vehicles scheduled to incorporate a host of engineering changes that have been approved, but could not be installed in earlier B-2s. Also, the entire six-aircraft test fleet has a retrofit schedule, a shift from the original planning.

Together, the six B-2s would fly approximately 3,600 hours at rates up to 40 hours per month in conducting the flight test program. Most of the hours would be flown by the last few aircraft that join the test fleet because the planned flight rate increases as each succeeding vehicle arrives at Edwards.

LOGISTICS TESTING—A NEW EMPHASIS

But flying was only part of the test program. All six bombers would participate in ground-based logistics testing, which would involve almost 10,000 separate tests and require more than 40,000 hours of dedicated aircraft time. Most of this work would involve validating and verifying more than 1,200 volumes of technical manuals that covered every conceivable maintenance action.

These manuals tell a technician everything from how to wash a B-2 to the details of changing an engine or removing a black box. That might seem like a lot of detail, but this information is a maintenance technician's bible, and is essential for taking care of an aircraft in the field.

Logistics testing also covers all support equipment used to work on the aircraft; confirms the viability of maintenance concepts; and quantifies several "-ilities:" reliability, maintainability, and supportability. When all logistics testing is done, B-2 program managers can be confident that SAC maintenance crews will be able to keep their new bomber fleet flying.

This aspect of a new aircraft's development has traditionally been relegated to a lesser importance during the flight test program, overshadowed by what was considered to be more pressing requirements, usually translated as *flying*. Flight hours typically were the management yardstick used to measure test program progress, so flying took precedence over the more mundane ground or logistics testing.

However, the Air Force repeatedly learned a painful lesson on each new aircraft program: When they reached the field, new bombers, fighters, tankers, and cargo aircraft couldn't start flying missions, even though they were considered operational. Why? Because maintenance crews were not trained, and they had no tech data, maintenance manuals, diagrams, and procedures, to tell them how to prepare an aircraft for flight. Typically, frustrated supervisors were caught between a commander demanding that his aircraft fly and a maintenance team that was essentially incapable of caring for the new birds sitting on the ramp.

Program managers were determined that this horrific scenario would not be repeated on the stealth bomber. Rather than defer logistics tests to the end of the flight test program, as had been done on other aircraft development efforts, they would be integrated throughout the B-2's flight testing. This would extend the flight program somewhat, but would ensure that necessary support would be in place when the B-2 reached operational SAC units.

THE PACE ACCELERATES

Planning for flight and logistics testing was hardly the only work being done at Edwards during the early days of the B-2 program. In fact, it often seemed like hundreds of things had to be done at the same time. Most were considered essential, and all had to be done before the CDR. As the pace grew more hectic, so did the strain on interpersonal relations.

* * *

COL. RICK COUCH:

My first secretary at Edwards was a very sweet person who rarely got excited. However, after working around me a couple of months as we frantically prepared for CDR, I think she started praying for my soul's salvation. For one reason or another, every now and then she would get mad enough to give me the silent treatment for a few days. About the second time this happened, I called her into my office and shut the door. I had her sit down, then told her I was going to show her how to deal with some of the stressful things we were encountering at that time. I placed a government-issue office-sized trash can [wastebasket] in the center of the floor and told her to watch carefully.

"When you're really mad, this is how you get over it," I explained. "You sit a trash can right here, then drop-kick that sucker across the room! I guarantee that'll relieve all your frustrations."

She seemed a bit shocked, but was starting to get used to being shocked around that place. She adapted, though, even if a bit more literally than I had anticipated.

About two weeks later, I looked up from my desk to see that sweet secretary—a bit tight-lipped, though—walk into my office and set a trash can in the middle of the room. Without a word, she "kicked that sucker across the room." I guess she was mad about something.

Her aim needed some work, though, because the wastebasket flew across the room and hit my deputy, who shared the office with me at that time. Until the day she left, every time that secretary brought a trash can into the office, we ducked for cover.

* * *

CHASE AIRCRAFT

Determining which aircraft should be used to chase the B-2 during flight testing was another of the major support issues to be worked by the Combined Test Force. A number of these aircraft would be needed to provide safety checks and photos of in-flight tests, flying in loose formation with the B-2.

The selected chase aircraft, ideally, would be able to fly for long periods without refueling to minimize the amount of tanker support required. In-flight refueling has become an excellent way to extend in-the-air test time, and is used routinely on major programs today to accelerate certain types of tests that consume fuel rapidly. However, tankers are an expensive and scarce asset that is used judiciously.

Another chase requirement was an ability to fly at speeds below 0.7 Mach above 35,000 feet. For most high-performance aircraft, that's too slow for comfortable flight at such high altitudes.

After assessing a variety of airplanes in the Air Force inventory, the test team decided the F-15 Eagle, the current front line air-to-air fighter, was best suited for B-2 chase work. The F-16 Fighting Falcon was a close second choice. Although there were plenty of F-4 Phantoms available, the venerable old workhorses were not well-suited for slow flight at high altitude, especially when carrying the three external fuel tanks they would need for prolonged B-2 test missions.

The Edwards B-2 unit prepared a briefing for higher headquarters, outlining how B-2 safety/photo chase operations would be set up. Rather than use a dedicated fleet of chase aircraft, the CTF would share the fighters with other Edwards-based units; they would be part of the base's support fleet. Flight crews assigned to fly the B-2 also would serve as chase pilots.

These issues were briefed to Edwards commanders, then up through the long Air Force chain of command. The flight test team originally requested approval for six F-15Ds. As the preferred aircraft, the two-seat D-model met all B-2 chase requirements.

Things went smoothly up through Air Force Systems Command, and feedback from the Tactical Air Command (TAC) indicated the request was going well there. The B-2 briefing team's final stop was Headquarters TAC, which had ultimate control of the Air Force's fleet of fighter-type aircraft. Prior to briefing the TAC commander, though, the B-2 team was told that F-15s were out of the question. They were already committed to higher-priority service.

* * *

COL. RICK COUCH:

We were told by TAC staffers that, if we were really serious about the need for chase aircraft, we should ask for F-16s. It was felt that several of the smaller fighters were available, whereas F-15s were not.

When we talked to the TAC commander in chief (CINCTAC), things took a turn for the worse. He practically threw us out of his office, explaining in no uncertain terms that Systems Command already had the equivalent of a wing of his fighters on its ramps, and he would be damned if he would give us any more. If we could explain what we (Systems Command) were doing with all the fighters we already had, we were welcome to come back and he would listen again.

It was back to the drawing board. It took us about a month to gather all the data about specific tests being conducted at Edwards and Eglin AFBs on every F-15 and F-16 under Systems Command's control. We retraced the briefing trail, and were accompanied this time to TAC headquarters by the B-2 program director.

For two days, we talked to every general officer and staff member that we thought might be of assistance. The most difficult task was convincing staffers that a critical requirement for B-2 chase aircraft was their ability to fly high and slow, and that the F-4 couldn't do that, especially with the three external fuel tanks it would need to stay with us.

Our meeting with the TAC commander went significantly better this time. We were prepared to make all sorts of promises about what we would do with and to the aircraft, but that proved unnecessary. CINCTAC patiently sat through our briefing, asked no questions, then said he would give us four F-16s to do with as we liked. If we needed more, come on back. The chase aircraft issue was resolved. We would fly F-16s.

* * *

CRITICAL DESIGN REVIEW

The CDR began in late October, 1985. Activities at Northrop, its subcontractors, the Systems Program Office, and the test force had been focused on this event for months. CDR was a critical program milestone, and was a major undertaking in and of itself.

The review was set up to assess all engineering and development plans that had any bearing on the bomber. Northrop's main task was to present evidence proving the contractor team was ready to start building the first aircraft. The companies were to demonstrate to Air Force satisfaction that all critical engineering for the bomber was completed, and that any areas of concern related to manufacturing had been addressed.

CDR was run a bit differently than an earlier, similar assessment milestone, the preliminary design review, or PDR. Following traditional precedents, North-rop and its contractor team had made a series of presentations to the reviewers, which also served to educate the Air Force team about program details. For CDR, they decided to depart from this format.

* * *

BRUCE HINDS:

We told the Air Force, "We expect you guys to do your own homework before you get here." When their teams arrived, we handed them all the paperwork and said, "Take a look at it and make your comments." It was intended to force government people on the program to get up to speed on their areas [of responsibility].

Looking back, though, I feel the real result was that our approach generated more questions and requests for actions [which were] formal questions that required formal responses. In some areas, it may have cut down on workload, but increased our work in other areas.

It worked best with those people who had been on board [working on the ATB/B-2 program] since before PDR, but there weren't too many of those.

Of course, CDR was much bigger than PDR, too. CDR involved hundreds of people; we filled auditoriums at CDR. PDR was [conducted as] mostly large group presentations. There were very few big meetings at CDR. Most of the time, everybody was broken off into working groups.

* * *

The Air Force flight test team reviewed all flight-critical areas of the design. Considerable attention was given to the fly-by-wire flight control system, propulsion system (engines and their installation), flight test instrumentation system, and any other areas that could have an impact on test activities. Northrop was commended for the way its people addressed the myriad Air Force concerns.

Northrop hosted the CDR at its Pico Rivera plant, which is about a 30 minute drive east of downtown Los Angeles. Most of the detailed CDR work was done in an area of the plant that immediately was dubbed "SPO West." Hundreds of documents were assembled there for the comprehensive review. These addressed everything from how Northrop intended to keep track of its engineering changes, especially with a subcontractor network scattered across the United States, to how the test program would be conducted.

* * *

COL. RICK COUCH:

More than 40 people from Edwards participated in CDR activities. We lived five weeks in the Los Angeles area, staying in a number of motels near Buena Park. Because the security folks dictated nobody would stay near Pico Rivera, which might tip off somebody that a major event was happening there, we were doomed to drive about 30 miles to and from Pico over some of the most congested freeways in Los Angeles. To this day, I marvel at the resiliency of LA commuters who do that every day of their working lives. After five weeks of it, I was ready to commit suicide.

We were working long hours during CDR, so there generally was no energy left for partying or hitting the bars after work. Again, the stereotypical image of hard-working, hard-partying "flight testers" was not borne out by fact. About the most exciting thing some of us did was get up early and run every morning.

One of the pilots' primary activities during CDR was conducting an evaluation of ATB performance and flying qualities, using Northrop's engineering development simulator. This was not the full-featured, motion-base simulator that would be used later to train pilots. It was an engineering tool used to work out bugs in the system by focusing on the essentials.

The airplane's flight control laws were still being developed, but the SPO felt they were far enough along for us to do a first-cut evaluation. We looked at basic flying qualities throughout the ATB's planned flight envelope, and assessed the cockpit avionics displays that were being planned. This gave us an opportunity to provide feedback about things we did and didn't like.

Even though we found some minor problems in the flight control system, we felt the evaluation went quite well, especially for that early development stage. We came away with the comforting impression that the airplane was going to be a good-flying machine.

Hours spent in a development simulator can be taxing, especially when trying to concentrate on a number of minute but important issues. This effort obviously was warranted, because, after all, what we decided in the simulator would show up on the airplane. If we missed something that could affect the bomber's operation in the field, it might be expensive or very difficult to change later.

In the heat of simulator battle, I was asked once to check something in a side-panel of the cockpit. I pulled out a couple of chocolate-chip cookies . . . and thought I had died and gone to heaven! One of the flight control engineers knew I had a weakness for the little fat-pills and had slipped them in before we arrived. After three hours of concentrated simulator work, those cookies made my whole day!

* * *

YB-49 FLYING WING EXPERIENCE —AND ADVICE

Getting a preview of the ATB/B-2's characteristics in the simulator was reassuring, but the test pilots and engineers also drew on the first-hand experience of former YB-49 Flying Wing pilots. Retired Air Force Col. Russ E. Schleeh met with the test group at Edwards after CDR, providing his perspective on YB-49 taxi and flight tests. Although his comments about Northrop's earlier flying wing were somewhat reserved, Schleeh helped the group better understand some of the problems the aircraft had encountered during its test program almost 40 years earlier.

Because Schleeh did not have a program security clearance, B-2-cleared personnel could not discuss current problem areas with him. Those who attended the sessions, though, were amazed to hear about some of the problems the ex-test pilot had dealt with on the YB-49. The smiles and nodding heads in the audience told any casual observer that many of those same concerns had already arisen on the B-2. Attendees had to be reminded repeatedly that "Col. Schleeh is not cleared. Watch what you say."

Max Stanley, the first test pilot to fly the YB-49, also provided excellent tips for B-2 pilots and engineers. Stanley was a very friendly, outgoing man who described in detail the performance and handling characteristics of Northrop's earlier flying wings. He allayed pilot concerns about the ATB/B-2's behavior close to the ground, saying he never saw a bad landing in the YB-49 and that the B-2 team should expect the same. He was absolutely right. The first landing of the new bomber on July 17, 1989, was smooth as glass.

* * *

COL. RICK COUCH:

Another issue resolved for the test group at CDR was the selection of a call sign for the B-2 Combined Test Force. While this may seem like a trivial concern, at Edwards it's important for other flight crews to immediately recognize radio call signs for each unit. For example, when a ground controller refers to a *Zoom* call sign, everybody knows it's an F-16. The F-15 CTF uses *Eagle* and the B-1 is *Wiry*.

Ideally, the call sign has some recognizable relationship to the aircraft being tested. We knew the ATB/B-2 would be large and dark-colored, so *Raven* was our first choice. Anybody familiar with the large black birds that live in the desert areas around Edwards AFB would understand the analogy to our B-2 . . . both birds are relatively big and sinister-looking. More importantly, both fly with impunity anywhere they please.

We submitted our choice to the Air Force office that monitors such vital issues, only to have it rejected. A squadron in Idaho was already using the *Raven* call sign. During CDR, several of us spent a few hours in a Los Angeles bookstore one night, looking through bird books for a fitting call sign. Nothing but *Raven* seemed appropriate.

Someone finally picked up a Russian-English dictionary and found that the Russian word for raven was voron. We applied for a *Voron* call sign and it was approved. Although *Voron* isn't a real catchy call sign, it's recognizable to other Edwards flight crews, and it has meaning for those who use it.

* * *

BACK TO WORK

With the completion of CDR, the B-2 program was set on a well-mapped path and schedule. Each group left the exhausting review with an understanding of what the new bomber would and would not be, and a list of things yet to be accomplished.

The Combined Test Force returned to Edwards with a number of tasks. Test instrumentation, data processing, Northrop's planned staffing levels for the CTF, delivery schedules for maintenance technical orders, and a weakness in systems engineering support for test integration are examples of issues that fell to the CTF for resolution.

Ordering test support equipment and the right number of aircraft spares was one of the top priorities after CDR. Approximately 860 types of support equipment, ranging from workstands to ground power carts, and 17,000 different spares items were identified as requirements. Once these needs were certified as valid, a lengthy process of deciding how to obtain them began.

In some cases, the only way to get an item was to have a contractor either make it or buy it. Make/buy decisions were based on cost and availability at the time the item was needed. In other cases, it made sense to obtain an item from the Air Force supply system.

The Air Force has a well-structured system of priorities when ordering from stock supplies, typically based on the importance of a particular program or weapon system. The B-2 program had a high priority, which generally assured the CTF would get most of what it needed to perform ground and flight tests.

The supply network also has a set of checks built into its procedures to ensure the system is not abused. Even with its high priority, the CTF's requests were always scrutinized carefully. Any hint of supply system abuse was enough for someone in the B-2 organization or at a higher command level to be called, requiring a justification for what was being requested.

* * *

COL. RICK COUCH:

We were ordering so much material through the Air Force [supply] system that, at one point, the Edwards base supply squadron automatically raised the priority of anything we ordered to make sure we got the support we needed when we needed it. This worked well . . . most of the time.

One day, I received a scorching phone call from the two-star general in charge of the Flight Test Center, wanting to know what the hell we were doing ordering 12 dozen black ballcaps on a priority one basis, one of the highest in the supply system. Leavenworth was mentioned as a possible next assignment, so I took an immediate interest in the black hats.

On our end, things looked legitimate. Different test units often obtain matching caps as a unifying, morale-boosting mechanism, and the Air Force supports the concept with material from its supplies. My guys had ordered the hats on a low priority basis, but the supply troops had seen the order was from the B-2 CTF and automatically jacked up the priority to the highest available to them.

Some conscientious soul in the supply system questioned whether those 144 ballcaps were really that vital to the national interest. His concerns were relayed to the general, probably with some choice words about a mad colonel working at North Base.

The problem was worked out and the caps were delivered under a more appropriate priority. When they arrived, I presented the general with his own black hat . . . just as a reminder.

* * *

THE CTF'S FIRST AIRPLANE

The KC-135 flying avionics testbed arrived at Edwards shortly after CDR ended. It had undergone extensive modifications at E-Systems' Texas facility, receiving higher-capacity electrical generators on all four engines and two additional Boeing 707 air conditioners. These alterations were made to ensure the aircraft would handle the extra electrical and cooling loads put on it by an interior that was full of avionics equipment.

The development versions of black boxes that would eventually find their way into the B-2 were flown and tested on this aircraft, saving hundreds of flight test hours on the bomber. By testing B-2 avionics in-flight this early in the program, the old KC-135 water wagon testbed was estimated to have saved about $100 for every $1 spent on it. If, instead, the same integration and debugging tests had been flown on one of the bombers during its flight test program, the extra work would have lengthened the process substantially and cost millions.

* * *

COL. RICK COUCH:
For a long time, the KC-135 testbed was the only flying operation we had at the CTF. Besides the obvious benefits it provided for avionics development, the aircraft gave us a chance to develop methods we would use for actual B-2 flight operations. The old water wagon . . . had its own personality and provided a few interesting moments, as well. Takeoffs on hot desert days at Edwards were always especially exciting. Takeoff rolls of [more than] 12,000 feet were not unusual under these conditions. Even with 15,000 feet of concrete in front of you, that KC-135 could make the Edwards runway look short before we got airborne.

* * *

THE REAL WORLD

The Air Force's recent painful experiences with fielding the B-1B bomber in the mid-1980s had a number of spinoffs that affected designers, planning and testing operations in the months following CDR. One of the operational test and evaluation (OT&E) managers recommended that several civilian and military engineers be sent to operational Strategic Air Command bases to see actual day-to-day bomber operations. To add a strong dose of realism to the project, it was decided they should visit one of the northern tier SAC bases in the middle of winter.

Each engineer was assigned briefly to different maintenance and operations squadrons on a rotating basis over a week's period, and was given real-world tasks to perform in the course of preparing aircraft for flight. These were eye-opening experiences for people accustomed to designing and testing aircraft from behind a desk or in a hangar at Edwards.

The engineers were outfitted with heavy gloves, boots, and parkas, then worked alongside regular Air Force mechanics or aircrews launching an aircraft in the middle of the night when the temperature was well below zero. One engineer later related his astonishment at seeing a B-52 crew chief load a drag chute in the bomber's aft parachute compartment, then grab an aircraft wheel chock and start pounding on the chute access door to get it closed. Another time, a similar chock was used to pound a KC-135 engine cowling closed.

Nothing could have made a more lasting impression on those engineers. Who, when designing a compact, aerodynamic engine cowling or parachute compartment, would ever have dreamed that a 200-pound mechanic would resort to beating on the door with a 50-pound wooden block, just to get the damned thing to close? But that's exactly the sort of thing a guy in the field will do to get the job done. The message came through loud and clear: Good designs could make the maintenance man's job significantly easier, and possibly avoid damage to the aircraft at the same time.

The engineers also returned with tales about the joys of deicing an aircraft using the standard government-issue deicing truck. Squirting heated deicing fluid on huge, frozen bomber wings when it was –40°F hardly qualified as the engineers' idea of a good time, but it is a fact of life for Air Force airplanes and maintenance troops every winter.

Surprisingly, the hands-on experience was so well received by those involved that the program was expanded to include contract and system program office engineers. Overall, the project was considered a huge success, thanks to a smart manager with a little foresight.

The experience provided a completely new perspective for people involved in the B-2's design and development, and has been reflected in the aircraft's maintenance philosophy. In other words, the B-2 will have built-in features that should make a tough crew chief's day . . . and save a lot of wear and tear on the Air Force's wheel chocks.

6

Building the
first B-2 bomber

THE CRITICAL DESIGN REVIEW WAS COMPLETED ON SCHEDULE. That fact, in itself, is normally enough to prompt a system program office to declare any program's CDR a success. For the B-2, the review also had highlighted many areas that required additional attention, and focused the various participants on specific tasks that were considered most critical.

The Air Force felt Northrop needed to strengthen its systems engineering department to ensure all aircraft components and subsystems would be integrated properly. This was particularly true of software, the computer programs that comprise the B-2's electronic brain. These programs, written separately for a number of aircraft systems, had to be able to work together without mutually interfering or locking up at an inopportune time.

Similarly, a number of essential operations analyses had not been completed. These were step-by-step checks that would make sure every component and function had been considered, nothing had been overlooked. Analysts were charged with checking every detail of the aircraft's operation to make sure each wire that was supposed to send necessary signals from one box to another had been accounted for and included in the mounting reams of design data. But until the ops analyses were finished, nobody could stand up and declare that the entire aircraft would work as advertised.

The design review also pointed out that a dialogue between all test-related organizations had not begun and that it needed to start soon. Several CDR participants expressed concern that the various Air Force and contractor test teams appeared to be poorly integrated. Apparently, there was so much emphasis and attention focused on getting the first aircraft built that little thought had been given to how it would be tested. Improved communication and integration of engineering and logistics organizations with the test community were encouraged.

Completion of CDR gave Northrop and its contractors the green light to start building the first aircraft. This was greeted with a mixture of relief, enthusiasm, and trepidation.

The B-2 would be a much different aircraft than any built since the 1940s, when Jack Northrop's Flying Wing designs were being tested. The mystique of being involved in resurrecting the wing design and turning ethereal concepts into hardware that would fly in a few years was exciting. This was "where it was happening" in the aerospace industry during the mid-1980s, and to be an engineer, manager, or mechanic on this program was considered a privilege.

More sobering, though, was the realization that an incredible job lay before this team. It did not take one very long, after being assigned to some aspect of the B-2 development process, to realize the magnitude of the task at hand.

MANUFACTURING: A NEW GAME

First of all, the B-2 would have to be built from the "outside in," and the first aircraft would have to be as accurate as the last one, in order to meet low observables criteria. There would be no hand-built prototypes on which to learn what worked and what did not. AV-1 would have to be built to production standards, just as every bomber after it, because all but one test aircraft would be returned to the active-duty fleet after the development program ended. Building to production criteria from the outset had never been done before on a brand new aircraft, Northrop claimed.

Because the exterior surface absolutely, positively had to be smooth and have precisely the correct contours to meet low observability criteria, there was negligible room for error in building any of the internal structure. Tolerances were tight, to say the least. If something was a few thousandths of an inch off deep inside the massive wing, it would be magnified at the surface. In other words, by the time other structure had been built on top of that first misaligned point, adding allowed tolerances along the way, the mistake on the inside would be seen as an incorrect curvature or mismatch of pieces on the skin.

Even basic aircraft building materials, tools, and techniques had to be revised for the B-2. In fact, more than 900 new materials and processes would be developed and used to build the bomber. The aircraft would use much more *composite* (reinforced plastic-like) material than a conventional aircraft because the carbon-based substances tended to absorb radar energy rather than reflect it. Sandwiches of different types of composite material and aluminum, or titanium, in some cases, would comprise much of the B-2 structure.

Making this material required new techniques. Many of the pieces were huge, requiring strips of composite tape to be laid at high rates before the whole piece changed temperature too much. That meant new tape-laying machines had to be designed and built before fabrication of the aircraft's thousands of components could begin.

Composites are a family of modern materials that use graphite fibers and special resins to create strong, lightweight panels and structural members for aircraft and other vehicles. Pieces of structure typically are built up in layers of flexible tape that contain these fibers and resins, oriented in well-planned directions to produce the desired flexibility and strength characteristics.

When a part has completed the build-up or layup process, it normally is encased in plastic bags and all the air evacuated from the bags by vacuum pumps. Several parts are put in a large pressurized oven called an *autoclave*, essentially a huge pressure cooker, and literally cooked and squeezed until they harden.

Aviation Week magazine, in its September 17, 1990, issue, described in detail how Boeing makes the 65-foot-long outboard sections of the B-2's composite wing, as well as a 50-foot aft center section. The Seattle-based aerospace manufacturing giant has built a special $400 million plant specifically to build composite structures, initially for the B-2.

The wing sections are cured "at about 350[°F] and 100 psi" in 25-foot-diameter, 90-foot-long autoclaves, believed to be the largest ever made for composite work, the magazine reported. "Many of the raw composite materials are stored in large freezers at the plant until just prior to use to increase shelf life and ensure the quality of the materials. Some composites lose their desirable characteristics if stored at room temperature," *Aviation Week* editor Breck Henderson wrote.

Tasks as normally simple as drilling holes in pieces of composites and other new materials became complex. The sandwich of composites and metal required an entirely new drill to be designed and manufactured. Rockwell's Allen-Bradley group came up with a computerized drill that could sense how hard the material was at each layer and automatically adjust the drill bit speed. This allowed millions of holes to be drilled as fast as possible, but greatly reduced the possibility of either breaking a bit, or, worse, ruining a piece of expensive material by making a lopsided or crooked hole.

Even fastening one piece of material to another was a chore. Special fasteners, not the standard rivets used in building aluminum aircraft for more than 40 years, had to be developed. Some of these fasteners were designed to withstand forces in the lengthwise direction (tension or compression) better than crosswise (shear). At one point, thousands of these fasteners were mixed up accidentally. The two types looked very similar, and many fasteners that were supposed to be installed in shear-sensitive areas wound up in places that had to take tension loads.

That apparently minor error, installing the wrong fasteners in the wrong place, would prove to be a major headache for the entire program for several years. The first B-2 flew a number of test missions before the full extent of the fastener mix-up was discovered, and the program test schedule had to be adjusted until the correct fasteners could be installed.

At the aircraft's exterior surface, every fastener had to be installed perfectly; not extending above the skin level and not sunk slightly below the surface; not cocked sideways with one lip sticking up and the other slightly lower.

If it was wrong, the fastener was drilled out and the whole process repeated until it was correct.

Holes in two different pieces of material had to be perfectly aligned so the fasteners that joined the pieces could be correctly installed. As a result, every hole in some areas had to be measured, inspected, and approved before the fastener could be inserted.

This attention to minute detail was dictated by one overriding guideline: The B-2's skin had to be *perfect*, or it would reflect too many strong signals back to an enemy radar station. If a reflected radar pulse—no matter how small— was detected, the aircraft could be found and the entire premise of the stealth bomber was gone. In other words, how perfectly the bomber was manufactured would directly determine how successfully it could perform its mission. The men and women building the airplane literally had the lives of Air Force crewmen riding on the quality of their detailed workmanship.

B-2 DESCRIPTION

This demand for manufacturing perfection was compounded by the sheer size and complex shape of the B-2. The aircraft is 172 feet wide, wingtip to wingtip, and 69 feet long. Standing on its landing gear, the B-2 is 17 feet high. It has a wingspan approaching that of a B-52 bomber, but the length of an F-15 fighter. Looking at it head-on in flight, with the gear retracted, the B-2 is relatively thin, roughly 10 feet, top-to-bottom, at its thickest point.

Tricycle landing gear are placed so the two main gear are 40 feet apart, enabling the bomber fleet to be dispersed, if necessary, to any airfield in the world that can accommodate a Boeing 727 commercial airliner. With a short takeoff and landing characteristic, the aircraft can use more than 700 airfields throughout the United States, as well as hundreds more around the world.

The fuselage blends smoothly into the wing, making the cockpit resemble a helmeted Darth Vader-like character peeking over a fence. A wrap-around windscreen slants almost to the beak-like nose of the wing in front, while blending sideways towards the wings' top surface.

Low-profile, jagged-edged engine inlets on each side of the raised fuselage feed air through curved ducts to four General Electric F118 powerplants buried inside the thick wing. Hot exhaust gases from the engines are directed through another complex duct, then shot directly aft, across a titanium-covered deck on top of the wing's aft section.

Behind the cockpit, the internal central fuselage area is dedicated to aircraft systems and large bomb bays capable of carrying both conventional and nuclear weapons. All bombs and missiles are carried internally to preserve the all-important stealth or low observable characteristics.

Most of the wing volume is consumed by fuel tanks, giving the bomber an unrefueled range of more than 6,000 nautical miles. With a single aerial refueling, range extends to 10,000 nautical miles, enabling the B-2 to reach any potential target on the globe. If adequate tanker support is available, only the crew's physical endurance will limit the aircraft's time aloft.

FLIGHT CONTROLS

The complex aircraft is a collection of flying computers, too. Approximately 200 computer processors are onboard, and they employ a total of 500,000 lines of *code*, or *programming*, even more than the space shuttle.

A quadredundant fly-by-wire flight control system relies on the latest in digital electronics to ensure the aircraft will fly well. This means there are no cables or pushrods connecting the pilots' sticks and rudder pedals to the large, barndoor-like flight controls hinged to the trailing edge of each wing surface. Traditional mechanical controls have been replaced by wires, sensors, computers, and actuators.

When a pilot pulls on the stick, a signal is sent to a computer that determines how much pitch change is being requested. The computer then sends a signal over a wire to another electronic unit that controls how far a hydraulic actuator moves the flight control surface. That deflection causes the aircraft's nose to rise and the aircraft starts climbing. Sensors throughout the aircraft "feel" that change and feed new signals back to the computer. This continuous loop between pilot, computer, flight control surface and sensors is, in essence, what keeps the aircraft flying "pointed-end forward."

A 4,000-psi hydraulic system, which is substantially higher pressure than that used by most civil or military aircraft, provides the muscle needed to move the big flight control surfaces fast enough to give the aircraft good response to pilot inputs. Hydraulic and electrical power are provided by pumps and generators mated to each of the four GE engines.

The seemingly oversized control surfaces and the bomber's very stiff construction were outgrowths of the Air Force's decision during the ATB proposal stage to redesign the aircraft for a combined high/low-level mission profile. The new design was tailored to a stringent *gust-loading* criteria that would ensure the aircraft could tolerate heavy turbulence and gusts that would be encountered during low-level flight.

A Northrop executive said, "Personally, I feel the structure is very much overdesigned, just to meet the [gust] spec. I can't tell you the [gust specification] number, but it's a big one . . . sort of a once-in-a-lifetime-of-the-fleet number. I can tell you that it's much more than a 2-g airplane. That's why it's so stiff, and why [the pilots say] it handles like a fighter. It doesn't flex like most big bombers' wings do. It also has those very big control surfaces, which can only help flying qualities. We have more than enough control authority with them."

Those control surfaces consist of *drag rudders* near each wingtip that create drag on either one side or the other, forcing the aircraft to turn in that direction. These large surfaces provide yaw or side-to-side control. When both sides are activated together, they act as speed brakes.

Inboard of the drag rudders are three sets of *elevons*, which are combined elevators (for pitch control) and ailerons (for roll control). At the center, directly aft of the cockpit, is a pointed control section dubbed the *beavertail*, but properly called the *gust load alleviation system*, or GLAS. This surface automatically moves in flight to counteract strong gusts that create a rough ride for the crew and add stress to the airframe.

The GLAS feature is unique to the B-2, as far as the author knows. It moves 11 degrees up or down, but will not roll sideways because the surface is not articulated in that direction. As a result, it will only affect pitch, but works with the mid-elevons to keep the aircraft body from trying to flex when it encounters a rising or descending gust. Although the GLAS does not move during taxi (it stays at an 11-degree down position), it is constantly moving when flying at higher speeds. The beavertail, or *turkey feathers*, surface also is designed to help the bomber ride out the massive gust front of a nuclear blast, as well.

All B-2 control surfaces are positioned automatically by onboard computers before takeoff; pilots do not set them for takeoff or landing. Even in crosswinds, the computer and its control laws are programmed to provide optimum initial control settings. Deflections of each surface can be changed by altering computer software settings, but the pilot still has no direct control over them.

For example, the outboard elevons could be set to deflect six degrees, the mid-span surfaces four degrees, and the inboard two degrees. As of late 1990, it has not been necessary to alter these pretakeoff settings in order to obtain good flying qualities, but the capability exists, if ever needed.

During high-speed flight, the computer also cuts out the powerful outboard elevons, simply because they are capable of commanding too much control power if activated at high Mach number speeds, where air *dynamic pressure* also is high.

The mid-wing elevons work together with the GLAS for gust load alleviation throughout the flight envelope. All elevons will deflect 30 degrees up or down, and the drag rudders or speed brakes will move ±70 degrees.

BLACK BOXES

Avionics are state-of-the-art, tailored especially for this aircraft. The cockpit is dominated by a number of television-type cathode ray tube displays that present all the flight information needed by two pilots. Similar displays show engine operation, fuel state, navigational data, and a wealth of other vital information. These computer-generated displays are designed such that information is available to the pilots immediately. Not only can they rapidly retrieve the data they need, many systems are operated automatically for them, requiring less pilot attention.

Overall, the computerized cockpit makes the job of flying the new bomber substantially easier. Enough so, in fact, that the Air Force expects a two-man crew to perform the same job as a four-man crew does in the B-1B bomber.

That issue, two-man versus a three-man crew, will not be totally resolved until the flight test program is completed. At the time of this writing, though, the Strategic Air Command most definitely intended to operate the B-2 with two pilots. Why? Because it's cheaper. People have become one of the Air Force's most expensive "systems"; eliminating one crew member per bomber saves a significant sum over the 20- to 30-year life of an aircraft weapon system. Thanks to computers, that goal is attainable on the B-2.

If the bomber's mission changes in the future, though, and a third crewmember becomes necessary, the B-2 is designed to accommodate another seat and more avionics equipment. Even an escape hatch zone has been stenciled on the skin, above the B-2's cockpit, showing where a third ejection seat would exit.

Having the flexibility to add another crewmember built in from the start shows that military planners recognize a combat aircraft must be adaptable to changing mission needs. Over its expected 10,000-hour airframe life, the B-2 might go through any number of variations, just as the venerable B-52 has.

Finally, offensive and defensive avionics will provide that extra ounce of insurance by waging electronic war against enemy radars, missiles, and fighters. These electronic countermeasures go to work only if the bomber is detected. Its primary protection mechanism is its stealthiness.

The B-2's performance and detailed configuration are still classified, and probably will remain that way for awhile. The Air Force has acknowledged that the bomber will fly as high as 50,000 feet and its top speed will be subsonic (less than the speed of sound). It will carry more than 40,000 pounds of nuclear and conventional weapons, including the SRAM and SRAM II (short range attack missiles), gravity bombs, and antiship weapons. With an optimized load of weapons and fuel, the B-2 will have a maximum gross takeoff weight of more than 350,000 pounds, placing it in the *heavy bomber* class.

DESIGNING AND FABRICATING A LOW OBSERVABLE AIRCRAFT

Building the B-2 to the necessary level of precision, a mandatory requirement designed to ensure its low observable design features were preserved in the final product, demanded a radical approach. Rather than create tons of paper drawings and blueprints, the entire B-2 design would be done in computer graphics. Every engineer's work would eventually be pooled and retained in a single three-dimensional computer database that could be instantly accessed by any other engineer or manager.

For example, if an engineer designed a cooling duct that had to fit through an opening in the fuselage frame, clearances could be checked on the computer screen by calling up the frame design. Tolerances could be verified and the drawing manipulated to make sure everything fit together properly.

Having the entire aircraft design in an electronic database had other advantages. Subcontractors at widely dispersed locations also could tap into that information pool and, in essence, get electronic copies of the latest design. Another advantage lay in the ability to make changes to the design.

A Northrop manager of *computer-aided design* and *manufacturing* (CAD/CAM) told *Aviation Week & Space Technology* magazine that the electronic change system for engineering's CAD drawings had reduced the number of problems with new parts fitting together the first time they were connected (*first-time fits*) by a factor of six.

This 3-D database contains detailed information about all of the aircraft's subsystems, wire harnesses, and components. It also has eliminated that mainstay of aircraft production, the *full-scale mockup.* Until the B-2 came along, manufacturers typically made a model of the aircraft out of wood, metal, and plastic. This model conformed to design measurements, allowing other parts to be checked for clearances, and wires or tubing checked for the correct length, bends, and interference. In effect, the computer database, because it can be viewed as three-dimensional images from any angle, is the mockup, in addition to being a depiction of the actual aircraft.

Switching to a computerized database and design system was a major departure for the aerospace business. Previously, even though CAD/CAM had been used for specialized tasks, much of an aircraft was still designed on paper and mylar sheets.

★ ★ ★

JOHN CASHEN, Northrop designer:
By going to the 3-D database, we tried to completely computerize the whole design process. It took a lot of equipment. As of a few years ago, Northrop had the largest IBM facility west of the Mississippi.

We had 10,000 people at Pico Rivera [Northrop's B-2 design and manufacturing facility], and, as far as I know, there isn't a drafting board in the place. All drawings, designs, and specifications are done on the computer. The design engineering department had over 500 3-D [computer] tubes, and a lot of 2-D tubes, as well.

Even on a massive scale, the system worked very well. Of course, it was backed up by a lot of testing and documentation.

★ ★ ★

NOT IMMUNE TO PROBLEMS

Despite the confidence Northrop, the Air Force, and all the major subcontractors had in their star wars computer database, problems were still encountered. Major structural parts of the aircraft were built in several large sections; Boeing (Seattle, Wash.) built the aft center and two outboard sections; Northrop (Pico Rivera, in the Los Angeles area) built the forward center section, as well as all wing leading and trailing edges; and LTV (Dallas/Fort Worth, Texas) constructed the two intermediate center assemblies, but shipped them in three pieces. All parts were shipped to Northrop's new Palmdale, Calif., B-2 facility at Site 4, Air Force Plant 42, for final assembly.

The first time all the major structural sections came together in Palmdale, there were a few minor problems in getting them to mate properly. These problems were attributed to needed refinements in the allowed tolerances, but were nowhere near the dreaded classic problem of not having the "rails meet in the middle." The common electronic database that was accessible by all the major subcontractors seemed to be working as advertised.

Even though it was built in three different locations, the structure fit together extremely well. The wiring, however, was another story. *Wiring harnesses*, consisting of hundreds of wires bound together in a single long, snake-like bundle, often turned out to be too short or long when workers tried to install them. Sometimes the gauge of wire was wrong, or the bundle would not fit in areas allocated for wiring runs.

Cockpit wiring was especially troublesome. One manufacturing engineer remarked that the B-2 had the highest density of wiring in the cockpit of any aircraft ever built. Consequently, the cockpit wiring was installed, ripped out, and reinstalled at least three different times.

* * *

BRUCE HINDS:
Wiring was a nightmare, especially on the first aircraft. Just the way it was made and installed, the wiring has been and always will be a problem until it gets changed out.

Wiring shouldn't have been that much trouble. Everybody thought it was a straightforward task, so they didn't put the most experienced people on it. It turned out to be a tougher job than anybody had suspected . . . it's just extremely [tightly packed], especially in the cockpit.

These problems paced manufacturing [on the first B-2], and, to some extent, it still paces much of the work on AV-1. [Because] that aircraft eventually has to go back to the [operational] fleet, it has to be brought up to production configuration, just so we can even test it. All [FSD aircraft] but No. 2, which will stay a test airplane, have to be brought up to production standard. That takes a lot of time.

* * *

Wiring headaches often were compounded by having several contractors build large pieces of the aircraft. For example, one wiring harness that ran from an outboard wing section to the aircraft's nose area was made by three different contractors. Boeing, LTV, and Northrop each built separate sections of the wing and aft/forward center zones of the aircraft. Each section had to include its own wiring. For large, many-wire harnesses, the possibilities for errors and interconnect problems at the joints were abundant.

One might ask, why bother to have so many companies involved in making the B-2? Wouldn't having a single contractor build the whole aircraft avoid these interface problems such as incorrect wiring harnesses?

It probably would, but in today's very costly aerospace environment, it makes good economic sense for manufacturers to work as a team on a large program like the B-2. No single manufacturer is at risk if the program should die or have major problems, and the costs of facilities are shared.

Almost 8 million square feet of U.S. defense industrial base facilities were dedicated to B-2 development, production, and testing as of late 1990. These are scattered around the country and include plants operated by Northrop, Boeing, LTV, General Electric, Hughes, and several government-owned locations. If Northrop had to expand its own facilities to do this same level of work, its cost during and after the B-2 program would be too much for one company to handle.

On this program, Northrop performs about 30 percent of the total B-2 manufacturing, and its team of partners and subcontractors supplies the other 70 percent. That split balances risk, while taking advantage of expertise developed by other contractors.

On the political front, a well-selected subcontractor network spreads B-2-related money across numerous congressional districts, extending program influence and its support base in Washington. That lesson was learned and applied very effectively by Rockwell International on its B-1B bomber program in the 1980s.

Frustrating wiring problems were occasionally the basis for criticism of the electronic database method of design. What must be understood, though, is that designers are not perfect. No matter how good their tools, whether paper and ink or computerized databases, there will be problems when the design is turned into hardware. A new aircraft design always has been, and always will be, a high-risk venture.

Realizing this, managers built procedures into the design control and release system that would accommodate inevitable changes to the original engineering drawings. The thousands of parts that go into an aircraft will never be designed perfectly the first time. Making necessary changes, though, while trying to build an aircraft, has always been a time-consuming problem that is to be avoided as much as possible.

Again, Northrop resorted to its electronic database to manage the change process. With every responsible organization in the change approval cycle having access to the database, changes could be made quickly, then checked and approved on-line in a matter of hours instead of weeks. Piles of paper did not have to move from one desk to another; the whole process was expedited by computer.

Still, the engineering change process threatened to bring construction of the first B-2 bomber to its knees more than once. The system of approval, even with computer assistance, was still cumbersome. Any design changes had to be reviewed and approved by Northrop, then transmitted to LTV and Boeing for implementation into hardware. The subcontractors, in turn, had to pick an appropriate time and place to incorporate changes into the production line.

Most of these changes were prompted when a new piece of hardware was being installed for the first time and it either did not fit or would not mate properly with something else. One of the most frustrating occurred repeatedly: A complex electrical harness with multiple bends would be painstakingly installed, only to find it was a couple of inches too short or too long. Nothing to do but pull it out and make a new harness. Splices were suggested, but that opened the door for potential in-flight problems during flight test.

LABORATORIES

To minimize the risk of numerous inoperable systems being installed in the first aircraft, Northrop and its subcontractors built a number of laboratories and system simulators. These were stand-alone replicas of a particular aircraft system, constructed of the same part-numbered hardware that would actually be in-stalled on flying versions of the bomber.

Laboratories and simulators emulated all the major aircraft systems: fuel, electrical, environmental control, crew escape, avionics, primary and auxiliary power, landing gear, flight controls, and hydraulic. The full-scale structural components and control-surface test lab even evaluated all the large pieces that would make up the airframe and large barndoor-like flight control panels.

* * *

BRUCE HINDS:
    At Northrop, the test organization was responsible for building all the labs. They had to get design engineering input, then build the labs around that design. Later, development groups used the labs extensively for iterative changes to a system. For example, the RCS [*radar cross-section*] labs were essential for iterative work . . . we did hundreds of thousands of RCS tests.
    RCS and wind tunnel tests, all the high risk areas, actually, were the most iterative. Others, like the ECS [*environmental control system*] were less so, mainly because those systems already had a lot of qualification testing done at the vendors. The electrical system lab was the least iterative; the system worked the first time we tested it.

* * *

COL. RICK COUCH:
    The most cosmic of all the labs was the *flight controls and hydraulic integration laboratory* [FCHIL, pronounced fickle]. It was commonly referred to as *The Iron Bird*, because of its skeletal, stripped down look.
    [Because] it was a full-scale, working mockup of the B-2's entire hydraulics and flight controls system, hydraulic lines ran everywhere. All dimensions were correct . . . every line was the same length and had the same bends as the real airplane did . . . forming a dimensional skeleton of the B-2.
    This lab could simulate environments that critical systems would see on the ground and in the air. It was constructed of both real hardware or simulations of certain equipment, such as the landing gear.
    A cockpit built into the lab allowed us to exercise the FCHIL by "flying" simulated profiles, just as if we were in an actual aircraft. Most of the cock-

pit was not what we would call "full fidelity." It didn't really look like an actual aircraft cockpit, but it didn't need to. However, the sticks and throttles were exact hardware . . . the same types that would be in the real bomber . . . so everything between the crew and the flight controls was exactly the same as what we would find in the full-size aircraft.

When we "flew" the FCHIL, the hardware and software responded like the B-2 would in flight. We could move the stick and watch the flight controls actually move, just like they would on the aircraft. At this stage of development, that was a real buzz for us pilots.

Building this lab . . . hooking all the bits and pieces together to emulate the B-2 configuration . . . took literally years of work. But it was time and money well spent. Engineers could see how things were coming together at every step of the process, making changes as necessary along the way. Components for the flight controls and hydraulics were meticulously tested . . . a process that took [more than] a year by itself. This time investment was worth every minute, though. It was much more efficient, and easier, to find problems, fix them, and retest the fixes in a lab like the FCHIL than it would ever have been on the aircraft.

★ ★ ★

There were numerous starts and stops throughout the FCHIL's development and operation, but, in the end, the lab finished its critical preflight testing about the time AV-1 was ready to fly.

The dedicated laboratories proved invaluable to B-2 development. By enabling full-scale sections of the aircraft, actual hardware and software, to be tested as a complete unit, engineers had a chance to get an early look at system integration factors. They could determine very quickly whether a system would work the way the designer intended. In some cases, lab test results confirmed that a particular design feature simply wouldn't work at all, or that the complete system did not function quite the way it was supposed to.

Potential failure modes and their effects could be evaluated in the safety of a ground-bound laboratory, providing confidence that a similar occurrence in the actual aircraft would produce predictable responses. Laboratories also gave an opportunity to develop checkout procedures that would be used on each aircraft before it flew, or following maintenance work during the test program. These dry runs ultimately saved countless hours of valuable on-aircraft time later.

Aircrews developed and practiced normal and emergency procedures in several of the labs, particularly the *flight mission simulator*, a full-scale replica of the B-2 cockpit, including all the standard controls and displays. This engineering tool was used to develop mathematical flight control laws, crew procedures, avionics, and display formats. The simulator had a six-degree of freedom motion base that duplicated all the pitch, roll, yaw, and bumps that an actual aircraft would experience in flight.

It also included a computer-generated visual system to create very realistic out-the-window daytime or nighttime scenes. In essence, it was the ultimate arcade video game, even though it had a much more scientific purpose.

For example, the flight mission simulator was equipped with an in-flight refueling scene that pilots agreed was the best they had ever seen. The high fidelity made them feel like they were actually flying behind a KC-135 tanker. This capability allowed crews and engineers to evaluate B-2 flight control systems under "high-gain, pilot-in-the-loop" conditions, such as aerial refueling, typical of what would be required in actual flight.

These simulators also allowed the B-2 test pilots to try maneuvers and procedures that could never be done in an actual aircraft, primarily for safety reasons. Practice sessions also provided added confidence that the B-2 would be a robust aircraft—relatively tolerant of failures and the stress of training and combat.

Overall, the labs were directly responsible for uncovering some "very interesting things," according to project participants, and contributed to a number of important engineering changes in the B-2. Before the aircraft ever made its first flight, the simulators had provided more than 750,000 hours of experience with these important aircraft systems. Another 50,000 hours were added prior to this writing—more than 800,000 hours of total testing. This was probably more than any other military aircraft had ever been tested, but it greatly reduced program technical risks.

As a result, the B-2 was actually a much more mature vehicle going into the flight test program than other aircraft are after months or years of flying. Those directly involved in the B-2 effort have been very pleased with how well flight testing has gone, so far. They point to the relatively few problems and high flight rate (number of flights per month) as proof that up-front work done in the labs is paying dividends in the more expensive and schedule-intensive flight test phase.

Throughout the next umpteen years of flight testing and B-2 operation, these laboratories will continue to justify their existence. They will allow problems discovered on the aircraft to be studied and solved *off-line* (in the laboratories) instead of tying up the aircraft.

Engineers can often duplicate a flight problem in the lab, while the aircraft continues with its test program. It would be extremely inefficient to ground the aircraft for troubleshooting and problem solving, and would delay the test program tremendously, just as it has on other aircraft development efforts in the past.

During the most intense laboratory testing phase, especially before first flight, the Air Force and contractor B-2 flight test community expressed concern about whether problems discovered in the labs were, in fact, getting back to the right people. It didn't make much sense to spend time and money uncovering deficiencies if they never found their way back into the system, so design changes could be made in the aircraft.

Problems could be quickly solved in the lab by changing a part, altering the software or changing test conditions, then rerunning a procedure. But these did not address the real design issues. Without a good feedback system to the designers, the same problems could show up on the aircraft years later, when solutions could be very time consuming—and atrociously expensive, based on previous experience. Without proper controls, the benefit of having a multitude of laboratories could be lost.

Northrop management repeatedly expended a lot of effort assuring its customer, and its own test personnel, that problems found in the lab were, indeed, being investigated and documented, and that needed changes were being made on the actual aircraft.

This skepticism from the test community, born of experience with breakdowns in the laboratory and flight test feedback system on other aircraft programs, probably will not be put to rest until the last B-2 finishes its final test mission at Edwards AFB. It is a concern firmly rooted in basic human nature, and an historical irritant to every aircraft program manager since the Wright Brothers first contracted to build airplanes for the Army.

EARTHQUAKE!

The Whittier earthquake that hit Southern California on October 1, 1987, rocked the B-2 program, but the impacts were never publicized at the time. Northrop's Pico Rivera plant was only a matter of miles from the quake's epicenter, a fact that grabbed the attention of everybody working on the program, regardless of their location. Pico was pretty much the engineering and manufacturing nerve center for the B-2 program at this stage, so there was a great deal of concern about the safety of people there.

When the first shock hit the Pico Rivera plant, lights went out and ceiling tiles started falling on the third floor of the plant. Because this is a windowless area, longer and wider than a football field and divided into dozens of offices, the place instantly became a nightmare of dust-filled darkness with debris crashing on desks and people's heads, a frightening experience by all accounts.

Miraculously, nobody was seriously hurt, but most people on the third floor were a bit shaken. That area suffered the most damage. Soon, though, concern centered on how the quake might have affected the first aircraft, which was under construction at the time. The forward center section of AV-1 was positioned in a manufacturing jig that was supposed to be earthquake-hardened. Still, there was considerable concern that something might have shifted and would cause problems later.

As soon as it was safe to get into that manufacturing area, engineers started taking detailed measurements of every part in the aircraft's center section. They determined, after about two days of work, that nothing had moved; the aircraft had weathered the quake just fine, they reported.

At Edwards AFB, buildings and equipment shook a bit when the tremor struck, but nothing serious happened. There were a few anxious moments for two maintenance men, however. They were working on the KC-135 flying testbed, which was suspended on jacks in the large B-2 test support facility hangar. When the building started shaking, the effectively airborne tanker started moving around on its jacks, threatening to fall off. The two maintenance men held their breath as the huge four-engine aircraft rocked and rolled a bit, then settled down as the shock passed. After a few seconds, buildings and aircraft were substantially calmer than a couple of fast-beating hearts and shaky knees a few yards from that KC-135!

INTEGRATED MAINTENANCE

As the first B-2 neared completion, the Air Force started integrating its maintenance personnel with Northrop's such that both military and contractor experience was gained in parallel. This maintenance concept had been discussed at the Critical Design Review, and all parties agreed that each dedicated maintenance team should be made up of half Air Force and half Northrop people. The Air Force half would be further divided into half Systems Command and half Strategic Air Command personnel.

The objective was to ensure that a trained cadre of Air Force maintenance troops would be available to support the bomber when it was turned over to SAC and sent to active duty bases. Although it seems like a simple concept, establishment of a Northrop/Air Force maintenance partnership early in the development program was a major departure from traditional military aircraft procurements. Normally, the contractor maintains his aircraft until it is signed over to the government customer. Once the Air Force takes delivery of that aircraft, uniformed crews take over the maintenance.

When Northrop set up its first maintenance training classes, both contractor and Air Force personnel attended, learning about the new bomber at the same time. The next step was to actually start working on the aircraft together.

As that day approached, some Northrop middle managers started getting cold feet. After all, how could they meet a stringent first-flight schedule if the whole maintenance force did not have the same do-or-die motivation as company troops naturally did? Maybe this wasn't such a good idea, they suggested. It could delay first flight, they argued, even though the long-term payoff might be desirable.

The Air Force Systems Program Office and the Edwards test force quickly started lobbying the senior Northrop program manager, who agreed to let the dual-maintenance plan go into effect. He assured his own people that he definitely recognized the risks, but felt the benefits to Northrop and the Air Force far outweighed those risks. Consequently, government/contractor maintenance teams started taking care of the B-2 almost a year and a half before it flew the first time.

As it turned out, both the Air Force and Northrop realized benefits from this approach. The Air Force got an early look at the aircraft, enabling its personnel to make inputs about design features that were going to impact routine maintenance on the bomber. Northrop received immediate, valuable insights from hands-on troops about issues that affected the aircraft's maintainability, and could modify designs and procedures accordingly.

Numerous Air Force, Defense Department and congressional visitors periodically visited the Palmdale Site 4 final assembly plant to see the first B-2s coming together during this time. Air Force escorts started pointing out that military and contractor technicians were working side by side, something these delegations just didn't see at other factories. This fact impressed enough people that Northrop escorts started making the same point. Such attention was rare for the maintenance teams, and had a very positive effect on their morale and sense of teamwork. Before long, these normally invisible troops were explaining in detail to any interested VIP the details of what they were doing.

CONCURRENT MANUFACTURING/CHECKOUT

As much as people had hoped to avoid it, the pressures of getting the first aircraft completed and in the air led to concurrent manufacturing and checkout. Ideally, an aircraft is built, then systems are checked out to make sure everything works correctly before first flight. However, a series of changes and unforeseen problems encountered on AV-1 compressed the schedule, reducing the ideal approach to impossibility. If the aircraft was to make its first flight by mid-1989, manufacturing and checkout would have to be accomplished essentially in parallel.

Concurrency meant a lot of headaches for people doing the actual work, though. Manufacturing technicians had to work elbow-to-elbow with checkout engineers and specialists, often in the same cramped quarters. Without question, this added new meaning to the term teamwork. It was a new mode of operation for most, and it caused any number of frayed nerves and problems.

For example, when mechanics were working three shifts a day, weekends, and endless, mind-numbing overtime, just to get the aircraft built, they could get a bit testy themselves, especially when the test teams needed to "throw everybody off the airplane" in order to run a series of checkouts. Often, for safety reasons, nobody could be on or around the aircraft when a test was being run, so manufacturing ground to a halt.

Testing rarely goes smoothly, so more time typically was absorbed than had been planned, leading to new schedules, compromises with manufacturing, and more frustration all around. Tests were halted because systems that were supposed to be completed turned out to be missing a critical part or section; or a connector had been removed by manufacturing to get something else installed. Just keeping track of what was done, what was "in work" (in progress) and what was ready to test was a massive chore, given the fluidity of such a large project. One senior manager summed it up: "This concurrent building and testing is the classic case of trying to put 10 pounds of potatoes in a five-pound sack!"

Somehow, though, managers, engineers, technicians, and government observers seemed to find a way around every stumbling block. Slowly, each day brought the B-2 closer to first flight.

WARNINGS—FROM INSIDE AND OUTSIDE

As Northrop and its team pushed to get the first B-2 ready to fly, a number of ominous warnings found their way to reporters and government officials. As an *Aviation Week* engineering editor, I received several of them: anonymous letters from inside the B-2 organization, plus a series of concerned messages and verbal warnings from an experienced engineer outside the program.

We weighed these carefully, discussing whether we should develop a story for our magazine from them or not. We knew that the Air Force and Northrop were striving to keep the B-2 program bathed in as positive a light as possible. Asking their officials to comment on the warnings would assuredly yield "poo-poo" answers. On the other hand, if there really were serious problems with the aircraft or the program, the letters warranted further investigation.

One anonymous letter, addressed only to *Aviation Week & Space Technology*, we finally decided was from a disgruntled Northrop employee working at the company's Site 4 final assembly facility in Palmdale. He assured us that he was not a "whistle- blower," but a taxpayer concerned about "lack of accountability on the B-2 program. It's enough to make [ex-Senator] Proxmire come out of retirement," he wrote.

His letter cited a number of incidents supporting a claim that Northrop management was unable to keep the program on track, and that the company's engineering decisions were unsound. Consequently, they had gone to Lockheed and Boeing "to solve elementary technical problems in the propulsion and structural systems," he claimed.

He alleged that "bickering between contractors" and internal organizations had become so prevalent that "the Air Force often has to step in to settle disagreements." Morale was sinking steadily, he claimed, largely due to excessive work schedules and poor management.

The unsigned letter closed with a charge of collusion and a chilling warning:

"It appears the Air Force turns its back on these daily fiascoes because of a perceived immunity to scrutiny, by hiding behind a classified veil (sic).

"Unless there is a congressional investigation before aircraft No. 1 flies, we may be attending an air crew's funeral."

Particularly unsettling to me was that some charges in this letter could be confirmed through independent sources, such as a retired general being hired by Northrop, then quitting in disgust shortly after he started work. Did that make the rest of the charges more credible, or not?

During the same period, in the spring of 1989, I was contacted by a senior engineering consultant who was adamant that the B-2 was unsafe. He had an impressive resume, having worked as a stability and control expert for a number of companies and government offices over a 30-year span. As a young man, he had been employed by NASA at Edwards AFB as a stability and control engineer, working on the agency's lifting body projects.

He said he had uncovered a potential instability in one of these vehicles, presented it to his superiors, and had been told his analyses were incorrect. He wasn't to worry about it. Chagrined, he had done as he was told, but was shocked to the core when, sometime after that, a pilot was nearly killed when his lifting body went out of control and crashed. The instability he had discovered, he claimed, was to blame.

The engineer explained that his primary purpose in bringing his B-2 concerns to me was to prevent such a reoccurrence. Secondarily, he wanted to transmit his analyses and concerns to the B-2 flight crew. "I swore back then that, regardless of what people thought about my theories and analyses, I would always make sure the pilots knew what I knew. Never again would I sit on important data that might save a man's life," he said.

Over the next three months, the man sent technical papers, his own detailed analyses and more letters to back up his periodic telephone calls. By then, he also was sending letters to a number of U.S. senators, stating his concerns. He asked for their support "on a subject important to you, me, the Air Force and the nation."

That letter continued: "The B-2 is a dangerous aircraft. The problem most apparent is roll coupling. This occurs when an aircraft rolls, and the rotation couples into the vertical or yaw axis. This has occurred on the F-100A, X-2, N-9M, YB-49 [Northrop Flying Wings], B-58 and possibly other aircraft. I see additional problems, but this roll coupling is the most dangerous." He also expressed concern about "the situation that led to the resurrection of the flying wing."

On a deeper technical level, he disputed the validity of modern flight control design that relied on modern *Kalman filtering* techniques. He believed that "classical" stability analyses were superior, and that the new methods would give incorrect answers. Further, simulators based on the fallacious models would fly perfectly fine, but the actual aircraft, subject to rigid laws of physics, "would not be fooled by the smoke and mirrors" of the new stability techniques.

I was convinced that the man was sincere and that his analyses made sense, but, without access to B-2 design information, I had no idea whether there was any substance to his concerns. After an in-house *Aviation Week* analysis of these letters and technical papers, I called Col. Rick Couch, who I knew was slated to fly the B-2, and told him about the man's concerns. He agreed to look at copies of the material sent to me and pass them along to Northrop's B-2 stability and control experts.

They assured the pilot that the outside consultant's worries were unfounded. They were confident the Northrop designs, analyses, and simulations were valid. He and Bruce Hinds would be flying a perfectly controllable aircraft that would act very much like the simulator they had been "flying," the engineers said.

Only after the B-2 had flown awhile did Col. Couch confide that the man's letters and concerns stayed on the pilots' minds for some time, despite repeated assurances from their own B-2 experts.

★ ★ ★

COL. RICK COUCH:

I had confidence in our guys, but you never know. After all, there was a group of engineers screaming that the [space shuttle] Challenger was going to blow up, too. Their bosses said, "No, everything's fine," and we all know what happened.

★ ★ ★

Regardless of the "trust factor," an engineer's confidence only goes so far when it's your tail riding in the new airplane, he observed. The final analysis is not on paper, but in flying the aircraft.

7

The B-2 combined test force comes to life

AT EDWARDS, POST-CRITICAL DESIGN REVIEW ACTIVITIES focused on forming the B-2 Combined Test Force (CTF) and building the facilities needed for flight and ground testing. The test group consisted of both Air Force and contractor, primarily Northrop, resources merged into a single organization that would eventually consist of almost 2,000 people.

A combined test force attempts to blend military and civilian managers, pilots, engineers, maintenance technicians, and support personnel into a smoothly functioning machine having a single objective: thoroughly testing an aircraft to ensure a good vehicle is sent to Air Force operational units. Not an easy task.

A combined test force defies every possible management tenet for an effective organization, and creates more than its fair share of unique problems. The B-2 test force consisted of three distinct groups, each made up of representatives from several organizations, which had their own chain of commands and responsibilities:

- Air Force Development Test & Evaluation (DT&E) group, which was charged with making sure the new bomber met contract specifications. These were the "developers." The group included individuals from the Air Force Systems Command and its in-house contractors, Computer Systems Corporation and Ball Systems Engineering; General Electric; and the Air Force Logistics Command.
- A contractor DT&E group, which consisted of representatives from: Northrop's B-2 Division, as well as a smattering of people from other Northrop organizations; Boeing; LTV; Hughes; and a host of other subcontractors. These were the companies that actually built the aircraft, and their people were on-site to ensure everything worked properly; if

not, they fixed the problem and made sure their home offices changed the original design to reflect the needed updates.
- An Operational Test & Evaluation (OT&E) group, which comprised Air Force Operational Test and Evaluation Command, Strategic Air Command, and the Air Training Command. These were the "users," the people who ensured the new bomber would actually perform the job it was intended to do, and could be supported in the field.

In the final analysis, individuals and their personalities make a CTF work. Without the correct mix of cooperative people—those having a get-it-done attitude—this type of organization would never be effective. Even then, friction is inevitable, and the CTF is, at best, a compromise designed to save government funds. It requires the right type of manager to handle its day-to-day direction, a tough job requiring the diplomacy and leadership of a United Nations secretary general.

As if the demands of integrating diverse groups into a single, efficient test unit at Edwards weren't enough of a challenge, the U.S. Congress periodically stepped in with its agenda for the B-2. These elected officials and their staffs might have had the best interests of the nation's citizenry at heart, but they invariably created new problems for the B-2 team.

For example, one of Congress' mandates was that the operational test and evaluation group should be independent of the other test force members. This flew in the face of what the CTF was trying to accomplish in the first place, which was to integrate all the organizations into a single unit. This did not preclude independence for the OT&E team, because they still were able to decide what tests they needed to conduct, and their reports were not subject to local review.

By combining development and operational objectives, the CTF concept avoided the staggering costs and time expenditures that would be required if many of the same flight tests were duplicated in development and operational evaluations. Sharing these expenses as an integrated test unit avoided unnecessary duplication, but did not inhibit the OT&E community's critical role.

In essence, Congress was dictating that the clock be reset to the days before combined test forces, which were created to save time and taxpayer money! Congress' intention, which was to ensure that operational testing was a truly independent, final check on the B-2's ability to perform its intended mission, was commendable and fully supported by all involved. But the proposed method was a throwback and not an economical alternative, especially in the days of strained defense budgets. Eventually, compromises were worked out and the test force gradually evolved into a functioning organization.

CREATING A CTF

The CTF was formed specifically to wring out the new bomber, find its faults and get them fixed before turning the first aircraft over to SAC. To do that required a tremendous amount of work, even before AV-1 made its maiden flight.

The B-2 was tagged early-on as one of the Air Force's top priority programs. Service personnel managers were asked to provide B-2 organizations with the best qualified engineering, maintenance and flight crews available, and they delivered the same, to both the SPO and Combined Test Force. Contractor personnel sent to the CTF also were some of the best available in the industry.

When assembled as a CTF, these were some of the hardest working, gung-ho people to attack a major aerospace project since the heady days of the Apollo program, according to those charged with setting up the organization. The early group was once characterized as "the type you could throw a bone to and they would come back with a whole cow."

The CTF initially was formed at the North Base area of Edwards AFB. Just as earlier secret projects at North Base had been over the years, this put the B-2 team out of sight and out of mind as far as the rest of the base was concerned. There, its members started the planning necessary to form the large CTF and a massive, multiaircraft test program. For the first few years, it seemed like planning was about all anyone ever did.

The fledgling CTF was housed in an old building that contained a huge classified vault. Built years earlier for the ultrasecret U-2 reconnaissance aircraft program, the vault was designed to secure sensitive equipment and documents. It was converted into a large office that, initially, held the entire CTF: director, his deputy, and a handful of support people.

As the first cadres of operations, maintenance, and technical people started arriving, the CTF expanded into other North Base buildings. Invariably, each was run-down to the point that significant work was required to make them habitable, a task that repeatedly seemed to interrupt more pressing issues.

The CTF, as it grew, started becoming fairly scattered, with people in a number of locations. When the KC-135A Flying Avionics Test Bed (FATB) aircraft and its support troops arrived, they were moved into a hangar on the Edwards main base, several miles from the North Base complex. Coordination became increasingly difficult and everybody on the CTF looked forward to moving into the new B-2 Test Support Facility (TSF).

The decision to build an entirely new complex for the B-2 test program at South Base was based on several criteria; security was one of the top concerns. Isolating the B-2 CTF on the south side of the primary runway, well-removed from the main Edwards complex, simplified the problems of physical security by limiting traffic in the area to only people involved in B-2 business.

Other areas of the base would have been remote enough, but lacked access to the main Edwards runway, another important criterion for determining TSF location.

The flight test workload at Edwards also was increasing, and every building along "contractors' row," which was a main taxiway running from NASA to the runway, would be filled to capacity in a few years. There was no way existing facilities could absorb 2,000 people, six bomber-size aircraft, and all the support equipment needed by the CTF.

Finally, Ridley Mission Control Center, the Edwards range operations facility that provides real-time and postflight data handling during flight tests of most aircraft on base, was operating near its full capacity. The massive data requirements the B-2 program would generate could only be accommodated by greatly expanding Ridley, which was not an optimum solution, given other B-2 requirements.

The most economical alternative that would meet all these needs was to construct a stand-alone complex specifically for the B-2 program.

Building and equipping the huge B-2 Test Support Facility under tight budget and schedule constraints was akin to creating another wonder of the world, or so it seemed for the people involved in the project. It would be dedicated to flight test support, have state-of-the-art equipment developed specifically for that purpose, and give the B-2 program capabilities far beyond those enjoyed by previous Edwards-based test efforts. Before the TSF project was finished, almost $180 million was spent preparing for both flight test and logistics test support.

The TSF was built on a 120-acre site in the old South Base section of Edwards. This originally had been the center of test activities at the sprawling desert base, until new facilities were built on the North side of the 15,000-foot concrete runway in the 1950s. Since then, several buildings had been moved across to the north side, while others were either destroyed or left to languish. In recent years, the few structures left at South Base had been used primarily by the base Aero Club and for storage.

The TSF project would include constructing four large new buildings, refurbishing three existing ones and adding all the infrastructure needed to support the facility: electrical, plumbing, water supply, and the like. A new aircraft parking ramp adjacent to the big hangars would be connected by a center taxiway leading to the main Edwards runway. An underground fuel hydrant system would feature two huge fuel tanks near the aircraft parking area.

Security would be inherent in characteristics of the buildings themselves, as well as through extensive lighting, and a stout fence surrounding the compound.

Military construction projects typically are nightmares of paperwork, red tape, funding constraints and mind-numbing bureaucracy. Add to this the often conflicting priorities of the parties involved, and one can begin to imagine the potential headaches for those at the center of a major effort like creating the B-2 TSF. The CTF leadership's primary interest, of course, was to ensure the facilities truly met the needs of the test group.

The Air Force Systems Program Office, while sympathetic to CTF priorities, was concerned most with holding costs to a minimum. These concerns, plus those of Northrop and other interested parties, were aired during a review of the TSF construction plans and relayed to the architectural and engineering firm charged with building the facility.

Key players in the TSF project included the Army Corps of Engineers, an Air Force regional civil engineer, the Edwards base civil engineer, the B-2 SPO, and the Combined Test Force. To expedite an already-slow process, a special project management plan was written to combine all these elements' interests. The stated purpose of this plan was "to meet the objectives of constructing the Edwards AFB Test Support Facility with minimum changes, at least possible cost growth, within schedule, and to meet the functional needs of the user."

Amazingly, all of these objectives were met. While many people were responsible for the TSF's construction, a good bit of credit goes to a dynamic 23-year-old Air Force civil engineer assigned to the test force. Being young and female, she initially was allowed to attend—somewhat patronizingly, perhaps —but not encouraged to participate in, many of the TSF planning meetings.

She immediately proved herself to be aggressive, quite smart, and totally dedicated to the project. In many ways, she became the driving force that kept any number of elements moving, never allowing "the system" to block necessary actions. Although others also were instrumental, she was one of the key players that brought the TSF into being on schedule and within budget.

A quiet ceremonial ground-breaking ceremony in May, 1985, marked the beginning of TSF construction. Massive earthmoving equipment started tearing up the area, only to hit the first problem: concrete foundations, old sewer pipes, and the like, from razed South Base buildings. Old plans in the base archives failed to document all these, and defunct systems were mixed with active utilities, which prevented simply ripping everything out.

Once these initial hurdles were passed, construction progressed extremely well for several months. Of course, there were a few anxious moments, though. When the first of several 422-foot steel trusses forming the "big hangar" were erected, they failed to meet in the middle. Despite frantic reviews of the plans and inspections of the completed steel work, a 6-inch gap remained at the top, where trusses were supposed to join at the peak of the hangar roof.

Apparently, the trusses had been manufactured to the proper specifications in the middle of a scorching Texas summer. When the sections were erected in the middle of a California desert winter, the difference in temperature caused the long steel segments to shrink, creating the 6-inch gap. Loosening bolts and adjusting each section of the truss "regained" the lost six inches.

MISSING EXPLOSIVES

During early refurbishment of two old round-top, quonset-shaped hangars in the new TSF compound, a detachment of the Edwards Security Police (SP) showed up one afternoon, announcing that it would be conducting refresher training for a few hours in the old hangars. The SP's canine corps would be trying to locate hidden explosives, so the contractors working in those buildings would have to leave. The foreman objected, but a memo produced by the base police proved they were authorized to use the facilities for their training.

The foreman stomped away to garner some higher-authority help from the Corps of Engineers, while the cops started hiding plastique charges. Once hidden, the trained dogs were sent in to locate the dangerous explosives. Meanwhile, construction was at a standstill.

By the time the foreman returned, the cops decided their training exercise was essentially completed, except for a small problem . . . they were missing one package of plastique. The cops concluded that somebody on the site had stolen the package; there was no other feasible explanation. More than 100 fuming construction workers—at the end of a long work day and not in the best of humor—were subjected to a tedious three-hour search. When open hostility between workers and SPs threatened to boil over, the cops gave up and allowed the construction crew to go home.

The security police were baffled by the plastique's disappearance. They were convinced one of the workers had stolen it. Although it defied logic that, if stolen, the package would be brought back on-site, the SPs decided to search every worker's vehicle as it arrived the next morning.

Of course, a horrendously long line of vehicles stacked up at the site's entrance and delayed the start of work that day as each car and truck was searched. Tensions again flared. One of the SP's dogs, spooked by one of the construction workers, promptly sank his teeth into the man's rear end, adding a bit of combat drama to the situation.

Finally, the dogs "alerted on" one truck. A detailed search uncovered the missing plastique in a worker's tool box, precisely where the SPs had hidden it for the training exercise. The construction worker about passed out as he recalled innocently locking and throwing his tool box into the truck and hauling it—and about a pound of high explosive—to and from home.

The contractor, however, got the last laugh when he charged the Air Force for time lost to the incident.

Other ironic moments punctuated the TSF's development, as well. A patio area between the CTF's huge main hangar and a multipurpose building was designed by an architect simply to take advantage of the space available. By incorporating a series of right angles to give the patio a visually interesting pattern, the designer innocently created a good representation of the B-2 bomber's wing planform. CTF pilots flying over the complex noted that the patio layout bore a striking resemblance to the right angle/parallel pattern of the B-2's wing leading and trailing edges.

A similar pattern was spotted in the layout of a patio area at Northrop's Pico Rivera plant. Everybody involved, however, swears that the architects never had a clue what the aircraft looked like; their designs just worked out that way.

Another strange twist occurred as a direct fallout of intransigent government bureaucracy. To meet federal and state requirements, the TSF obviously incorporated design features geared to physically impaired employees who might someday work at the site. However, logic went south when California officials insisted that building plans include provisions for a handicapped pilots' shower!

A senior Air Force pilot said, "Although many of our test pilots might arguably be considered mentally impaired, I'll guaran-damn-tee you they are all physically sound!"

TECHNICAL EQUIPMENT

After the TSF buildings were erected, the considerable effort that had been expended in planning how the facility would be laid out and equipped slowly evolved into reality. The TSF's physical features had been designed specifically for testing the B-2. That same philosophy extended to equipment installed in the buildings.

Members of the B-2 test force, assisted by several acquisition specialists shared with other organizations, procured the technical gear they would later be using: computers, telemetry systems, radios, and the like. This was a radical departure for the Air Force, which typically takes user requirements and turns over the procurement responsibilities to a group outside the CTF. Not this time, though.

To maintain control over the process, ensuring what was bought was exactly what was needed and that everything would play together, the CTF's technical experts participated actively in the acquisition. They wrote the specifications for CTF gear, then worked with contractors and Edwards' procurement officers to ensure delivered products matched the requests.

Equipment dedicated to test data acquisition and processing was designed to be a generation beyond what was already installed across the base at Edwards' Ridley Mission Control Center. Ridley was built in the early 1980s and was still considered a relatively modern, efficient facility. However, it was designed to support several aircraft test programs at once. On any given day, Ridley's control rooms and computers could be supporting real-time F-16 or B-1B tests, while processing data from F-15 tests run the night before, for example. It was a cost-efficient, matrix-type facility geared to support a number of users simultaneously.

The B-2 system, on the other hand, was to be self-contained and dedicated to only the bomber program. It was tailored to handle the tremendous amount of data that would be accumulated during the six-aircraft test program. Because it was dedicated to B-2 work, data reduction, and *turn-around* (the time between acquiring the raw data and when the processed versions are turned over to the program's engineers) would not be held hostage to other program priorities.

This, too, was a departure for the cost-sensitive test community, but highlighted two important issues: First, how important Congress, the administration, Defense Department, and the Air Force considered the B-2 program, and, second, the criticality of testing schedules.

* * *

Col. Rick Couch:

The system needed a tremendous capacity for manipulating test data in real time [while the aircraft was flying and performing test maneuvers]. And it had to be easy to use . . . what we call *user-friendly interfaces.* As it turned out, this system performed better than anyone could ever have hoped, thanks to the efforts of many dedicated engineers, mathematicians, and computer scientists. These folks did an incredible job, which usually went unnoticed by most.

* * *

The TSF's technical equipment was highly integrated, which required considerable coordination between Northrop, the Air Force, and a host of contractors working on a number of subsystems. These elements varied widely, including everything from a state-of-the-art telephone system that handled secure (classified) and open conversations, to specific facilities and equipment for ground-certifying nuclear and conventional weapons loading techniques, to storage and tracking of B-2 spare parts and test equipment.

At the heart of the data handling system was IFDAPS, the Integrated Flight Data Processing System. Developed by Computer Sciences Corp., IFDAPS was an updated version of an existing system used at Edwards' Ridley mission center. It processed all real-time mission support and postflight data generated by B-2 flight and ground tests.

While the aircraft was in the air, IFDAPS received a radio signal (known as *telemetry,* or TM) containing up to 10,000 items of information, then converted the ones-and-zeros of this digital TM stream into engineering data (such as knots of airspeed, feet of altitude, pressures in pounds-per-square-inch, and the like). Processed data were displayed on high-resolution Megatek television screens in a control room.

Real time meant that engineers monitoring those screens could see what was going on in the aircraft, which was flying several miles away, within a second or so of when something occurred. Electrical, hydraulic, structural, and other engineers in the ground-based control room could select what they wanted to monitor in real time and what they would simply store for review after the flight. The data available to these engineers presented a better picture of the aircraft's health at a particular time than even the aircrew had in flight.

Further, engineers in the room could talk to each other over a sophisticated internal communication system without bothering the pilots. Individuals manning certain engineering positions also can talk to the pilots over preassigned radio frequencies, providing additional insights and directions for the crew. Test pilots first introduced to IFDAPS or other real-time systems say they feel like a whole room full of engineers is flying with them in the cockpit.

Before the first B-2 flight, the TSF control rooms were configured specifically for tests that would be conducted on that mission. Extra positions were set up to permit additional engineers to monitor more parameters than would normally be the case on a test mission. This also kept specialists immediately available to provide specific expertise, if it was needed, to solve a problem that cropped up in flight.

Training on IFDAPS operation for personnel who would man these stations was accomplished through special classes for engineers; during aircraft engine runs; on practices for the first flight; and throughout the taxi tests. Checkout of the control rooms after equipment installation was a major task, especially the process of making sure calibration data matched properly with telemetry streams transmitted from the B-2. Without the right calibrations, the values of displayed aircraft parameters would be meaningless.

A package of computer software known as the Flight Test Management System (FTMS) also provided a critical link between the TSF and the test aircraft. Consisting of two parts, FTMS provided several critical computerized capabilities: The FTMS Support Section automated day-to-day administrative tasks: security and maintenance records, personnel files and training records, and facilities maintenance tracking.

The Operational Section of FTMS assisted engineers in planning the actual aircraft test missions throughout the program. It contained a detailed list of all the *data points* that had to be flown to accomplish a particular test objective, as well as the associated instrumentation needed for that test. In the past, just keeping track of what tests needed to be done, which had been completed, and what instrumentation was needed was a tremendous task, often dominating several people's time every day during active testing periods.

With FTMS, a flight test engineer planning a particular mission would check the desired test points to be flown, and FTMS provided information about the required instrumentation, whether the aircraft currently was configured with that equipment, and was it working or not. Once a flight plan was set up, FTMS provided an optimum instrumentation setup to ensure all the data for that mission could be acquired. Consequently, the aircraft, test planning, and instrumentation configuration were tied together through the FTMS common link. The computerized system currently serves a very important bookkeeping function, which would be extremely time consuming and costly to perform manually.

One of the most important time-saving resources built into the TSF was the Flight Test Avionics Laboratory. Patterned after a similar Edwards facility that supports avionics testing on other modern Air Force aircraft, the B-2's lab allows realistic ground testing of avionics hardware and software.

Across the runway, Edwards' integrated avionics test facility has repeatedly proven its worth on the B-1B, F-15, and F-16 test programs. The lab permits black boxes and associated software to be tricked by the computer's wizardry into "thinking" they are flying. Thus, the function of avionics systems can be verified on the ground before flight, saving countless hours in the air. Further, any electronics problems uncovered in flight can be duplicated, isolated, and corrected in the lab before retesting the system on a subsequent flight. Depending on the hours involved in solving a problem, avionics labs are estimated to be 20 to 100 times more cost effective than testing and troubleshooting avionics systems only in flight.

The B-2 FTAL occupies about 26,000 square feet of TSF floor space and emulates most avionics systems on the bomber. The lab at the Edwards B-2 test site also is patterned after a similar development facility Northrop built at its Pico Rivera plant a few years earlier.

The test community has proven time and again that contractor lab priorities often conflict with those of flight test. An on-site avionics lab dedicated to flight testing greatly enhanced the speed and efficiency of an aircraft test program, particularly on software-intensive systems. Without it, a fly-fix-fly situation typically developed, which disrupted the planned test schedule and proved extremely inefficient.

To save time and money on each test mission, and reduce the number of confirmation flights needed for avionics work, a dedicated lab made sense. Each flight could be flown with the confidence that all the systems and their software were working properly before takeoff.

FINAL TOUCHES

Construction of the TSF essentially completed, the B-2 CTF started moving from North Base into its new quarters. Somewhere around moving time, putting up a flag pole in front of the B-2 TSF became a personal priority for Col. Rick Couch. It would serve as a visible sign that the CTF was indeed in business, as well as a focus of patriotism for the people working there, especially because they were somewhat isolated from the rest of the base. Securing a flagpole through routine Air Force supply channels was one option, but would take time and require a pile of justifications. It was hardly critical to the program, so its priority would be low.

* * *

COL. RICK COUCH:

When Northrop heard we were looking for a flagpole, one of their managers walked into my office and said there was one at the Palmdale Site 4 production facility that might be available. The SPO approved, so I approached Northrop's site manager about the flagpole. He not only was willing to let us have the pole, but offered to help move it to Edwards for us. Getting it "planted" was the next hurdle.

One of our facilities engineers dutifully went through "the system" by talking to Edwards' overburdened civil engineers, only to be told they might get to it in about six months. To our rescue came a construction contractor who already had a crew working at South Base. He volunteered to help us set the pole and, three days later, we raised our first U.S. flag in front of the CTF.

After first flight, several CTF maintenance troops presented me with a flag that had been flying at the CTF on the day of our first B-2 flight. That meant a lot to me.

* * *

KEEPING IT LIGHT

Moving into the TSF prompted a few incidents and "crimes" that now serve as interesting memories marking the shift in CTF operations. The heinous Bartles & Jaymes kidnapping actually involved the entire CTF before the "crime" was solved.

The CTF's flight operations section had obtained a poster of the two elderly Bartles & Jaymes marketing characters sitting in lawn chairs, displaying their finest wine coolers. The poster had been dressed up a bit by the flight ops troops, and ostensibly was prominently displayed to "protect the classified" information stored there. However, the poster was "kidnapped" one night and a ransom note left in its place.

For about a month, flight ops was without the calming presence of the two laid-back B&J gentlemen. A flurry of ransom notes and attempts to "free" them ensued, punctuating the turmoil of moving hundreds of people and their equipment into a new facility. The case was closed when negotiations culminated in an acceptable ransom and surreptitious drop: a case of B&J wine coolers left in the CTF parking lot. Only a handful of people ever knew who the high-ranking "kidnappers" were.

Furniture and equipment moved into the TSF and piled temporarily in orderly blocks set the scene for a baffling caper involving the organization's security force, as well. Security guards at any highly classified facility are deadly serious individuals who do not take their jobs lightly. At the B-2 TSF, they took great pride in how they performed their services, especially in knowing everything that was going on there. But security's very seriousness also made their guards irresistible targets for the bright minds of a hand-picked CTF populace.

One of the security guards routinely patrolled an area called the "bull pen" where boxes and crates of systems and control room furniture were stacked during the move. All was well in this area when the guard performed his routine check late one night.

An hour later, he returned to find that someone had put up street signs identifying the natural lanes created by the stacks of furniture. Memory Lane, lined with all the computers and word processors, joined Voron's Mine Road, where the flight operations desks were located. Roughly 30 signs had been erected by someone, although the guard was not aware of anyone entering or leaving the facility during that time.

The guard and his colleagues were stumped. How did the signs appear? To this day, the B-2 security section has yet to determine who the "Little ol' Sign Maker" was.

Tons of concrete, steel, and equipment comprised the test support facility, but people were the CTF. Accordingly, the full gamut of joys and sorrows that are inherent to any large organization were experienced by the people who worked on the B-2 test program in the early days. Some of these were amplified by the unique security circumstances in which CTF personnel found themselves.

A guard gate was constructed a few hundred yards away from the TSF on the only road leading into the site. This served to keep the curious from driving right up to the facility's security fence and staring, taking pictures, and the like. The gate's designers decided to build a sturdy "tank trap" directly in the middle of the road as protection for the guards, who stood between the traffic lanes during times of high traffic flow. The 5-foot high, 6-foot long, 1-foot wide brick and concrete barrier also was intended to slow the speeders who routinely blew by the gate during site construction, before the gate was manned.

Early one morning, one of the CTF's brightest PhD. engineers miscalculated the width of the new guard-protector and sideswiped it as he breezed through the unfinished gate. The monument to security guard safety was barely scratched, but an insurance company decided the engineer's old sports car was totalled.

As if that wasn't embarrassing enough, the engineer was subjected to unmerciful ribbing from his fellow workers, simply because he was so bright, and more than a little sensitive about the incident. He was once described as "the kind of person who routinely saw the world in three dimensions while the rest of us were still trying to understand just two of them." With that reputation, nobody was about to let him forget the day when an immobile security wall reached out and touched him.

VERY IMPORTANT VISITORS

The B-2 program's mystique also attracted a steady stream of official visitors to the various facilities. At the CTF, these included congressmen, their staffs, Government Accounting Office (GAO) watchdogs, SPO officials, Air Force general officers, and various high-ranking civilians. Each visiting cadre was given briefings that comprised general overviews of the CTF's purpose, a summary of the flight and logistics test programs, and information tailored to any specific requests and needs. Most were given a tour of the facilities, as well.

One Defense Department visitor focused on the flight rate planned for the test program, and the state of each aircraft that would be delivered to the test team. Although CTF personnel acknowledged that their plan was aggressive, they explained why they were confident it could be accomplished. The visitor left, however, convinced that the test force would not be able to execute the planned program. He took that opinion to the highest program and department levels.

Needless to say, his concerns got plenty of attention. For different reasons, though, he was right; the program would have been tough to complete on the test team's advertised schedule. His concerns resulted in a complete scrub of the entire test program and, ultimately, a restructured flight test plan. When repackaged, the new version was more in line with the flight rates experienced by other large aircraft test programs. It also made better use of each test B-2 and provided allowances for unknowns that are always encountered on a test program.

Having said that, though, initial B-2 flight tests paint a different picture. In retrospect, with the benefit of more than 45 flights on AV-1 and AV-2 as a basis for hindsight comparison, it seems that conservatism might have been unwarranted.

* * *

BRUCE HINDS:

The Air Force had some doubts about our original plan. They were concerned that [the CTF] couldn't generate the 28 hours per month fly rate we had planned. I thought we could. As it turns out, we're running at about that level, and doing it even earlier than I thought we would.

The [revised flight rate] was based on the Air Force's experience with the B-1. Northrop realized that, after it was cancelled [by then-President Carter], there was a tendency to stretch out B-1 work, just to keep everybody [in that test organization] working. So, the B-1A had incredibly low flight rates during the interim years before the B-1B came along. After the B-1B started flying, there was still a lot of that organizational inertia built-in, at least for awhile.

I was sure we could do better than that. Our basic premise was to fly each aircraft once a week, then keep the airplane up as long as we could on that flight. Now [late 1990], we're just about doing that. We fly till the crew wears out.

* * *

The ubiquitous General Accounting Office staffs that visited the CTF were somewhat intimidating, and they knew it. They had very little knowledge of flight testing, but made a real effort to learn as much as they could in a short time. GAO staffers quickly found that flight and ground testing are not as simple as they appear at first glance. Analysts realized that a tremendous amount of resources was required to support testing, there were a number of limitations on how the program could be done, and the matrix of tests required to determine the B-2's capabilities was staggering.

To their credit, the GAO staffers worked hard to understand the testing process, and their probing questions impressed CTF leaders. Unfortunately, their reports sometimes misinterpreted what they had been told, causing extra work for the CTF to unravel the misconceptions. The majority of GAO concerns, though, were expressed in a forthright and professional manner.

A visit to the CTF by the four-star general that headed the Strategic Air Command literally created a big stink, the likes of which should never be repeated. The visit was seen as a highlight for SAC troops assigned to the CTF, and an opportunity to shine for the boss. Consequently, a special effort was made to ultraclean every area where the general might show up. Floors were scrubbed, carpets vacuumed thoroughly, and everything arranged as if it were standing at attention for inspection.

The commander was scheduled to address his troops at an all-hands gathering in the main hangar. The white-painted floors, despite everybody's best efforts at keeping them clean, still looked grubby. Borrowing a special Air

Force steam cleaner designed specifically to thoroughly scrub hangar floors, the B-2 maintenance teams jumped into the five-hour job.

About two hours later, all the fire bells in the hangar started sounding off, alerting everybody that they had about 10 seconds to clear the area before a deluge of water and fire suppressant was released. Right on schedule, the protection system dumped thousands of gallons of "the most God-awful, foul-smelling concoction imaginable," leaving about a foot of water standing on the hangar floor, according to witnesses. The stench was absolutely terrible, and was still detectable when the SAC chief arrived.

Evidently, heat from the steam cleaner had been sufficient to set off the fire protection system. Subsequent steam cleanings were religiously preceded by temporarily switching the alarm and deluge system off.

GOOD TIMES AND BAD

As the first B-2 was taking shape and the CTF starting to grow into its new desert home, considerable time and effort were spent on getting ready for the first flight. People, though, not hardware or software or buildings, were still the lifeblood of the B-2 program. With a workforce of about 10,000 at Pico Rivera, 3,000 at Palmdale, and about 1,200 at Edwards, personnel issues were necessarily a major element of the program.

The remoteness and special circumstances of those assigned to Edwards operations prompted CTF parties at least twice a year, a spring fling that involved entire families, and a Christmas party for adults only.

The high point for many at the CTF, though, was the open house for families after the TSF was completed. CTF members finally could show their families where Mom or Dad worked: offices, the highly technical control rooms, and huge hangar. That event featured tables loaded with food, games for the kids, dancing, and even a B-1B bomber for everyone to eyeball. It wasn't quite a B-2, but it was at least related.

Senior CTF managers and their staffs dealt with the usual spate of personnel problems that afflict any large group: off-duty drinking, domestic issues, and illnesses. But several tragedies that occurred during the hectic period leading up to first flight were unusual and deeply affected everybody on the test force.

In October, 1988, one of the CTF's young facilities engineers started suffering from severe headaches and was diagnosed as having brain cancer. The CTF had gone through hell trying to get the 25 year-old a clearance to work on the program in the first place, simply because he was younger than most others on the test team. A quiet individual, he had proven to be a real asset to the organization, and had grown close to several of his younger coworkers.

Surgery did not eliminate the deadly cancer and doctors only gave him approximately six to eight months to live. But hope was renewed when a Canadian medical research clinic suggested that a new treatment for that type of cancer was showing promise. The procedure was not approved in the U.S., so his insurance would not pay the heavy costs associated with going to Canada for treatment.

The young man's parents provided the necessary means to get the treatment, and he returned to the CTF with the cancer in full remission. He married and started rebuilding his life, confident the cancer was defeated. About a year later, though, the deadly disease came out of remission with a vengeance. Despite heroic efforts to move him close to Boston, his parental home, the young man died in Lancaster, California, near Edwards AFB. The traumatic loss struck just as the test force was at its busiest, during checkout of the B-2 for first flight.

Another maintenance man in the CTF lost a young son to bone marrow cancer after a lengthy battle. That also happened during the frantic period surrounding first flight, adding to the pressures and emotional stress experienced by the entire test force.

A traffic accident claimed another life, as well. Two-lane desert roads that connect the remote Edwards Air Force Base complex to several communities in the south end of the Antelope Valley are dangerous at best. Repeated admonitions from Edwards' leaders to *drive carefully* on these back roads do little to slow the speeds most people drive on the long and boring, isolated stretches of sun-beaten pavement.

On his way home one afternoon, a Northrop B-2 maintenance employee was struck by a motorcycle rider doing about 80 mph. The two-wheeler drifted across the centerline, hit the man's car, and smashed through the windshield, killing the drivers of both vehicles.

Tragedies such as these were not unique to the B-2 program, but they were a part of it. They served as poignant reminders that, in an unusual, special way, the rigors of building and testing this particular aircraft also had bound together the lives of all those involved.

Constructing the test support facility and putting the test force together were major milestones in the overall B-2 program. Thousands of people were involved at all levels, focused ultimately into the day-to-day activities of those assigned to Edwards. Through their tireless efforts, all the pieces came together correctly, and the TSF became a show piece for the program. It and the assembled test team were ready to receive the first B-2 and get on with the test program.

8

Rollout

IN APRIL, 1988, THE AIR FORCE STARTED LIFTING the veil of secrecy that had surrounded the B-2 program for years. A relatively accurate artist's rendition of the bomber in flight was released, providing the American public its first look at the mysterious aircraft. The service also admitted for the first time that the aircraft would be tested at Edwards AFB.

The fact that it was a flying wing surprised very few people, but the B-2's highly blended wing and body, smooth curvature, and serrated trailing edge were radical departures from most bomber designs. The B-1B had hinted at some of these features, but were a full generation away from those of the B-2. Stealth technology was visible now, and, rather than removing some of the mystique that had surrounded the B-2 program, the artist's drawing piqued the nation's interest even more.

The Air Force dropped another public relations bombshell when it announced that a formal, although highly controlled, rollout ceremony would be held sometime later that year, followed shortly thereafter by the first flight; actual calendar dates for rollout and first flight would be provided later.

When the B-2 sketch was released on April 22, 1988, everybody on the program knew the bomber's first flight was already going to be almost a year late. Optimism and an underestimation of work yet to be completed were at the roots of these delays, and program officials were acutely aware of how quickly scheduled dates could slip.

Many felt that open discussions about and commitments to a scheduled flight date would only backfire if the date slipped, as it had before. But most agreed that it was time to start releasing selected information. Taxi tests and the first flight could not feasibly be carried out in secrecy; releasing specific bits of information now would pay dividends later.

* * *

COL. RICK COUCH:
At Edwards, we had heard talk about an impending news release, but,

the day it actually happened, we only learned about it 15 minutes before the press conference convened in Washington. We quickly passed the word to our CTF personnel, to make sure they wouldn't be surprised by friends and family when they went home that evening.

This was a major departure for us. Before April 22, our people had been ordered to neither confirm nor deny any speculation about the B-2 or that it would be tested at Edwards. After April 22, people could discuss only what had been approved for release. Now we were faced with distinguishing between what was releasable and what was still classified to avoid inadvertent disclosure of sensitive data.

Further, the idea of a formal public rollout was so inconsistent with the heavy security we had lived with for more than five years that I could hardly believe it was even being considered, let alone planned. It was, though, and it seemed to some of us that half the world was going to be invited to attend the event.

* * *

Despite the planned shift to a heightened public profile for the program, activities at Pico Rivera, Palmdale, Edwards and Wright-Patterson AFBs, and the major subcontractor sites continued as before. Rumors, some later confirmed as fact, continued to filter out that construction of AV-1 was proceeding relatively well, although problems continued. As mentioned earlier, wiring harnesses had to be pulled out and replaced in the cockpit area. The windscreen transparencies were stressed in their frames. The wing leading edge, a complicated labyrinth designed to dissipate radar energy, became a knotty manufacturing problem.

Production employees went to seven-day work weeks, and daily overtime for many became the norm. At Palmdale, the number of cars parked in the parking lot at Site 4, where the No. 1 B-2 was being built, steadily increased.

Boeing, which produces a number of major structural elements such as the outboard wing and the aft center body sections, advertised in Southern California papers for mechanics, inspectors, structures and jig builders, electricians, and production expeditors. Boeing representatives rented several rooms at the Desert Inn Motel in Lancaster, Calif., to serve as makeshift employment offices. Local aerospace workers that had been displaced from Rockwell International's Palmdale plant as B-1B bomber production wound down quickly lined up to fill out applications and wait for a brief screening interview.

Speculation that Boeing would take over B-2 production was fed by corroboration in official circles that the Air Force had become impatient with Northrop's handling of the program. Newspapers, magazines, and television reporters pestered Northrop and the Air Force for details and confirmation, but the official word was simple: Northrop would remain the B-2 program's prime contractor.

There was, indeed, some internal discussion about Boeing assuming a larger role in the program, but Northrop retained its key position. In fact, Boeing had its own problems, and the Air Force was well aware of them. The Seattle-based firm had fallen behind on some of its production tasks and had been unable to complete the wing sections before they were to be shipped to Palmdale. Consequently, Boeing hired local workers to complete electrical, fuel system, and other manufacturing on the wings after delivery to the final assembly site. Obviously, this was not the optimum approach from Boeing's point of view, but it allowed other time-critical work on the first bomber to continue.

PLANNING AND GROUND TESTS

The Edwards test team, plus their SPO counterparts at Wright-Patterson AFB, Ohio, and Northrop, were still focused on detailed test planning. Each Northrop test document, called a *flight test work order* (FTWO), was about 300 to 600 pages long, laying out all the necessary information for flying individual test points.

Approximately 85 FTWOs will have been written before the B-2 program ends. Writing and reviewing these were monumental tasks that absorbed considerable time. Program officials estimate that all FTWO reviews consumed about 18 months. Similar documents, called *logistic test work orders* (LTWO) governed thousands of ground tests. More than 10,000 of these were generated and reviewed.

Part of the Edwards team focused on planning the first few flights, trying to think of all possible contingencies and preparing an action plan to deal with them. To a person not familiar with the process, the amount of preparation that goes into a major test flight is absolutely mind-boggling. Hours of planning each step of the flight—from before engine start through takeoff, performance of in-flight tests, landing, and shutdown—are necessary to ensure all data are obtained efficiently.

The proper instrumentation parameters must be activated at just the right time to acquire data on a particular test, and the test must be flown in a specific way. *Test cards* used by the flight crew and ground test controllers are written to ensure all activities happen on schedule. These are organized as step-by-step checklists and followed religiously, although the order of testing might be shuffled to accommodate aircraft or flight condition changes.

Test maneuvers are preceded by setting up *initial conditions*, such as required airspeed, altitude, and trim condition. Test points are grouped to take advantage of previous or following test conditions. For example, if one test ends at a high airspeed, good energy management planning would call for a subsequent test point to begin at a high airspeed. Or, that speed might be advantageously used in climbing a few thousand feet before starting the next test, trading airspeed energy for altitude.

Time management also is a key criterion. Instead of simply flying in circles while waiting for a tanker to reach the refueling altitude, a flight test engineer might plan some "hip-pocket" communication or navigation system tests to fill the waiting time to advantage.

Added to the detailed flight planning are additional scheduling tasks necessary to secure range tracking, air refueling tankers, and airspace commitments, then double-checking to be sure they are available when needed. Put these all together and a person starts to understand why it might take weeks to plan for a specific flight of a long-endurance aircraft like the B-2. Because the B-2 was expected to fly more than once a week at times, many people were dedicated to this detailed planning process, ensuring test missions could be formulated in parallel.

Also during this time, flight test personnel were supporting a variety of ground test activities. Engineers, pilots, and maintenance technicians were either conducting, assisting, or reporting on testing being done in the B-2 laboratories. These support tasks were integrated with actual practice sessions, often using the laboratories, to prepare key people for the first flight.

FLYING THE TIFS AIRCRAFT

The *total in-flight simulator* (TIFS), one of the most valuable tools for training the B-2 test pilots, also supplied excellent data for flight control system design. Bruce Hinds, Northrop's chief B-2 test pilot, Col. Couch, and other designated B-2 pilots flew the highly modified Convair NC-131 to evaluate control law implementations.

The Calspan Corp. TIFS aircraft is a tremendous flight research tool, but, visually, it's also an ugly creature, at best. Imagine an old airliner sitting quietly on the ramp, then imagine a two-propped C-131 ramming the first aircraft from the rear, destroying all but the cockpit area of the first. If the first aircraft's cockpit area was then simply bolted to the "chin" area of the C-131, creating a two-cockpit vehicle with one behind and above the other, you have a fair mental picture of TIFS.

The top or aft-most cockpit (the NC-131's real one) is occupied by Calspan Corp. pilots, who serve primarily as safety observers. If the test pilots up front run into a problem that ultimately could be hazardous to the aircraft, the Calspan crew can automatically disengage the research system and take over control of the aircraft.

Through the magic of electronics, the lower-front cockpit can be configured to "feel and fly" like almost any other aircraft. For the three B-2-related evaluations flown on TIFS, the test pilots first crawled on their knees through a tunnel to enter the forward cockpit. There, they found a flight deck configured with several basic B-2 features. A center control stick and left-hand throttle quadrant had been installed, and the windscreen had been altered to emulate the B-2 cockpit's visibility.

TIFS had the advantage of putting it all together for the test pilots, giving them an opportunity to preview the B-2's handling in an actual flying environment.

* * *

BRUCE HINDS:

TIFS is a very good motion and visual simulation. It gets rid of the 80 to

100 millisecond lags that are inherent in even very good ground-based simulators. You also add in the "white knuckle" factor with TIFS . . . pitting your pink body against the ground. This [ensures] real "pilot gains." Things that we may have seen in the ground-based sim, and thought were *no-factors*, became more important when seen in the TIFS. [Other modern, fly-by-wire aircraft programs] have discovered the same thing, using TIFS.

There are some limitations to TIFS . . . mainly its computer size [capacity]. We had to simplify some of the B-2 software quite a bit, putting in a lot of linear extractions, so it would run on the TIFS computer. We "linearized" a lot of functions that were actually curves in the real aircraft's [flight control system]. That's the only way TIFS could handle the software.

* * *

The first TIFS flights identified several important aspects of the B-2 flight control laws, such as the stick *feel gradient*, that needed to be changed to improve safety. Later TIFS flights confirmed that several changes made to control laws had completely corrected the problems.

* * *

COL. RICK COUCH:

A second TIFS session proved very interesting, because we discovered several anomalies when flying in *ground effect*. In essence, ground effect refers to how the aircraft behaves when flying in the cushion of air under an airplane just before landing. [The ground effect model was not included for evaluation during the first TIFS session.]

The problem we ran into was planting the aircraft precisely where we wanted it on the runway. Our landing performance became unpredictable . . . and that is *not* the way we wanted the aircraft to fly.

The harder the engineers worked to figure out what to do about the landing dispersion problem, the more confused the issue became. There were a lot of arguments about whether the problem lay in the TIFS simulation . . . maybe it didn't really simulate the B-2 . . . or in the aircraft's set of control laws. I always voted for the simulation problem, but the issue remained an open question until we actually flew the B-2 for the first time.

* * *

BRUCE HINDS:

One of our pilots got into a pretty good PIO [*pilot-induced oscillation*] due to ground effect. The aerodynamic model [the computer program that simulated the B-2's aerodynamics] that we were running at that time was the best we had from wind tunnel testing, but it really wasn't representative of the B-2. To me, it seemed very "sharp-edged," where handling characteristics changed sharply when the airplane got close to the ground.

It caused what I called the "skipping rock syndrome," like going from air to water as we approached the ground. As we got into ground effect, the aerodynamic [model] seemed to change enough that the airplane would almost skip, then sink down a bit. It was controllable, but not really a desirable response.

After that session, we decided this could be a problem, so we made an adjustment to the flight controls. We later threw it out, because we found that, in the actual aircraft, ground effect was no big problem at all.

* * *

As Couch and Hinds described, TIFS evaluations had their exciting moments while the B-2 pilots sorted out what was good and not so good about the control law implementations. Of course, they were not alone on these flights. Other hardy souls that put up with hours of repeated landing tests and maneuvering included the Calspan safety pilots who kept the "real" aircraft functional and safe.

Another courageous group consisted of data system operators who sat in the back of TIFS, running the computers and data acquisition systems that constituted the real heart of the unique testbed. Unable to see what the B-2 crews were doing up front, the operators could only listen to the pilots' comments and heavy breathing as they flew repeated approaches to landings.

Several Northrop and Air Force engineers also rode along, keeping a written log of what tests were being done at what time, as well as what the pilots were saying about the aircraft's handling. These logs and notes were used to recreate the flights later, when each landing was carefully reconstructed and reviewed.

Most of these recording engineers had never been involved in a flight test before. They must have had a few anxious moments as they watched the B-2 pilots make multiple approaches, trying to induce flight control system glitches by putting it through unusual conditions. Besides being a real asset to this phase of testing, the engineers also acquired a healthy appreciation for problems the pilots later faced during B-2 flight tests.

A FLIGHT TEST LEGEND'S INFLUENCE

While preparation and detailed planning were foremost and directly responsible for the success experienced so far in the B-2 test program, more than a few "breaks" also came from unexpected quarters. One of these was credited to Brig. Gen. Charles E. "Chuck" Yeager, a retired Air Force test pilot best known as the first man to successfully fly supersonically.

Each B-2 CTF pilot routinely flew proficiency flights in the F-16, which later would be used for safety and photo chase. Exercising his standing right to periodically fly with Edwards test pilots, Yeager took the controls of an F-4 Phantom and joined the B-2 pilots' formation one day during the period before the bomber's rollout.

After the flight, Yeager asked one of the B-2 test pilots to join him at the Edwards test operations building. Once alone, Yeager started talking about the Northrop B-2 Division's organization and how it was affecting the overall test program. Although Yeager was known to be a long-time consultant to Northrop, the CTF pilot had no idea whether the retired general had ever been given security access to the B-2 program. Although uncomfortable with Yeager's direct approach, the young CTF pilot did his best to appear cooperative while avoiding specifics.

It was surprising how accurate Yeager's assessments were, though. Inside the B-2 Combined Test Force, there had been frequent discussions about Northrop's organization, which placed its flight test unit under control of the engineering department. Although normal for Northrop, this was considered an aberration in the aerospace industry. The concern was that this arrangement could make it very difficult for the flight test team to fairly and objectively evaluate an aircraft's design.

The thinking went, "If your boss designed the aircraft, and believes it is as close to perfect as it can get, are you going to be the one that tells him the design has some serious problems?" More than one messenger has been shot in the heat of flight test-versus-engineering battles in any number of companies. The organization at that time was hardly conducive to impartial flight test evaluations. An independent test unit, separate from vested interest pressures, was the norm at other companies and military test units.

Although nobody knew what had sparked Gen. Yeager's interest, he supposedly left Edwards AFB and went directly to T.V. Jones, Northrop's president and CEO, and told him that his B-2 organization was wanting. Whether Yeager's comments were responsible or not is unclear, but, shortly thereafter, Northrop launched an internal review of its engineering/flight test organization.

The resulting recommendation called for an independent flight test unit headed by a vice president of the B-2 division, equal in stature to the VP of engineering. This arrangement ran counter to Northrop's prior history, and was a traumatic institutional change. But it was carried out professionally and ultimately was judged a benefit to the entire B-2 testing program.

PREPARATIONS FOR ROLLOUT

As completion of the first B-2 drew closer, attention again turned to the impending rollout. Initial plans centered around an indoor rollout ceremony, keeping the aircraft in a large hangar and moving it only a short distance. For a number of reasons, an outdoor event in November eventually surfaced as the final plan. Picking a precise date was a considerable challenge, because the rollout needed to occur between major steps in the manufacturing and checkout process to avoid significant schedule impacts. Also, November weather in the California high desert can be rather fickle, raising the spectre of a wind-blasted ceremony in the middle of a sandstorm.

Its location at Edwards AFB, about 25 air-miles from the Palmdale rollout site, gave the B-2 CTF a contributing role in the event, even if by default. The test unit provided people for a number of tasks, and made plans to receive the many aircraft that would arrive with dignitaries. Edwards also provided the Air Force honor guard and police to assist with crowd control and other security issues.

Early planning for the once-in-a-lifetime B-2 rollout got off to a rocky start, but finally settled into a smooth operation when the proper people became involved. Still, there was something almost surrealistic about preparing to show off the bomber after so many years of silence and secrecy.

From the very start, it was mandated that the number of people attending the event would be strictly limited. The invitation list was restricted to certain organizations, and only a specific number of people from each. Edwards-based units received authorization for approximately 20 people, neatly eliminating most of those who had been heavily involved in the program, working very hard for years. More than just feelings were hurt by this process; morale and test unit cohesiveness also were inevitable casualties. The situation was mitigated somewhat by installing television sets in several CTF briefing rooms so employees could watch the rollout ceremony.

Restrictions on the number of attendees were dictated by available space in the selected rollout area, according to event officials. A set of bleachers had been erected to face Site 4's engine run building, where the aircraft would emerge during the ceremony. Invited guests would be seated in each "arm" of the V-shaped bleachers. Reporters covering the rollout would be located at the V's vertex, in a special section directly in front of the aircraft, 180 feet from where the aircraft would stop when pulled from the hangar.

An approximately 30-foot high platform constructed behind the press section would give photographers and TV cameramen a more pleasing topside angle than would be available looking directly at the aircraft nose. Areas along the side of the rollout quadrangle would be limited to an Air Force band on the south side and a standing-room-only area for Northrop and other contract workers on the north.

The layout effectively prevented any views of the aircraft's serrated trailing edges or engine exhaust areas. The selected location also shielded the aircraft from outside viewing along a public road that bordered the Site 4 plant area, roughly 200 yards away from where the B-2 would be positioned.

Security for the entire event would be tight. Everybody realized that a new nuclear bomber aroused significant emotion in many, and risking a demonstration or even an attempted terrorist attack was to be avoided at all cost. As a result, considerable attention was devoted to determining who could attend the rollout and how they would get into the viewing area.

The possibility of traffic jams around Plant 42 and the Palmdale Regional Airport was high enough that provisions were made to airlift any attendee who fell ill to local hospitals by an Edwards-owned helicopter. To expedite air traffic into the Palmdale area, special arrangements were made with the FAA's Los Angeles Air Route Traffic Control Center (ARTCC) to avoid delays.

Planners knew there would be any number of jets and turboprop transports arriving, carrying government and corporate VIPs. Once they neared Palmdale, the LA ARTCC would hand the aircraft over to Edwards approach control, which would sequence them into the Palmdale traffic pattern as quickly as possible. During the ceremony, the airport would be closed to takeoffs and landings.

As the November 22 rollout date approached, the guest-of-honor, B-2 No. 1, had moved into the final checkout process. The instrumentation system was being installed and checked, and Edwards support functions were already being activated, preparing for the test aircraft's arrival at the base.

Every contractor manager and ranking Air Force officer hoped the rollout would be simply a brief interruption between checkout and start of taxi tests. Later, some of these same people estimated that the rollout was responsible for delaying aircraft assembly by approximately one or two months. This was caused by a sense that "the aircraft had to look good for rollout at the expense of finishing internal jobs. That's typical of rollouts, though . . . the airplane's always unfinished and the event is never 'noninterference,' as it is billed to be ahead of time," one executive said.

Unfortunately, a number of knotty manufacturing problems complicated rollout preparations. Fuel tank completion was the primary issue. Fuel leaks experienced by the B-1B bomber, a source of much frustration and reams of negative press, definitely made managers paranoid about the same thing happening on the B-2. Consequently, the decision was made to devote excruciating attention to properly sealing all fuel cells and system components. If a problem arose, time was taken to review it and find a way to mitigate the concern.

Delays were accepted in order to make sure the fuel system was completed as well as humanly possible. Those efforts later paid off. Through the first two phases of flight testing, AV-1 experienced no fuel leaks—absolutely zero. This is a phenomenal record for a new aircraft, and is excellent testimony to the people who meticulously sealed every tank crevice, joint, and fastener.

THE B-2 UNVEILED

Rollout day dawned crisp and pleasant, with only light breezes and a brilliant blue sky to greet arriving dignitaries and press. Still fearing massive traffic jams around the airport, several attendees from Edwards flew to the Northrop facility at Palmdale aboard an Air Force helicopter. A table with coffee and donuts set up in an adjoining hangar greeted the arriving VIPs.

Press reporters and TV crews were ushered into a temporary building set up behind the reviewing stands. They were given media kits filled with news releases, a schedule showing who would speak when, and refreshments. Both reporters and VIPs were given white baseball caps with a logo commemorating the rollout.

The attending press corps was restricted to certain publications, networks, and local TV stations. Print publications (newspapers and magazines) were limited to a single reporter, who also served as his or her employer's event photographer. Television crews were limited to a reporter and a cameraman.

These restrictions caused any number of battles: Air Force and Northrop public affairs officials found themselves pitted against the heavyweights of several TV networks. Ultimately, exceptions to the original dictums were made and all the major television entities were represented at the event.

Late in the morning, hundreds of invited visitors and media representatives were directed to their seats in the V-shaped bleacher complex. Air Force uniforms, most with stars, eagles or silver leaves on the epaulets, were mixed with well-tailored corporate suits and bright dresses. One reporter noted that 41 generals attended the event. A sea of white baseball caps shielded much of the crowd from a bright desert sun, and emphasized the fact that dignitaries were packed together like the proverbial sardines. Off to the north side, about 1,000 Northrop and subcontractor employees gathered in the standing-only zone.

Although the usual pomp and flair of a military aircraft rollout was evident, it was significantly scaled down from the massive events that had become the norm in recent times. "The B-2 will be shown, but only barely," was the stern message stated in the event's body language, which seemed diametrically opposed to reasons for even having the rollout.

There was little doubt that this was a public relations blitz prompted by a desire to generate more popular awareness of the aircraft and, hopefully, some grassroots support for the B-2. Air Force and contractor leaders obviously were concerned about rough political roads the aircraft acquisition would be travelling in Washington over the next few months, and the program needed all the help it could get.

A huge United States flag hung alone above the closed engine-run hangar doors, the only decoration on the facility. Armed Air Force security policemen with German Shepherd attack dogs were prominently positioned throughout the open area in front of the stands.

The white, scrubbed-looking concrete apron in front of the hangar was adorned with a five-point Air Force star, formed by five blue cutouts of the B-2's planform. Each B-2 cutout was positioned with its nose to the center and its wings forming half of a star point. The stylized star was a clever design, enough so that most of the ceremony had passed before many attendees actually recognized that the logo was created by B-2 cutouts.

The ceremony began when an official rollout party walked to a simple raised platform to the left of center stage. Secretary of the Air Force Edward C. Aldridge Jr., Air Force Chief of Staff Gen. Larry D. Welch, Northrop Chairman T.V. Jones, and B-2 Program Manager Brig. Gen. Richard Scofield each spoke briefly as part of the ceremony.

Finally, Northrop's Jones turned and gave the signal to open the hangar doors, saying, "Jack Northrop, we salute you," acknowledging the contribution made by the company's late founder and designer of its original flying wings. As the band played "Stealth Fanfare," a rousing tribute written by Air Force Tech. Sgt. Alan Yankee especially for the rollout, two large hangar doors separated and moved slowly horizontally, revealing the sleek gray aircraft. Then a tug slowly towed America's newest bird of prey into the open. The bomber literally emerged from the dark and entered the light, the first time sunshine had touched the aircraft. Until then, it always had been moved between buildings at night.

The crowd immediately broke into a spontaneous round of applause, accompanied by subdued "Oohs" and "Aahs." The B-2 struck most observers as both radically different and sinister-looking. One reporter muttered, "It's Darth Vader."

For those who had worked so hard to bring the aircraft to this point, the unveiling was a spine-tingling, emotional moment of button-popping pride. Those in attendance could now turn to spouses and say, "There's what I've been doing for the last few years." Wives, in particular, were finally face-to-face with "Lady-M," the "mistress" that had occupied their husbands' time. Many had long ago come to the uneasy conclusion that there really must be another woman in their man's life. To them, the latest in America 's nuclear arsenal probably was a welcome relief.

Hundreds of cameras snapped off thousands of pictures, and TV crews kept miles of videotape running over the next half-hour or so while the aircraft posed silently. Reporters unaccustomed to operating sophisticated cameras agonized under the knowledge that, not only did they have to accurately capture the facts of the big day, they also absolutely must bring back stunning photos for their next issue. Clearly, the real story here was the visual event. People out there wanted to see pictures of the B-2, so the more the better.

LOOK-DOWN, SHOOT-DOWN

The entire rollout event had been choreographed to prevent reporters and, subsequently, everybody else in the world from ever seeing the aircraft from behind. Only the front side could be photographed. At that time, Air Force security officials still considered the sawtooth-shaped aft edges of the flying wing as sensitive information.

However, the aircraft was, indeed, pulled completely out of the protective hangar, revealing the entire planform to any Soviet satellite positioned overhead. All but one media reporter/photographer attending the event accepted the fact that nobody, except the Russians, would get pictures of the forbidden trailing edges and engine exhaust areas.

Before the rollout ceremony started, Air Force and Los Angeles sheriff's department helicopters continuously maneuvered at low altitude around the Site 4 rollout area, projecting a menacing aura of strict security. A few propeller-driven twin-engined aircraft wandered over the area, apparently for a quick look at the B-2 site, but immediately departed. I was convinced our *Aviation Week* plan was doomed. Those helicopters were obviously there to chase away unauthorized flyers.

Finally, though, almost unnoticed by everybody in attendance, a small Cessna 172 appeared, orbiting several thousand feet overhead, tracing a lazy box pattern against the brilliant blue sky. The helicopters made no move to chase the Cessna away, preferring to stay low, it seemed. At that time, I knew we had done it; we had pulled off the unthinkable and scored a tremendous journalistic coup.

We *Aviation Week & Space Technology* reporters in the Los Angeles bureau assumed that, because the aircraft would be shown outdoors, the Air Force evidently didn't care that Soviet intelligence satellites saw the B-2's trailing edges. Then why shouldn't the American public?

Consequently, Mike Dornheim, *Av Week* engineering editor and a licensed pilot, rented the Cessna, then flew it over the rollout ceremony while photographer Bill Hartenstein clicked off about five rolls of film, using a 600-millimeter lens to compensate for the 172's altitude.

Dornheim had expected to be hassled by FAA controllers or Air Force aircraft, at the very least. For self-protection against possible charges of FAA rules violations, he tape recorded all voice communications between his Cessna and the Palmdale tower.

He later said his biggest preflight concern was to avoid all the other aircraft he expected to see flying over the rollout ceremony doing the same thing. He even brought along Keith Coble, a friend, just to help spot other airplanes in the area. Dornheim was surprised, and elated, when he found himself alone, legally flying above the airport traffic area where FAA rules permitted.

The following Monday, *Aviation Week* readers were treated to exclusive look-down views of the B-2, clearly showing the "forbidden" wing trailing edges, engine exhaust ducts and the bomber's full planform.

Although no official government response to the look-down pictures was received, *Av Week* reporters were surprised at the breadth of feedback. One Air Force officer predicted that "somebody's head will roll because of your pictures." Another shrugged and responded, "Hell, we figured you guys would do something like that."

William G. Hartenstein

Look-down photo of the B-2 rollout was shot by an Aviation Week & Space Tech-nology *team flying overhead in a rented Cessna 172.*

Northrop

Side view during taxi tests highlights the B-2's beak-like nose structure when the nosegear is down.

Northrop

Shortly after main gear liftoff, the B-2 bomber is airborne on its maiden flight.

USAF

More than 40 years after the YB-49 crashed there, a new Northrop flying wing glides over the Mojave Desert on its first flight.

Northrop

July 17, 1989: 8:29 a.m.: Touchdown, a picture-perfect landing at Edwards AFB, and the first flight was concluded successfully.

The B-2 heads for the main Palmdale runway in preparation for high-speed taxi tests. Day-Glo orange patches (made of radar-reflective material) on the wing leading and trailing edges were added to increase the aircraft's radar cross section, making it easier for ground stations to track the bomber during flight. Later, the patches were painted dark gray.

Northrop

Straight and level, B-2 pilots prepare to conduct a test maneuver. Rogers Dry Lake is at top of photo, with the Edwards test complex spread along the lakebed's shoreline (right).

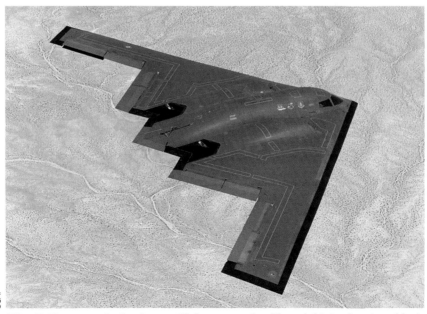

The B-2's unusual planform will become a familiar sight to desert residents around Edwards AFB, with six aircraft devoted to the flight test program through the early 1990s.

Refueling door open, AV-1 approaches a KC-10 tanker. Sawtooth-edged engine inlets and multiple air data ports around the cockpit are visible. A circular star-gazer port (for celestial navigation) is at the right edge of the cockpit's shadow.

Refueling tests continue as a KC-10 and B-2 cross over the Edwards AFB runway. The B-2 Combined Test Force complex is located to the left of the runway.

Northrop

Cockpit of the No. 1 B-2 shows several cathode ray tube displays, fighter-like control sticks, and left-hand throttle quadrant (only one set visible). Orange-outlined displays and control panels are unique to flight test aircraft and will not be installed in production bombers.

Northrop

Production line at Northrop's Palmdale Site 4 final assembly facility (early 1990). The second, third, and fourth flight test aircraft are visible here, with AV-2 in the foreground. Leading edges and unfinished engine inlets were covered with plastic for security protection during the photo session.

B-2 Air Vehicle No. 1 (AV-1) taxis from its hangar shortly after sunrise on July 10, 1989. Gull-wing doors atop each engine inlet allow more air to be drawn into the powerplants during slow-speed ground operations.

Landing gear hanging, the B-2 climbs steadily. Flight control surfaces are faired with the wing contours. Auxiliary air doors remain open during engine high-power settings.

Back in the air, second flight, ready for first landing gear retraction: everything worked perfectly. Drag rudders are partially opened for yaw and speed control.

At Edwards AFB in late 1990, B-2 No. 1 (left) displays its new low observables (LO) exterior following a lengthy surface preparation period. B-2 No. 2 (right), which will remain a flight test aircraft, has not been configured with production LO surface.

Upon nose liftoff, all trailing edge surfaces are faired with the main wing's contours. Side view accentuates the B-2's large underbelly. The bomber is capable of carrying more than 40,000 pounds of conventional or nuclear weapons.

Test control room at the B-2 Combined Test Force gives Air Force and contractor engineers instant access to data telemetered to the ground from airborne B-2s during flight tests.

With Col. Rick Couch at the controls, the B-2 lifts off from Edwards AFB on its second flight.

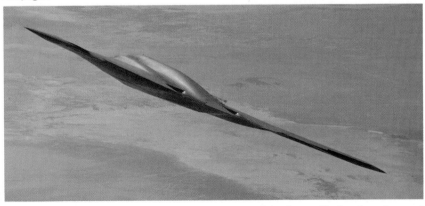

For a large aircraft, the bomber presents a surprisingly small visual, radar, and infrared signature from aft viewing angles.

Proponents and critics agree on one point: The B-2 stealth bomber is a radical departure from earlier aircraft, and will be remembered as a turning point in air vehicle design.

9

System checkout
and taxi tests

AFTER THE B-2'S UNVEILING IN NOVEMBER, 1988, the world's aviation community anxiously awaited the next most significant event of the program: the bomber's first flight. Air Force and Northrop senior officials were necessarily vague about when that would happen. The same phrases were heard over and over, driving reporters to exasperation:

"It'll fly when it's ready."

"We don't have a strict schedule."

"When we're satisfied that everything is working right, and it's safe to fly, we'll fly."

At Palmdale, the number of cars in the Site 4 parking lot seemed to increase sharply in the late spring of 1989. Inside the well-guarded facility, three shifts of workers scrambled to finish building the first test aircraft, then meticulously check every system out. Often, checkouts were done on one system while manufacturing technicians finished installing others.

Schedules and time estimates dictated what would be done and when. Essential tasks were identified and given priority over things that could be done later, or even deferred until after first flight. The steadily increasing pressure was felt by everybody, from the SPO director to the physically small men and women crawling through AV-1's fuel tanks, sealing every possible source of leaks.

As people worked long hours, fatigue set in and congenial personalities took on a sharp edge. Stress was a constant parameter throughout the Air Force and contractor B-2 organizations, exacerbated by an increasing din of criticism in Congress. The dominating thought and action for B-2 leaders was first flight; only that would quiet the critics who claimed the bomber would never fly and was astronomically overpriced. The aircraft had to fly as soon as possible.

JOHN'S CORNER

Outside the huge Site 4 facility, speculation about what was going on inside was neither confirmed nor denied officially. Rumors abounded in May that the B-2 would taxi "any day now," and the crowds of airplane enthusiasts that convened at the intersection of Avenue N and Sierra Highway—John's Corner—swelled accordingly.

A vacant lot at that corner was fortuitously located about 100 yards to the west of Palmdale Regional Airport's east-west runway. The broad concrete strip was also the longest of Palmdale's two runways, and would probably be the one used for initial taxi tests. The Air Force had remained silent about when the tests would be conducted, so an around-the-clock watch was informally set up at the corner.

John's Corner was owned by John MacWhirter, a crusty, fiercely patriotic retired Marine Corps character. For several years, John, or BJ, as most knew him, had been the host-by-default for a cross-section of Southern California aviation enthusiasts who simply liked to watch airplanes. Because Palmdale's Air Force Plant 42 was home to several of America's exotic military aircraft, the corner was a natural gathering spot for dedicated airplane watchers.

On any day, John's oversized faded-white step-van was perched on a raised concrete slab that had once been the foundation of a building at the corner. It was surrounded, at times, by everything from Cadillacs with car phones to beat-up Volkswagen Bugs. People stopped briefly during their workday travels to check on the latest B-2 rumors and hear BJ's current, usually off-color, jokes. It was not unusual to see a Los Angeles County Sheriff's Department patrol car in the group, the deputy writing up reports as he kept a sharp eye on the heavy traffic flashing by on Sierra Highway. Everybody also monitored the imposing buildings across the road, inside the chain link, barbed wire-topped fence that surrounded Air Force Plant 42.

Back in the early 1980s, BJ had displayed and sold aviation T-shirts, posters, and other memorabilia from the van, giving him a good reason for being there. But hot winds that swept the desert landscape every afternoon periodically ripped the posters, scattered trinkets, and deposited fine sand and dust on his wares.

Eventually, the business excuse was abandoned. John really just liked being out there, flying his large U.S. flag and sharing aviation lore, and lies, with his "guests." When asked by a stern Midwestern woman why he sat out there in the desert heat from first light until dark, every day, John unleashed a well-rehearsed, polished spiel that usually baffled the inquisitive soul even more.

"I just happen to like airplanes. A lot of people up here do. We show our support for the pilots who fly these unique aircraft by being here when they take off, waving at them, flying the flag," he would explain. "We also have a lot of respect for the people who build and maintain these aircraft. This is our way of saying 'Thanks' to them, too. Besides, we have a great group of people that drop by here. We share a love of airplanes and have a good time watching them."

"But what do you *do*?" the perplexed visitor would ask.

"I watch airplanes, talk to people, drink a little beer, and have a good time," BJ would respond. If pushed, he might admit that he had a part interest in a hot-air balloon business that sold rides during the cool, early morning hours. Of course, he had his Marine retirement pay, and he usually had a new venture of some type either in the formative stages or just underway. During the spring of 1989, BJ announced that he was in the car-detailing business, and promptly painted the giant step-van a canary yellow to prove it.

First-time, casual visitors rarely learned about John's active-citizen record, or his big heart. Like the time he rushed to a woman's aid when she skidded to a stop in front of his van, screaming for help. Her child was choking on a piece of hard candy, and she was at least five miles from the nearest medical facility. Panic threatening to take over, she had seen the group of cars and the big van at John's Corner, and remembered reading in the local newspaper that the "airplane watchers" typically had citizens band (CB) radios. Somehow, she knew they could help.

Before stunned onlookers could move, BJ had pulled the child from the car, dislodged the candy, and started mouth-to-mouth resuscitation. Seconds later, the boy was breathing normally. John's heroism was recognized by local leaders and newspapers, which recapped earlier incidents where he and his makeshift group had assisted with car accidents on Sierra Highway.

At other times, BJ had alerted Plant 42 guards by radio when people were seen trying to climb the perimeter fence. On one occasion, he ran across the four-lane road and physically accosted a young man seen climbing out (yes, out) of the plant early one morning. The intruder was a runaway, and had tried to locate his father, who worked the graveyard shift on the airport. He had wandered freely around several aircraft for hours, despite generally tight airport/plant security.

Still, most out-of-town visitors to the corner departed, shaking their heads and muttering about "crazy Californians." How could anyone waste his or her time just sitting on the corner, watching a Lockheed SR-71 Blackbird take off and land once a week? Sure, the occasional TR-1 spyplane, maybe a lumbering four-propped P-3C, a Rockwell B-1B bomber, a fighter from Edwards or George AFB, or a three-ship formation of C-130 Hercules transports would liven things up, but that was hardly an occupation!

Regardless of any reasons for being, John's Corner became the hot-spot center for trading B-2 rumors during the late 1980s. A strange network of construction workers, businessmen, nurses, transients, and reporters kept informal tabs on vehicle movement, hangar door openings, and general activity around the Northrop Site 4 plant.

People driving by the plant would report their observations over CB radios to the small crowd at John's Corner, which was quick to embellish those tidbits and create rumors of major imminent events. Big John, or "BeeJay" in CB lingo, fielded the radioed reports and passed them along to those with incoming requests for information about "what's happening over there?" The radio traffic, at times, could get pretty lively as interest in the B-2's activity heightened.

One afternoon, a hard-nosed Plant 42 security chief pulled up to the corner, outside the fence that marked his domain, and chastised BJ for reporting aircraft flight activity. In no uncertain terms, he explained that such activity was tantamount to spying and, if he had to, he'd see that every damned man jack on the corner went to jail in order to stop the radio traffic. He almost caused a riot on the spot, but most people grudgingly obliged and curtailed their reports somewhat. Or so it seemed. Really, key players in the watcher game simply resorted to their own simple code and the information continued to flow.

Whether Mr. Security knew it or not, BJ was well-connected enough that he probably could have created some heat of his own for the well-meaning, but a bit rude, security chief. The corner was frequented by any number of well-known personalities, ranging from TV stars and the lieutenant colonel in charge of Plant 42, to Pete Knight, former X-15 test pilot, retired Air Force colonel, and the current Palmdale mayor. BJ also had pictures to prove that several many-starred generals had stopped to say hello, as well as retired General Chuck Yeager, and local politicos.

But BJ's down-home patriotism and strong sense of fair play overrode any tendency towards political pressure or more-immediate Marine-trained responses to rudeness, and the security man was spared a lesson in the fine art of foxhole-brand profanity. As any regular to the corner knew, nobody, but nobody, told BJ what he could and couldn't do on his own land, unless he wanted to do it.

Almost nothing inside the Plant 42 complex escaped the watchers' notice, and often led to well-publicized speculation, or outright errors. For example, on September 22, 1988, exactly two months before the B-2 rollout, the Edwards test group flew its KC-135 flying testbed from Palmdale. The practice mission was set up as a dress rehearsal of the B-2's first flight, and involved all the various players and organizations that would participate in the actual event almost 10 months later.

Edwards and Plant 42 officials dutifully reported the KC-135's early morning takeoff as a routine test mission. Still, the next day, a local newspaper suggested that the B-2's first flight had occurred that morning. If the validity of several B-2- related tips nine months later were any indication, the erroneous press report might easily have stemmed from sources at the corner of Avenue N and Sierra Highway.

By June, 1989, John's Corner often drew up to 50 cars at 4 a.m. on Saturday or Sunday mornings. Ever the gracious host, John would move through the crowd, introducing himself and welcoming new visitors to his turf. On one early morning watch, almost 150 people strained eyes and ears to determine what was going on when vehicle lights kept moving around the Site 4 area, roughly one mile from the corner. Dozens of binoculars trained on the far end of Runway 7/25 monitored the movements of water trucks, street sweepers, and small pickups that wandered about with flashing amber lights on top.

Hushed conversations would stop instantly as one of the watchers saw another vehicle moving beyond the wire gate that separated Site 4 from the Palmdale taxiways. Was that it? Was the B-2 finally moving? Expectations soared with each tidbit, only to plummet when an innocuous panel truck would emerge. Little did the sleepy drivers of those vehicles know that their every movement was being watched by hundreds of eyes.

WATCHING AND WAITING

However, May, June, then the first weeks of July passed without anything more exciting to see than a concerted effort to keep the Palmdale runways clean. This, in itself, was B-2 information, no matter how insignificant it might seem now. We knew the aircraft had FODed (*foreign object damaged*) at least one engine during ground runs inside the engine run dock, and flight test officials probably were extremely sensitive to FODing another powerplant during initial taxi tests. Cleaning the runways seemed to indicate taxi tests would happen any moment now. But the bomber never appeared.

Despite strict, very tight security at Site 4, B-2 rumors started somewhere, then raced through the surrounding communities at the speed of a desert wildfire. Security officials must have steamed when a carefully planned night move of a B-2 between hangars at Palmdale was greeted by an impromptu audience. The rumor mill said an aircraft was to be towed under cover of darkness from Site 4 to a Lockheed structural test facility at the west end of the airport. Friday night was the supposed target.

Imagine the confusion when security guards, driving pickups and four-wheel drive vehicles around the wide-spread airport grounds, reported that night-shift workers at Rockwell International's B-1B plant were lined up outside their buildings, waiting for the B-2 move.

Some had brought folding lawnchairs and snacks to enjoy while they watched during their work breaks or lunch-hour. Others squatted on the ground or sat on the concrete, leaning against the huge hangar doors. A constant flow of people ensured somebody was always watching the B-2 plant across the runway while others were working. Clearly, the word was out.

At about 2 a.m. on another night, irritated security forces inside the Plant 42 compound requested that Los Angeles County sheriff's deputies chase away a carload of watchers they had discovered opposite the Site 4 buildings. Located at an odd corner notched into the southeast side of the airport grounds, the car was outside the fence, but positioned such that any B-2 leaving Site 4 would be clearly visible. The fence's exterior was plastered with signs warning the curious that photography and loitering at the corner were prohibited.

Deputies dutifully asked the car's occupants why they were there, recorded their names, addresses and occupations, then told them to get the hell out of there. Within hours, airport and B-2 officials knew that Mike Dornheim, *Aviation Week* engineering editor, and Bill Hartenstein, photographer, had

been in that car: the same duo that had flown over the bomber's rollout ceremony in November.

Whether these incidents ever altered any plans for moving the B-2 at night
is unknown. Eventually, aircraft were moved to the Lockheed hangars for structural testing. A few watchers saw the move, but, by the time it actually happened, most had tired of all-night vigils and had given up. People who had to
work the next day could only tolerate a night or two of fruitless watches before
conceding that the aircraft might have to just slip by without their knowledge or
participation.

In any event, the watchers might have prompted the Air Force to grudgingly permit the news media to cover taxi trials and the first takeoff. As one Air
Force captain said, "We decided we might as well have you guys in to watch
instead of hanging over the fence everywhere. At least this way, we can keep
you all in one place and, hopefully, avoid somebody getting hurt, or interfering
with our tests."

CHECKOUT

Behind the Site 4 fences, activity was reaching a feverish pitch as taxi tests, and
the all-important first flight, rapidly approached. Systems checkouts were
being run around the clock. More than 100 detailed test procedures were being
conducted while instrumentation systems accumulated thousands of data bits.

The flight control system checkout procedures, for example, were extremely detailed, requiring all interfaces to be working, as well as the primary
flight control hardware and software. Inevitably, problems were uncovered.
That's why testing was being conducted in the first place, to find and fix any
existing problems. When a fault was discovered, engineers would halt the testing until they could figure out why something did or did not happen a certain
way, then decide how to correct the discrepancy.

Quality control inspectors followed every move. They were ultimately
responsible for ensuring engineers conclusively proved the system worked the
way it was designed. They, probably more than any other participants in the
process, knew the importance of reconciling the actual aircraft configuration
with the approved design. All simulations had been done with systems set up to
conform to the design. Now, aircraft checkouts had to guarantee the real B-2
did the same. Without that assurance, all analyses and simulations would have
little relevance to the way the flight vehicle behaved.

Landing gear checkout was particularly laborious and time-consuming.
Clearly, proper gear operation is considered of vital importance for any new aircraft. Before the B-2 could be certified for taxi or flight, all gear struts, wheels,
brakes, and associated hydraulic and electrical systems had to be painstakingly
exercised. For an aircraft as big as the B-2, extreme care had to be used when
retracting or extending the landing gear for the first time.

Because most new-aircraft testing traditionally uses a *build-up technique*,
starting with the simple and proceeding to more complex and critical tasks, ini-

tial gear cycles were done at reduced hydraulic pressure. Using very little hydraulic power allowed the gear to be moved slowly and carefully to each new position. Ensuring the gear sequenced correctly, with all necessary clearances between gear components and the aircraft structure, consumed several weeks.

Once engineers were confident the gear would slowly retract and extend safely, hydraulic pressures were increased to the full 4,000 psi. Higher pressures not only caused the gear to react much faster, but, in turn, caused the entire aircraft to react. Snapping several thousand pounds of landing gear up and down caused the airframe to shudder and vibrate substantially.

Every experienced big-aircraft Air Force maintenance chief has felt his heart leap into his throat the first time he jacked a B-52 or C-141 off the ground, then raised the landing gear. For the B-2, with its higher-than-normal hydraulic system pressure, the response was particularly dramatic. As a result, safety managers and test engineers switched to a different type of jack, just to make sure the B-2 would not fall off its supports during *gear swing* ground checkouts.

Although hundreds of pretaxi tasks contributed, fuel tank sealing was probably still the central job that paced aircraft completion. Past history had proven that every new military aircraft has problems with fuel leaks; that's just the nature of the beasts. Any number of full-scale development programs were repeatedly interrupted by knotty fuel leaks that appeared overnight. Testing was always suspended if a leak was deemed sufficiently large to present a fire or explosion hazard.

Aircraft that use integral fuel tanks (cavities formed by the aircraft structure itself, as opposed to a rubber-like bladder liner inside a metal tank) were notorious leakers. All metal panels and fasteners that form the walls of integral tanks must be sealed with putty-type substances before fuel is loaded. If the tank leaks after the aircraft has been fueled the first time, much more stringent procedures are required to drain, evacuate fumes, and repair the leaking spots. The work typically must be done in a special hangar and, to minimize the danger of fire or explosion from trapped fumes, other work on the aircraft is prohibited. All that takes time, too: time the B-2 program could not afford.

However, necessary time was allotted to carefully sealing every joint, fastener, corner, and seam in the narrow, yet huge tanks. Men and women performing this task were as dedicated and as tireless as any professional mechanic that ever built an aircraft. As mentioned in previous chapters, their efforts paid off.

The decision to start fueling the bomber for the first time was not made lightly. Those who had sealed and inspected every inch of the tanks were confident they had done everything they possibly could. Now was the moment of truth. Thousands of gallons of JP-5, a kerosene-based military jet fuel, were pumped into the tanks as inspectors crawled over and under the hulking bomber. Others watched anxiously, waiting for the inevitable drip or seep to start.

A few fuel line fittings had small seeps, but these were not considered leaks and were quickly repaired on the spot. Finally, someone declared that the impossible had been done; the aircraft did not leak. (Later, after the initial 16 rigorous test flights, B-2 No. 1 still had not experienced its first fuel leak, which is a testimony to the thousands of hours spent meticulously sealing and inspecting the tanks.) That investment has paid countless dividends, and is one of many key factors that has allowed the flight test program to progress rapidly and smoothly.

The fuel system was then thoroughly checked out, which involved completely defueling the aircraft, pumping out more than 150,000 pounds of JP-5. Throughout the process, all tank quantity and temperature probes, valves and pumps were checked to ensure they performed properly. Even though the same tests had already been performed in the B-2 fuel system laboratory, they were repeated on the flight vehicle to verify the system would work properly.

With fuel system checks completed, the first aircraft was subjected to final ground vibration and ground resonance tests. These involved literally shaking the aircraft vigorously, then recording how the vehicle responded. Characterizing this response was of vital interest to engineers responsible for the flight control system software and the aircraft's basic structural integrity.

Aircraft designers take great pains to ensure an airplane does not have any resonance modes that could be excited by normal flight. These vibrations can be set up when air flows over the skin, by air turbulence, or simply by moving the flight controls a certain way. If the airframe or control surfaces resonate, the aircraft could *flutter* at a rate sufficient to tear the structure apart in the air. Flutter is one of the most dreaded reactions an aircraft can have, and engineers do everything possible to make sure it does not occur.

Only flight testing can verify that the aircraft is free of destructive flutter modes, but ground vibration/resonance tests are necessary to identify any suspect areas or frequencies. Ideally, when the airframe is plucked, struck, vibrated, or shaken, all the vibrational responses will *damp out* (die down to zero) on their own.

* * *

COL. RICK COUCH:

Personally, I had worried about GVT/GRT [*ground vibration* and *resonance tests*] and how long they might take. I had watched the Fairchild T-46 trainer program struggle through the same tests, and that was a relatively simple airplane compared to the B-2. Fortunately, the very talented B-2 flight control and structural engineers had their collective act together, and GVT/GRT went extremely well. In short order, the data from these tests cleared the aircraft to fly. That was a major step that brought us closer to first flight.

* * *

The next big hurdle was ground engine runs. Checkout and systems safety specialists insisted that flight crews be in the cockpit for these runs. This was a judicious decision, because it capitalized on the pilots' experience with other aircraft, as well as on the B-2 training they had received. Ground-run crew chiefs were capable of conducting the tests, but having pilots onboard was deemed an extra dose of prevention. That decision proved correct before the tests were completed.

Engine run tests required the participation of many pilots, managers, test conductors, technicians, and mechanics. In some ways, the operation was akin to sailing a large ship or filming a movie: many people, all doing the right thing at the right time.

In the cockpit, two pilots were assisted by a technician that helped locate and activate more than 200 circuit breakers. Outside the aircraft, but still inside the *engine run dock* (ERD) test cell, six maintenance personnel scanned the aircraft for abnormal leaks or events that could not be seen from the cockpit. Another 10 people in the run dock control room monitored the bomber on television monitors, poised to activate emergency fire equipment or respond to any other anomaly that might occur during the tests.

Next door, in a special mission control room, the test conductor and about 24 engineers scanned data streaming from the aircraft's instrumentation system. Twenty-five miles away at Edwards AFB, another 40 or more engineers monitored even more data beamed from the aircraft. Another 10 engineers tracked the B-2's flight control and avionics systems via cables that tied special vans (located outside the hangar doors) directly into the heart of the two systems. These specialists could literally monitor every ONE and ZERO that raced around in the complex, digital systems.

Coordinating all these players required a single communications network that linked the cockpit with every other location. Additionally, each group had its own communications net, enabling side discussions about observations or problems without drowning out essential cockpit communications.

The initial startup problems with this extended communications network were frustrating, but an efficient protocol was quickly worked out so the tests could proceed. With so many people on the cockpit communications net, though, a chronic problem that plagued the engine runs was poor reception at the pilots' position. Hearing messages and directions, particularly while the engines were running, was difficult at best. For whatever reason, this reception problem was never solved, even though it "drove the aircrews batty," according to one pilot.

The actual engine run tests were conducted amid an atmosphere of anxiety, excitement, and frustration. Problems with the aircraft, technical support systems, and the engine-run building itself hampered the tests, but each was solved as it arose.

Tests were very detailed, progressing from simply starting and operating the engines in a stand-alone manner, to operation of every system in the aircraft that relied on the powerplants and their accessory drives. Once preliminary checks were made, every person was in place, electrical power checked and rechecked, it was finally time to hit the start button for the first time.

* * *

COL. RICK COUCH:

After all the preparation, I can't overstate what an absolute thrill it was to be sitting in the B-2 that night, watching as Bruce [Hinds] started engines for the first time. That was a once-in-a-lifetime event, and it wasn't lost on us. For this type of aircraft, that moment would never be repeated . . . the first B-2 engine start. In an instant, the powerplant was spinning up, and the aircraft "came to life" for the first time.

* * *

The engine run tests had their good and bad moments, as was expected. Each engine accessory drive experienced a leak of some kind, slowing things down to where it took almost a full day to get all the powerplants running. The leaks were nothing serious, the type of manufacturing-related anomaly that is typical of new aircraft. Several were nuisance leaks like those seen after a standard engine change on many in-service military aircraft. Together, though, they stretched the test period hours beyond what had been expected.

During one of the early runs, ERD control room engineers saw sparks flying out of the No. 3 engine tail pipe and ordered an immediate shutdown. An inspection showed that something small had gone into the engine, causing foreign object damage (FOD) to compressor blades near the forward end of the turbofan.

This was a major setback, forcing an engine change in the middle of testing. The change was complicated by an investigation aimed at determining where the damaging object had originated. Although never proven for certain, the FOD culprit was believed to be a piece of debris from the run dock's ceiliing.

Engine power settings above idle revealed several unexpected problems with the ERD facility. The building was designed to prevent the ear-splitting roar of four B-2 engines running at high power from reaching the outside world, while simultaneously providing physical security for the aircraft during powerplant tests.

Steel walls of the 26,000-square-foot test bay were lined with acoustic absorption panels. A bank of large inlet silencers above the run dock doors allowed up to four million cubic feet of air to be pulled into the building and fed to the screaming engines. Exhausted hot air was then diverted through two massive ejectors and a series of diffusion tubes at the back of the building.

At high power settings, a diverter wall running the full length of the exhaust ejectors started disintegrating. The wall was installed so one of the two engines that lie on each side of the B-2's main fuselage section could be run alone without causing a backflow that might affect the other engine. Tests were halted again while building maintenance experts tried to fix the problem. After a few days of unsuccessful welding and repair, they decided to simply remove the diverters, a task that consumed about two more days. Tests showed the modification was successful; with diverters removed, the ejectors worked fine. As a result, diverters also were removed from the engine run dock ejectors at Edwards AFB.

Once basic engine runs and interface checks were completed, the aircraft entered a planned downtime to finish a number of manufacturing tasks. These included some cockpit work and installation/checkout of the environmental control system (ECS), which were required before the final round of engine tests could begin.

The ECS is an especially critical system on the B-2. It not only directly affects pilot comfort through cockpit heating and air conditioning, but it supplies essential cooling for the all-important avionics systems.

When engine run tests resumed, checking out the ECS was a top priority. Test engineers were relieved to find the system worked quite well, requiring only minor changes in its operation. During an engine test one night, though, the ECS failed for no apparent reason, causing an immediate panic.

* * *

COL. RICK COUCH:
Since the ECS was being driven by the engines at the time, we scrambled to get ground air conditioning back on the aircraft as fast as possible to avoid frying the avionics. The ground crew worked frantically to get the air conditioners hooked up, but the harder they tried, the more things seemed to go wrong.

In the cockpit, the CRT displays started going crazy. It was obvious that major damage to the avionics black boxes was imminent. We shut down everything as fast as possible, but before we could get it all done, none of the avionics seemed to work correctly.

About five minutes later, we finally had cooling air hooked up. Everybody was afraid to turn the avionics equipment back on, knowing full well what the impact could be. At worst, some of the only B-2 processor chips in existence at that time might have been fried to the point they would never work again. At best, it would take days to sort out what had gone wrong and decide what had to be replaced. We just knew something had to be damaged.

After checking all the available data, test controllers cleared us to turn the systems on again. We carefully brought all the units back on-line, testing every possible system as we did. No problems showed up. Not one thing was damaged!

The incident served at least one positive purpose . . . it gave us a healthy appreciation for how "robust" the avionic system was in this airplane.

* * *

During this intense checkout period immediately before taxi tests, work days were extremely long, and fatigue was taking a heavy toll on everybody involved. The test pilots were intimately involved throughout this phase, so they maintained the same brutal schedule as others on the checkout teams. Bruce Hinds and Col. Rick Couch settled into a night-shift schedule of 6 p.m. to 6 a.m. They now admit choosing this shift because more seemed to get accomplished while senior managers were at home, allowing the work force to concentrate on getting the aircraft out the door.

* * *

COL. RICK COUCH:

Our scheduled 12-hour workdays were extended by test briefings and debriefings held at each end of the shift. And, of course, there was always that urgent meeting that one of us had to attend at other times.

By the end of the first engine run block, both Bruce and I were exhausted. I had lost about 15 pounds, mainly because all our meals seemed to come from a candy machine. It was never convenient to leave long enough to get real food. At one point, I got concerned that we would both come down with rickets if we didn't start eating better.

Throughout this time, we still had to maintain our flying skills through proficiency flights in the KC-135 avionics testbed and the F-16 chase planes, which just added to our overall level of fatigue.

Of course, we weren't the only ones in this shape. About 10 other B-2 CTF pilots were maintaining the same sort of schedule. The engineers working checkout and engine run tests were on an even worse treadmill. Some of them not only had to be there during the scheduled test periods, but also travelled back and forth between Palmdale and Pico Rivera to review all the data. I don't know how they ever survived.

* * *

BRUCE HINDS:

During ground checkouts and engine runs, the aircraft performed great, but those were some awfully long days for everybody.

Rick and I took the late shift. Rick seemed to work all day and night, too, but I tried to avoid that. Yes, I saw him nod off a few times there in the cockpit [during a test]! And, of course, there was definitely a lot of peanuts and Cokes. He's right . . . we ate out of machines most of the time.

* * *

Between the first two engine run test phases, during a planned downtime, Hinds and Couch were given one more chance to fly the Calspan Total In-Flight Simulator (TIFS) aircraft. The sessions were technically billed as a final practice before first flight. However, they also provided an opportunity for B-2 engineers to get one last look at the bomber's flight controls and the aircraft's behavior in ground effect during landing.

Each pilot was given two flights to evaluate a matrix of test conditions that covered all aspects of the control system's ground effects model. Everything seen in earlier TIFS and simulator flights was confirmed once again. The pilots finished the TIFS sessions with a fairly good idea of what to expect during landing on the first B-2 flight.

BATTLES ON THE HILL

Through June and into July, 1989, Congressional and media interest in the B-2 program ran high. Fierce battles in Congress resulted in a House Armed Services Committee proposal to cut $800 million from administration budget requests, and barely headed off an orchestrated attempt to kill the program outright. Representatives from California, Ohio, and Connecticut blasted the program for its high costs, calling the expenditure of $22.4 billion up to that point, mostly for research and development, a "serious mistake," according to the July 3 issue of *Aviation Week & Space Technology.*

Powerful congressmen such as committee chairman Representative Les Aspin (D-Wis.) attempted to preserve the Bush administration budget, but were overridden. Aspin tried to defer the budget recommendation vote until after the bomber made its first flight, pointing out that termination of the program was "the wrong thing to do at this point."

Not only did his efforts fail, but the committee proposal carried an additional requirement: no procurement funds be released until Defense Secretary Richard B. Cheney certified to Congress that the B-2 could meet its "performance milestones." That translated into proving the aircraft truly was stealthy and could evade Soviet radars to complete its intended mission.

Ironically, it was the concept of meeting milestones that substantially delayed the first B-2's completion. For example, a major milestone for AV-1 was moving the aircraft from the Site 4 assembly building to the engine run dock. That move was intended to indicate that a certain amount of work was completed and it triggered a big progress payment to the contractor team. Naturally, Northrop managers pushed hard to make that move happen as soon as possible.

When AV-1 was towed over to the ERD, though, it was nowhere near ready for engine runs, and had no business leaving the assembly area. That meant a lot of extra equipment had to be moved across the ramp to the ERD, just to continue building the aircraft. Technicians then had to work in a more cramped, less-suitable location.

Yes, the contractor made his milestone, and the customer was happy about it, but the schedule suffered in the long run as a result. One executive estimated that meeting the move-to-ERD milestone added six to nine months to AV-1's manufacturing and checkout schedule!

Fortunately, program leaders appear to have learned from that particular mistake. Subsequent flight test aircraft are not tied to a milestone-triggered method of payment. Performance is rewarded, now, not making an artificial milestone.

The executive who estimated delays caused by the premature move said, "Milestones are OK as long as everything happens like it's supposed to. When it doesn't, milestones really hurt . . . they cost time and money. There are no 'must-have' caveats on milestones, so things are rarely finished when the aircraft is forced to move on to the next stage.

"Having to move Ship 1 to the engine run dock was very inefficient. But, [Northrop] got paid, because it moved," he added.

Interestingly, Congressional debate over the B-2's future in late June and early July focused on cost, not the strategic need for a new long-range bomber.

Sticker shock was touted as reason enough to kill the $70 billion program for 132 aircraft.

This focus on cost seemed to catch the Defense Department and Air Force off guard. For years, any congressional official who wanted a serious look at the B-2 program was given access to it, including cost figures. Nobody raised a fuss while the program was highly classified, but, as soon as its existence became public knowledge, congressional critics started screaming.

Defense Secretary Cheney, in testimony before the House committee, took the stately body to task over this apparent hypocrisy. A number of committee members, he said, "have had all the access they need, certainly in recent years, on the cost of the program. Now is not the time for the committee to suddenly decide it's got sticker shock and we can't go forward."

Air Force leaders reacted to public criticism by pointing out the many technical advances that had emerged from B-2 R&D: the thousands of testing hours done on the aircraft; the risk reduction efforts already completed; and the planned schedule for evaluating the bomber, which ensured that considerable hard data would be in hand before Congress committed to producing more than 20 percent of the bombers.

In the California desert, the Air Force/contractor test team bore the brunt of pressure created by the debate in Washington and hammered home daily in the press. Work continued at a feverish pace to get the aircraft into taxi tests and through the first flight. At this point, each day's delay added more fuel to the budget fire created by congressmen who wanted to kill the program in the summer of 1989.

The Air Force knew that keeping a low profile was no longer possible, or advisable, for the bomber program. Past efforts to limit information flow appeared to now be backfiring, forcing the B-2 community into a defensive posture, always scrambling to respond to the latest barbs. This realization might have helped USAF public affairs officers (PAO) convince their leaders that the media should be allowed to cover the taxi tests and first flight.

Earlier, Air Force PAO representatives had suggested that a press conference after the first flight would be a great idea. Hinds and Couch, the two test pilots, were less than enthusiastic about the prospect, preferring to stick to their expertise, flying and testing aircraft. Ultimately, they conceded that meeting the press was a small price to pay for the privilege of flying that historic first flight.

To prepare the pilots for their introduction to the media, a PAO expert suggested that Hinds and Couch attend a DOD class that prepared senior defense officials to deal with reporters. It might have been a good idea, but nobody followed through with it. Consequently, just before taxi tests began, PAO officials sat down with the pilots to go over typical press questions and suggested responses.

* * *

COL. RICK COUCH:
The session with PAO gave us some insight into what we should expect

in a press conference, but the list of expected questions and proposed answers was ridiculous. I wish I had saved that list of answers. They were demeaning to everybody involved . . . like "the B-2 bomber is Number One!"

I was really put off by the lack of real substance being offered, and I'm afraid my displeasure showed. My attitude came back to haunt me a few days later, when my boss told me to be more cooperative with the PAO folks. That didn't help my disposition much, either. I'm still not sure who brought the matter to my boss' attention.

* * *

FINALLY—READY TO GO

By July 10 the aircraft was ready to begin taxi tests. Although not 100 percent complete, the checkouts had reached the point where these critical preflight tests could be conducted. Every possible safety-related aspect had been reviewed and rereviewed to make certain that nothing had been overlooked.

The pretest briefings that preceded each taxi test were events in themselves. The first mission briefing was held three days prior to the first taxi, covering all engineering aspects, test objectives, security plans, test cards, health and status of the airplane at that time, discussion of any outstanding maintenance discrepancies, control rooms status, instrumentation system configuration, projected weather, and all emergency procedures. Approximately 48 people were identified to attend this briefing, but, prior to first taxi, more than 100 showed up. That prompted new paperwork, a list of people authorized to attend these briefings.

The day before a test, another briefing was held to update the status of the previous meeting. Although it was a shorter session, it drew up to 130 people because all the pertinent control room engineers attended. During taxi tests and prior to the first flight, these briefings were held in a large hangar, just to make sure all the players could attend.

On the day of a test, a preflight briefing was held for the B-2 pilots and any supporting aircrews that might be involved in that day's operation. The 30-minute briefing provided a final status update on every aspect of the test. Separately, engineers from several of the key disciplines held their own meetings in parallel with the preflight briefing to review their particular systems and go over any limitations that they expected might affect flight operations.

Taxi tests were a critical part of all B-2 flight test activities, just as they are for any new aircraft. In general, taxi tests mark the first time an airplane moves under its own power. This new dynamism also marks a shift from engineering projections and predictions to hard-core data about how the aircraft actually behaves.

Although nobody mentions it, these tests also are the first chance to damage the aircraft in a dynamic situation if things go wrong. Without question, passing taxi tests successfully is a prerequisite to flying.

For the B-2, taxi tests meant real data could be obtained about ground handling characteristics: brake, wheel, tire and nosewheel steering operation; and airframe response to movement across the ground and to flight controls activation.

A build-up approach was to be followed, just as it is in most flight tests. Initially, only slow taxiing would be done, gradually increasing speed to just below liftoff velocity. Data were to be reviewed at each step before advancing to successive, more demanding tests. Tire and brake temperatures would be watched carefully, as would the bomber's aerodynamic reactions to increasing speed.

In the "outside" world populated by the media and B-2 watchers, the Air Force announcement that press representatives would be allowed inside the gates of Plant 42 to monitor the tests was greeted with relief. Many of us reporters had devoted considerable time to keeping track of obscure movements around Palmdale's Site 4, as well as the abundant rumors about the aircraft's taxi schedule.

The change in Air Force attitude towards press coverage ended early morning vigils and expensive aircraft rentals, too. Since early May, 1989, I had fallen into a pattern of driving completely around the sprawling Plant 42/Palmdale Regional Airport complex early every morning, seven days a week. I talked to the crowd of dedicated watchers at "John's Corner," and routinely tapped a number of contacts who might have some scrap of information about when the bomber could emerge from its windowless engine run facility.

Aviation Week and CBS both rented light aircraft numerous times, typically on weekends, when the most reliable rumors seemed to predict the B-2 would taxi. From just before dawn until about 8:30 a.m., the two small Cessnas would wander slowly back and forth across the Palmdale airport, well above the air traffic area, yet low enough to tell whether anything was happening around Site 4. Contrary to what some may think, this activity was perfectly legal, and only reflected the American public's hunger for information about the radically different stealth bomber.

Many an early morning vigil ended with a number of watchers congregating at "Crazy Otto's" in Lancaster for breakfast. We discussed what had been seen from the air, trying to make sense of the two vans positioned in front of the Engine Run Dock doors, for example. Obviously, they were for instrumentation of some kind, because heavy cables were seen running through a narrow gap in the hangar doors. Now and then, observers had heard the muffled rumble of engines running inside the dock, but, as long as those vans remained in position, the aircraft was hardly about to taxi. Nothing to do but stay alert and keep watching.

For better or worse, the desert's normal pattern of rapidly rising temperatures and increasing winds each day limited the most serious monitoring of Site 4 to the early morning hours. Flight test engineering experience and good judgment said that was when the first taxi tests would be conducted. Night tests were considered a possibility, but a remote one. Nobody in their right mind would risk damaging a multi-million dollar B-2 by trying to taxi or fly it for the first time at night, just to minimize the chances of anybody seeing it, we believed.

The persistent crowd at "John's Corner" also may have been a final factor that convinced the Air Force to allow media inside the fence for taxi tests. "Bee-Jay" and his network of B-2 enthusiasts were not about to let the nation's newest bomber slip away into the dark without somebody seeing it and sounding the alarm. It may not have been as politically effective as the pressure exerted by the major TV networks, newspapers and magazines to open up the events, but the die-hards at "John's Corner" probably played a small part in the decision.

B-2 ON THE MOVE

In the wee-hour darkness of July 10, pre-approved reporters from bonafide news organizations started arriving at Palmdale Regional Airport's south entrance. Reporters were directed to a roped-off area in front of Plant 42 headquarters, and left to stand in the desert scrub a few feet from a taxiway. The spot provided a clear view of the airport's two runways, several broad taxiways and—about a half-mile away—the south doors of several Site 4 hangars.

At 4:45 a.m., still well before daylight, Bruce Hinds started the B-2's engines, alerting every reporter and photographer on the airport. Nothing more happened for another 1 hr. and 45 min., but the shrill sound of engine noise rising and falling periodically kept everyone's attention locked on the sand-colored buildings.

Finally, the low, gray bomber taxiied from behind the paint hangar and slowly made a series of turns onto the main east-west taxiway. Hundreds of contractor employees lined the fences of Site 4, cheering as "their baby" inched past them. The aircraft slowly moved to the west, directly towards an equally ecstatic crowd that overflowed "John's Corner" and threatened to block Sierra Highway as passing cars pulled off to watch.

For the B-2 pilots, this was the culmination of countless safety reviews and last-minute discussions about compressing the tests. Three tests were planned—very low speed, medium speed and high-speed taxis. Because checkouts had delayed the taxis far longer than anticipated, tests were combined. If everything went alright, all testing up to 90 knots would be completed on the first day, followed by tests up to nosewheel liftoff speed the next day. A quick review of the data would precede a planned flight on the third day.

This approach compressed the required data and safety reviews considerably, and was considered to be extremely high risk. Still, after much debate, it was decided that the aircraft and its systems would dictate the schedule, and nobody could change that.

Hinds and Couch conducted engine checks and three taxi tests over a four-hr. period on July 10. As Northrop's Chief B-2 Test Pilot, Hinds handled the aircraft from the left seat, while Couch assisted and monitored all systems from the right seat.

Although the slow speed tests were completed successfully that day, not everything worked completely as advertised. Part of any series of first tests is necessarily spent waiting on one thing or another, and that was the case on July 10.

During one of these periods, the pilots were advised that the "hot mic" feature of the onboard instrumentation system had failed. A "hot" microphone simplifies communications between the B-2 pilots and engineers in the test control center by automatically broadcasting everything said in the cockpit. The transmissions are made over a telemetry link without the crew having to depress a push-to-talk switch repeatedly. The system also ensures pilot comments are recorded for postflight analysis.

* * *

COL. RICK COUCH:

There is a downside to this hot mic feature, though, because it transmits EVERYTHING we say. After being told the hot mic was inop and we would have to transmit everything over the UHF radio, the test controller asked us to stand by for a moment. Then he didn't say a word for what seemed like an eternity.

Finally, frazzled nerves and frustration got the best of me, and I shared some frank opinions about the delay and engineers in general with Bruce. I didn't mince words, and chose liberally from my limited vocabulary. A few choice four-lettered gems about summed up my feelings at the moment.

Of course, Murphy was working overtime that day. Somewhere along the way, the instrumentation technicians had restored hot mic telemetry, but had never gotten around to telling us. Unbeknownst to us, my blue comments had been transmitted loud and clear to the control room.

Next day, the two-star general in charge of Edwards' test center noted that I had really impressed the four-star commander of Systems Command with my abuse of the English language. I didn't have a clue what he was talking about until the Test Director informed me that everyone in the control room—including the visiting generals—had heard my whole tirade.

* * *

On the 65-knot run that day, Hinds observed that considerable brake displacement was required to get the desired braking force and deceleration. The test had been started from a spot near the runway midpoint, where an earlier run had terminated. This seemed appropriate, in the interest of saving time, but forced Hinds to taxi into the runway overrun before he could stop the huge aircraft.

* * *

BRUCE HINDS:

Bear in mind, the aircraft was still being built at this time. When we did low-speed taxi tests, it was not capable of flying; it hadn't cleared all the final wickets yet.

The low-speed taxi worked out well, although we found that brake forces were a lot higher than we had found necessary in the simulator. In the sim, we had planned all our brake checks with about 100 percent pad [safety margin] for brake power. During the first runs, I used that [pad] up in a hurry! I was actually standing on the brakes during the 60 knot point on runway 25.

Later, we learned more about what was really going on there. One, we found that the brakes took a lot more 'burn-in' than we thought they would. Two, it took a lot more force on the brakes than we'd expected to get the required pressure at the wheel/brake mechanism. I'd push on the brakes to about the same pressure we'd practiced in the sim, watch the deceleration, and see that wasn't enough. So, I'd push a bit harder, and see that still wasn't doing the job. All this was taking time.

Three, we had put a smoothing function into the air data system software so we wouldn't get a lot of airspeed fluctuations all the time. It was a damping routine designed to avoid flight control problems. [The flight control system uses air data signals for many of its automatic functions.] This smoothing routine, though, caused about a 6-9-second delay in the airspeed readout presented to the pilots.

At light gross weight, we'd accelerate pretty quickly, just like in the sim. We'd get up to our target speed of 65 knots, pull the throttles back to a predetermined setting, then glance back down at the airspeed. Whoa! We're at 75 knots! It was strictly due to that airspeed delay caused by the smoothing function. The air data system was working fine. Since then, we've gotten that out so we don't have as much delay.

Of course, we didn't have time to adequately explore all this before the high-speed taxi two days later, so, on those tests, we were also 10 knots higher than we intended."

* * *

Post-taxi reviews pleased the B-2 engineering team tremendously. Data proved that critical systems were working normally, and that the aircraft was "robust"—capable of handling the rigors of flight operations. In particular, the flush-mounted air data sensors and their associated boxes, as well as the flight control system seemed to be operating as intended (airspeed smoothing function notwithstanding, since nobody had determined it was a problem at that time).

HIGH-SPEED TAXI RUNS
—AND THE "ALL TERRAIN BOMBER"

Prior to high-speed taxi tests, the aircraft had to pass all checkouts and inspections necessary for it to be declared flight-ready. These precautions ensured that, if the bomber became airborne during its high-speed taxi, it could be flown directly to Edwards AFB.

The possibility of an inadvertent first flight was not remote—it had actually happened on the General Dynamics YF-16's high-speed taxi test in 1974. A disaster was avoided when GD test pilot Phil Oestricher elected to lift off after a roll control problem caused the wingtips to bang the ground repeatedly as the aircraft rocked left and right, and threatened loss of the fighter. His quick assessment of the situation and professional airmanship saved the aircraft and, possibly, his own life.

On July 13, the day of the B-2's high-speed taxi, a number of false starts repeatedly delayed the tests. Final closeout of the critical preflight inspections, which certified the test aircraft was airworthy, took longer than expected.

★ ★ ★

COL. RICK COUCH:

We had planned to start taxiing at first light, but when I walked into the engine run dock, I could see there was no way the airplane could be ready for another few hours. We knew that having the aircrews hang around seemed to keep people hustling, so I wandered over near the ERD door and sat down where I could see what was going on around the aircraft.

About five minutes later, I noticed I was talking to seven aircraft mechanics who also were standing or sitting around by the door. These guys were part of the launch crew, so I asked them why, in all this chaos, was a major portion of the "first team" standing around watching instead of helping get the aircraft ready. They said they were tired of having their managers trying to do the mechanics' work for them, then turning around and hollering at them when things weren't done right!

To say the least, that highlighted the confusion and strain people were experiencing in trying to get everything done at once when there was too much to do and not enough time to do it.

★ ★ ★

A series of complications compounded these problems, delaying engine start until mid-afternoon on the 13th. By then, the temperature had soared to 110°F and a 12-knot tailwind threatened to scrub the nosewheel liftoff test—the final hurdle before first flight.

A last-minute decision to press on with the high-speed taxi test almost proved disastrous. At best, it was definitely embarrassing. With a slight tailwind, Hinds accelerated down runway 04, lifting the nose about four feet off the concrete. He then gently lowered the nose before applying brakes and deploying the large drag flaps to slow the bomber.

★ ★ ★

BRUCE HINDS:

By the time we got out [on the runway], it was hot and the winds were all over the place. Winds recorded by the ground stations [at various spots on the airport] probably were different than the winds the aircraft was experiencing. It felt like we had a little tail wind when we did the high-speed run.

During braking, the aircraft pulled to the left pretty well, so it tended to veer off to that side some. It took quite a bit of rudder to counter it. (We saw the same thing on the next couple of flights.) We still had the braking problems, so, with all these different factors at work, we barely got stopped on the concrete. We were off to the left side and couldn't turn that way, towards the taxiway, so I decided to pull into the overrun. I had done the same thing two days earlier with no problem.

Bad idea! It was hot, so the asphalt [in the overrun area] was soft, thanks to 110 degree temperatures. We had been up since 5 a.m., so maybe my judgment wasn't at its best by 5 p.m., either. Anyway, it all added up to a mistake. Things had gone wrong all day long, so it was a fitting end to a very long day, I guess.

* * *

Everything looked fine until the crew pulled into that runway overrun to turn around after the high-speed test. The blazing sun had softened the overrun's asphalt, causing the B-2 to sink up to its hubs. Hinds quickly added power, but the huge aircraft was stuck. Rather than chance damaging the landing gear, Hinds and Couch told the control room to send help and they shut the engines down. Maintenance crews later dug the aircraft out and towed it back to its hangars.

During the crew debriefing with engineers and maintenance personnel in the cavernous engine run building, Hinds professionally recounted all details of the taxi tests, then closed by saying: "Well, now I know that ATB doesn't stand for 'All Terrain Bomber!' " The B-2's original moniker—the ATB—had taken on an all-new meaning.

10

First flight

TRANSITIONING FROM INITIAL B-2 TAXI TESTS to first flight in less than a week required a mixture of expertise and outstanding skill on the part of hundreds of engineering and maintenance specialists. It also took a fair dose of blind faith, incredible luck and, perhaps, even a little divine intervention. Under the circumstances, B-2 managers were more than happy to accept all the help they could get, no matter what its source.

The frenzied activity leading up to first flight created an almost surreal situation, given that people from all over the globe were watching. Through the camera's steady eye of Cable News Network (CNN) and the interpretations of daily and weekly publications, anybody who was interested knew what was about to happen at Palmdale's Site 4.

Interest was heightened by televised congressional budget debates concerning whether the B-2 should be funded in 1990 or not. As mechanics worked feverishly in Palmdale, critics in both the House and Senate hammered their lecterns, declaring that the aircraft was too expensive and wouldn't fly anyway.

PRACTICES FOR FIRST FLIGHT

Despite the skepticism in Washington and other quarters, the test team felt well-prepared to fly. Their practices for this singular event had begun even before the B-2 was rolled out in November, 1988, and they had worked out every detail of the flight. All they needed now was the B-2.

Four dress rehearsals of the first flight had been conducted within the previous year, using the KC-135A Avionics Flying Testbed for three trials and an F-16 for the other. Prior to rollout, two practice missions were flown on September 22 and November 10, 1988. As the actual first flight approached, another two practices were flown on May 13 and June 7, 1989.

Each practice mission was flown from Palmdale to Edwards AFB, accompanied by chase aircraft and following exactly the same profile planned for the initial flight. Three premission briefings were conducted over a three-day period (designated the T-3, T-1, and T-0 briefings), and control rooms were manned by the same engineering contingent that would be in place on the big day. Even simulated airborne emergencies were included for added realism.

The first such practice, on September 22, 1988, sparked local radio reports of a mysterious aircraft that had flown from Palmdale in the early morning hours. A local Lancaster/Palmdale newspaper also reported that the B-2 might have taken off the same morning.

These practice sessions were valuable in that they highlighted areas of the complex support structure needing additional attention before the actual first flight. For example, by simulating ground emergencies such as a brake fire and a hazardous material leak, the exercises revealed a weakness in ground communications. These deficiencies were resolved well before the B-2 was ready to fly.

FIRST ATTEMPT

Despite the pressures and madness of the preflight environment at Palmdale, the B-2 was declared ready to fly on the morning of July 15, 1989. Reporters admitted to the Plant 42 grounds at about 4 a.m. set up their camera tripods among the weeds and desert dust beside Runway 04/22. Hands thrust deep into jacket pockets, they then stared numbly at the bright lights across the runways, waiting for the huge bomber to appear. Privately, some half expected that it wouldn't show at all. First flights were notorious for delays and cancellations.

In a brightly lit hangar, final preparations were made and briefings completed. Pilots were told that a fuel pressure drop at the engine inlet, which had been seen during high-speed taxi tests, had been resolved. Fuel boost pump failure had been ruled out by post-test checks, so engineers concluded that the problem had stemmed from excessive fuel temperatures. After all, outside air temperatures were well over 100°F when that final taxi test was run. To make sure the pressure problem did not recur, engineers had adjusted the system to ensure that additional cool fuel was mixed with the hot fuel.

Preflight, engine start, systems checks, and taxiing to the runway all went smoothly. After the "last chance" inspection near the takeoff end of Runway 04, the pilots conducted a run-up test on all four engines. Advancing throttles to a high power level approximating that required for takeoff, the low fuel pressure problem showed up again. During a 32-minute period, repeated checks confirmed everybody's worst fears: fuel pressure was inadequate for first flight.

★ ★ ★

COL. RICK COUCH:

To everybody's great disappointment, and with half the world watching on TV, we taxied back to the run dock. The first flight was aborted. Nothing else to do but turn the airplane back over to the engineers and let them figure out what was wrong.

Just as we were taxiing back to Site 4, we noticed a commotion at the other end of the airfield. Bruce and I could see security vehicles and people running all over the place, but didn't really know what was going on.

* * *

Dignitaries, workers, and reporters also were disappointed to see the bomber slowly taxi back to its hangar. But attention was diverted for a short time when people holding hand-held aviation-band radios heard the Palmdale tower first tell an aircraft to leave the local airspace, then, a moment later, to land straight ahead. To everybody's astonishment, a single-engine Cessna 172 touched down on the same runway the B-2 had, moments before, planned to use for takeoff—in the opposite direction!

Only half-jokingly, an Air Force public affairs colonel turned and yelled from about 30 yards away, "Scott, is that an *Aviation Week* airplane?!" Every reporter in the area faced my direction, most wearing accusatory expressions.

"No way!" I yelled back. "We may be sneaky, but we're not stupid!" That seemed to satisfy the colonel, who laughed and waved an "OK."

A swarm of no-nonsense security officers surrounded the wayward airplane and directed it off the runway, onto the grass median. Even from a distance, it was apparent that the officers saw no humor in the situation and were handling it as if a plane load of terrorists had just invaded the airport. As TV cameras followed every move, a subdued man and two scared children were marched to a nearby car as their aircraft was pushed well clear of the runway.

Stern questioning and a few quick phone calls confirmed the intruder's story. Brian L. Green, a 35-year-old private pilot, had become lost on a 100-nautical mile flight from Porterville to Agua Dulce, Calif. His destination airport was hidden in hilly terrain about 12 nautical miles southwest of Palmdale.

Green knew he was lost, saw the large runways of Palmdale below him, and decided to land and ask directions. He had no inkling that he was dropping into the biggest aviation event in the world that day.

Not knowing what airport he was seeing, Green couldn't tune his radios to the correct tower frequency. Naturally, controller admonitions went unheard. He looked for, but never saw, any red light—the universal DON'T LAND signal—from the tower, so he landed. Needless to say, he never noticed the big, gray bomber sitting at the other end of the runway, either.

Once security officials decided the pilot's story was legitimate, the whole atmosphere changed. Air Force officials gave him and his young passengers an autographed B-2 photograph and a B-2 patch as a souvenir of the most unfortunate landing in the hapless pilot's logbook. Slightly red-faced, Green was released and allowed to fly back to Porterville the same day.

Back in its hangar, B-2 No. 1 was descended upon by puzzled engineers and maintenance technicians. An hour or so of poring over computer printouts and strip charts uncovered the problem: A pressure drop across the fuel-to-oil heat exchangers was too high, indicating something was clogged. Filters were removed and the culprit found: fine lint, similar to what a person would find in the lint trap of a household clothes dryer.

Engineers speculated that the lint had come from cotton overalls and booties worn by technicians crawling around inside the fuel tanks during the sealing process. Ironically, the overalls and booties were worn to prevent dirt and fibers from a worker's street clothes being left in the tank.

In short order, all four heat exchangers were replaced and an engine test run performed. Everything looked good; the problem was solved, and the aircraft was ready to fly.

A Northrop flight test manager later said the whole incident actually was a blessing in disguise. The entire team had been pushing hard for days, and there was an air of uneasy tension throughout the Air Force/Northrop organization on that Saturday when the first flight was attempted. While the heat exchanger problem was being fixed, everybody else had time to double-check their own areas of responsibility. Some even had time to take a few hours off over the weekend and get some much-needed rest.

SECOND TRY

By Monday, July 17, the aircraft was ready to fly again. Even in the press area—a roped-off section of desert a dozen yards south of Runway 04/22—reporters could sense the air of confidence from Air Force and Northrop officials. Families and dignitaries, positioned about 50 yards away from the press area, seemed more relaxed than they had on Saturday.

A 6:30 a.m. takeoff had been planned to take advantage of the desert morning's normally calm air conditions and cool temperatures. The B-2 test pilots were scheduled for a final crew briefing with the safety/photo chase pilots who would be flying F-16s beside the bomber, watching for any anomalies and filming the historic flight. Because that briefing would take place via telephone link between Palmdale and the test control rooms at Edwards' B-2 support facility two hours prior to takeoff, Hinds and Couch rolled out of bed at approximately 3:30 a.m.

* * *

BRUCE HINDS:

When I got up that day, it didn't really hit me that this was to be a special day. We had done so much checkout and simulator work that it all seemed pretty routine. We knew what we were going to do, and we had practiced enough contingencies, that I felt pretty confident we could handle anything that came up.

For example, we had looked at any number of critical situations . . . engine out, loss of control, hydraulic systems out, four-engine flameout . . . I knew how much altitude I needed to get back into Palmdale or make it to the Edwards [dry] lakebed. If we could be at 4,500 feet over [the intersection at] 90th Street East and Avenue J, I knew we could make it to the lakebed. (In fact, we actually were well above that altitude then.) If we flamed-out all four engines, we would be like the space shuttle, in that altitude and speed determined where we had to land.

* * *

The two test pilots and Palmdale-based test conductors planned to call from a Site 4 briefing room and finalize details of the flight with the test director, chase pilots, and air refueling tanker crew at Edwards. Couch, who lived in base housing at Edwards, jumped in his car well before daylight and headed for Palmdale, about 50 road-miles away.

* * *

COL. RICK COUCH:

I was running right on schedule . . . until I got to the security gate leaving Edwards. I couldn't believe it . . . the Air Force Security Police had a random drug search in progress. I waited nervously while Major, the drug-sniffing police dog, meticulously inspected my car and me.

Now, I knew there were no drugs in that car, but, at that time of morning, on one of the biggest days of my life . . . . Who knows what Murphy might have in store? Can you imagine what the papers would say if Major had "alerted" on my car? He didn't.

Free again, I was now behind schedule. I wound up driving well over the legal speed limit, just to make sure I got to the briefing on time. That might have been the most hazardous thing I did all day, as it turned out.

* * *

The full-blown engineering briefings (T-3 and T-1) had been completed earlier, reviewing all the significant details about the planned mission profile. Those were conducted in the Site 4 paint hangar after the aborted first flight attempt, and had included the "cast of thousands" mentioned previously. Consequently, the preflight phone briefing was fairly short. Final directions were not particularly complex—collect as much data as safely possible in approximately a two-hour flight.

That time limit was dictated by desired fuel reserves. If anything went wrong during the tests, fuel equated to flight time. Plenty of fuel would allow the bomber to stay airborne, giving engineers time to sort out a problem and, hopefully, come up with a "fix" before the aircraft had to land. Of course, because the entire aircraft was a new "system" that had never flown before, a long flight was risky. In case fuel supplies ran low, however, a tanker was on standby to provide emergency in-flight refueling.

The first flight's success criteria were soberingly simple: "A safe first landing is a safe first flight." Anything beyond that would be gravy.

For several years, the B-2 test community had debated whether to retract the gear or not on the first flight. Proponents on both sides of the argument offered good reasons to back their viewpoints. Raising the gear would reduce drag and allow the aircraft to climb faster. Handling also would probably be better without the huge gear doors providing extraneous surfaces in the airstream that could affect flight characteristics significantly.

On the other hand, leaving the gear down eliminated one major safety concern. If the gear was retracted, then failed to extend, a wheels-up landing was inevitable. Nobody wanted to even think how that might turn out, to say nothing of the damage that would be done to the only test aircraft in existence. Politically, such an incident also would be suicidal to the beleaguered B-2 program.

In the end, technicians simply ran out of time to complete final ground checkouts of the gear retraction and extension mechanism and that decided the issue. Although the landing gear was declared safe for flight, retraction was out of the question until final checks could be completed. It was decided the gear would be pinned in the extended position for first flight, preventing either intentional or inadvertent retraction.

* * *

BRUCE HINDS:

The gear situation was representative of the way problems [finishing the aircraft] kept nibbling away at our margins . . . all the things we had built in to give us a safety edge. When we started out, we had maybe four or five levels of things we could fall back on. But, by the time we actually flew, maybe we had only one level left.

For example, we were told late in the game that we'd have to leave the gear down. That changed our glide capability quite a bit, because the landing gear added a lot of drag. If we lost three engines out by Harper's Lake [a dry lakebed east of Edwards], we couldn't make it to the Edwards runway. So, we had to adjust our plan.

Fortunately, the B-2 was so robust that there was always a Plan B. But we were down to the last level of redundancy in a lot of areas. We couldn't tolerate losing any more.

* * *

The planned mission profile called for taking off from Palmdale's Runway 04, which put the aircraft on a northeasterly heading, aimed directly at the Edwards restricted airspace. Officials were concerned that, until the bomber reached the Edwards-controlled zone, other aircraft could fly into the same flight corridor used by the B-2, endangering the expensive bomber.

The primary worry was that somebody might try to fly close enough to take pictures, which could pose a safety hazard to the B-2 or its chase aircraft. Terrorist attacks and the possibility of interference from radical antinuclear activists were not ruled out or treated lightly. A conservative approach based on prevention of potential trouble and protection of the No. 1 bomber guided the mission security plan.

The Federal Aviation Administration and its air traffic controllers were responsible for keeping other aircraft out of the area along the B-2's intended flight path. They restricted all airspace the B-2 would fly through, and agreed to advise the test crew of any aircraft approaching the area. Everybody involved intended to make sure the B-2 did not have a midair collision on its maiden flight.

Once airborne, the flight test plan called for climbing straight ahead to 10,000 feet, then conducting checks of basic aircraft systems in an area north and east of the Edwards AFB complex. All tests would be done at that altitude, aimed at collecting as much data as possible about the aircraft's handling qualities and systems operation.

The test area was selected so the bomber would always be within gliding distance of either the dry lakebed runways on the Edwards airbase, or one of the isolated dry lakes nearby. To ensure these dried, hardened-mud lakebeds (that once had been expansive prehistoric lakes) would support the B-2's weight, aircrews assigned to the B-2 Combined Test Force were sent by helicopter to survey each lakebed firsthand.

Finally, the preflight briefings were over and it was time to get on with the first flight. Both pilots were anxious to get to the aircraft and have plenty of time to take care of any last-minute problems that might arise. With luck, they would be airborne by the scheduled 6:30 a.m. takeoff time.

* * *

COL. RICK COUCH:
As Bruce and I prepared to go out to the airplane, I reflected back on the previous first flight attempt a few days earlier and tried to not get my expectations up too high. The normal mode for this type of operation is to build the whole organization's momentum, with everything and everybody peaked up for the flight. If something goes wrong, and the flight is scrubbed, it really pulls the rug out from under all of us. It's a huge emotional letdown.

On that Monday, we were well aware that the most simple glitch could take the wind out of our sails and put us on hold again while a problem was worked out. We had seen it happen before. If not the aircraft itself, then the instrumentation or data acquisition systems could act up. Although they really aren't essential to aircraft operation, they are critical for the flight test. There's usually no sense in flying the test if you can't gather data.

Workers who had spent countless hours with Bruce and me in recent weeks came by to wish us luck. These were welcome, heartfelt gestures, but they made me uncomfortable for reasons hard to explain. I appreciated them, don't get me wrong. But, the idea of accepting their good wishes, then maybe having to experience the disappointment of another cancellation, made the thought of facing these folks right after that too much to handle, somehow. I just wanted to go to the airplane and get on with it.

* * *

Couch's concerns were unfounded. Engine start and systems checks went smoothly and the aircraft was ready to taxi earlier than expected. When the huge wing-shaped bomber taxied from behind the Site 4 production buildings at 5:52 a.m., its speed appearing to be higher than on the first flight attempt, there was a definite confidence in its movements. Ground crew motions also looked crisp and efficient. Communications and telemetry links with the control rooms at Palmdale and Edwards were excellent. Everything was falling into place.

As Hinds and Couch taxied past their ground crew, positioned beside the taxiway, a crew chief held up a big sign that read "Next Fuel Stop - 25 Miles." The message was surrounded by signatures of all the people who had worked on the first aircraft.

At the takeoff end of Runway 04, final checks and a brief engine runup double-confirmed that the heat exchanger problem was fixed. Final communications and telemetry data verifications completed, the pilots notified the test controller that they were ready to go. Now, they waited for a go-ahead from each of the discipline engineers who carefully perused the streams of data coming from the idling aircraft to ensure every system was a "go."

* * *

COL. RICK COUCH:

I later found it interesting to watch the videotaped version of what was going on at that moment. Television reporters covering the event were trying to fill the dead time with some sort of continuous commentary, whether they knew what was happening or not. One TV reporter explained that we were going through a long, detailed, before-takeoff checklist, and that's what was taking so long. In fact, there are only 15 items on the B-2 takeoff checklist, and they take about two minutes to complete.

What we were really doing, of course, was waiting for each aircraft subsystem engineer to give the okay for his system. It took awhile to poll the entire group.

The reporter also made some statement about the B-2 cockpit being as big as a racquetball court. I agree that the cockpit is large and roomy compared to a lot of other airplanes, but it doesn't have a lot of room to play racquetball!

* * *

Finally, the go-ahead was given from the test controller and the big bomber taxied into position on the end of the runway at 6:27 a.m. Its oversized barndoor-like trailing edge surfaces drooped, partially deflected to improve lift during the early part of the takeoff roll. Winds were light and variable, less than 5 knots. Throttles were advanced on all four of the powerful GE engines, their blast kicking up a dirt cloud off the end of the runway.

Couch started the countdown for brake release, transmitting over the radio. This helped the two F-16 chase pilots time their approach as they descended toward the runway, positioning themselves for a *rolling pickup* abeam the B-2. In the left seat, Hinds scanned his cathode ray tube displays, while Couch did the same on the right. Again, everything looked good.

Near the end of the countdown, the Edwards control room lost radio contact with the flight crew, even though a check moments earlier had confirmed communications were good. "Lost comm" was an automatic abort situation, so the test director at Edwards pressed his microphone button and called "Abort! Abort! Abort!"

Those in the control room and in the chase aircraft heard the abort call, but Hinds and Couch did not. Couch called "zero," Hinds released the brakes and the B-2 was moving down the runway, accelerating to takeoff speed.

Both pilots and a cockpit tape recording confirmed that the TD's abort call was never received. Apparently, an intermittent communications problem in the control room, which had occurred before, was the culprit. Engineers in the Edwards control room have said they heard the TD's abort call, confirming that it was made.

At the prebriefed 140-knot speed, Hinds pulled the stick back, lifting the bomber's nose from the concrete just 21 seconds after brake release. He was aiming for a 7.5-degree pitch attitude, but the main wheels left the ground at 6.5 degrees. The big bomber was airborne for the first time at 6:37 a.m. Pacific Daylight Time, climbing straight ahead into the blazing desert sky.

At 65 knots during the takeoff run, the huge flaps had slowly retracted to the trail position, fairing into the sleek wing, and producing minimal drag. At the moment of liftoff, the big drag rudders were repositioned to their more aerodynamic flight mode, as well.

Rousing cheers and waves from an excited crowd parked on 50th Street East, along the eastern boundary of the Palmdale Regional Airport, greeted the big bomber as it roared overhead. Plant 42 security forces and Los Angeles sheriff's deputies had erected sawhorse-like blockades along both sides of the road to keep people from parking there, but they had little effect.

Swarms of visitors from all over southern California had arrived before dawn to see the historic takeoff, and they weren't to be stopped. The blockades, each with a big NO PARKING sign attached, were kicked over or moved so people could park beside the roadway or drive into the shrub-covered desert east of the street. Deputies tried to convince people that, for their own safety, they should leave the area. But hundreds of aviation enthusiasts were not to be deterred—they would take their chances that the B-2 would not crash in their midst shortly after takeoff. Rather than risk a riot, the deputies gave in and, instead, turned to keeping people away from the airport perimeter fence.

John "BJ" MacWhirter and his colleagues had moved John's Corner for the day. BJ and his followers, acting on a hot tip that said the bomber would take off on Runway 04, established squatter's rights just east of the Avenue M and 50th Street East corner the night of July 16. BJ's canary yellow step-van was a beacon drawing others to congregate there the next morning.

When the B-2 roared into the morning sky, shadowed by two white-and-orange F-16 chase planes, John and a professional photographer friend struggled with bulky cameras, doing their level best to record the moment. Theirs was "the perfect spot" to get a shot of the bomber's underside. They had growled at and chased away plenty of intruders that had tried to bull their way into the same area for the same reason over the past 12 hours, and here was the moment of payoff.

Maybe it was the sleepless, raucous night, or the abundant beer that flowed freely, but award-winning photography suffered that morning. BJ tried to track the bomber's overflight with one bleary eye glued to a video camera viewfinder, the other wide open to personally watch the event. Too bad the lens cap was still on. His photographer buddy, armed with more sophisticated gear, had his camera jam at the critical moment. Both had hoped to get the shot for *Aviation Week's* next cover.

In the press compound adjacent to Runway 04, banks of motor-driven cameras clicked off thousands of frames and several hundred feet of videotape during the short takeoff run. As the B-2 climbed away from them, the low morning sun casting a golden tint across the top of the broad dark-gray wing, even normally jaded reporters cheered.

Behind the press crowd, the B-2 program office's public affairs officer was waving a large U.S. flag, and trying to hide tears of joy. Beside her, a local TV anchorwoman, known for her excellent musical talents, was singing "The Star Spangled Banner" at the officer's request. An Air Force Systems Command public affairs chief stood at button-popping attention and saluted, pride written all over him.

Down the line, invited dignitaries, as well as Bruce Hinds' and Rick Couch's wives, children, and other relatives, hugged each other, clapped, and cheered. Across the runway, the crowd of workers and guests at Northrop's Site 4 set up the loudest cheers of the day. Thousands of hours of grueling work, lost sleep, missed birthday parties, and deferred vacations were forgotten in this moment of unbounded exhilaration.

In that crowd, many also cried unashamedly. John Cashen joined them. As one of the B-2's designers, he had seen the aircraft go from an idea to this emotional instant of liftoff. It had taken almost exactly 10 years, and the trials and turbulence of those years finally had culminated in this moment. The first goal had been attained.

Among the cheers, a lot of one-liners also were being coined:

"By God, WE DID IT!! The B-2 most definitely WILL fly!"

"America still has 'The Right Stuff.'"

"We are damned proud of what this nation can do, if we just set our minds to it!"

People hugged each other, shook hands and pounded others on the back.

FLIGHT TEST

In the air, the two test pilots still had a problem to deal with. The communication loss during takeoff roll was compounded by Glitch Number 1, which occurred right after the main gear lifted off the runway. The B-2's radio systems were designed to automatically switch from using antennas on top of the fuselage to those on the underside. This should have ensured that the most optimum signal was sent and received during conversations with ground controllers.

This transfer was supposed to be triggered by a *squat switch* that activated when the aircraft's landing gear broke ground. The switch worked as advertised, but a programmed software reconfiguration scrambled the radio system. The lower antenna was being used for data telemetry, so the pilots were trying to transmit into nothingness. For approximately 10 minutes, it was impossible for the B-2 pilots to communicate with the outside world. Hinds and Couch could talk to each other, but to nobody else.

Going through a troubleshooting routine, the pilots cleared up the problem, and reestablished communications with the chase pilots and test controllers. That first successful radio call to the test director elicited a massive sigh of relief in the control room.

Bruce Hinds had concentrated on flying the bomber into Edwards' protected airspace while Couch sorted out the radio problem. Hinds liked what he was finding. The big aircraft handled just like the simulator, if not better. He climbed to 10,000 feet, careful to hold the speed below 200 knots, the designated maximum for this first flight.

Once communications problems were resolved, the two pilots started a series of maneuvers that, together, were called *integrated test blocks*. From a steady, trimmed position, Hinds performed a number of standard flight test handling qualities tests: pitch, roll, and yaw doublets; bank-to-bank rolls; pull-ups and push-overs; stabilized turns, and wind-up turns.

Tests were conducted at 180, 150, and 140 knots, with each pilot flying two maneuver blocks. Hinds performed tests at 180 and 150 knots, then Couch completed a 180-knot point and concluded with a 140-knot block.

Because the landing gear was still locked in the down position, and gull-wing doors on top of each engine inlet were left open to ensure adequate air flow to the powerplants, top speeds were intentionally held to about 190 knots, about 10 knots fewer than the flight's established limit. Data from the handling qualities and performance maneuvers were automatically collected and beamed to the ground, where engineers also could monitor exactly how the aircraft was responding to Hinds' inputs.

Because the same maneuvers had been rehearsed in the B-2 simulator, the real aircraft's response could be compared immediately to the simulator-predicted version. Getting a good match between predicted and actual data was important. If they did not match well, then the extensive work done in the simulator to achieve excellent handling qualities would have to be reexamined, and more flight tests would have to be done in order to optimize the simulator.

* * *

BRUCE HINDS:
> One of the first real surprises to me was when we got into some turbulence. If I had thought about it a bit more, I would have expected the reaction . . . sort of undulating in the pitch axis. It was a strange feeling, sort of like going across ocean waves in a boat, slowly pitching nose up, then nose down. Almost a rocking in pitch.
>
> Because the simulator [has motion limitations], it didn't really heave or give the full sensation we got in the airplane.

The flight controls were doing what they were supposed to do . . . decreasing load factor [Gs] on the big wing by automatically decreasing angle of attack. That's just the way vertical turbulence affects this aircraft. It's just a different feeling than we're used to getting in other aircraft.

Later, other pilots had similar comments, saying "I'm not sure I like this pitch motion. It's a lot like riding in a boat."

* * *

Gradually, as millions of data bits flowed from the airborne B-2, through computers and onto display screens in the Edwards control rooms, engineers learned what the pilots already knew: The B-2 matched the simulator extremely well. With that declaration, managers and design chiefs started smiling for the first time.

The maneuver blocks completed, Hinds and Couch simulated an engine-out glide to collect basic performance data, then checked the speed brakes in their landing configuration. Each pilot then practiced a "landing," descending to a designated altitude as if it were the runway.

* * *

BRUCE HINDS:

It didn't take long to determine that it was taking about two degrees less pitch attitude to hold 180 knots than we had seen in the simulator. We figured that meant we had more [landing] gear drag than had been anticipated.

After a couple of hours I knew we had more gear drag . . . we were burning more fuel than we had expected to. That changed the landing technique we had planned.

In the simulator, we always had plenty of energy as we crossed the [landing] overrun and had to pull the power clear back to settle onto the pavement. With the extra drag we were seeing in flight, though, we decided we'd better not do that. So, I planned to hold the power on until we were over the [runway] threshold, then slowly pull the power back to check the speed bleed-off rate and see how the airplane responded.

We did a simulated approach at altitude and this technique seemed to work pretty well. Actually, it wasn't really an "approach," we called it an *idle descent* on the test card. What I really wanted to do was see how it handled in a simulated four-engine flameout situation, what we call an SFO [*simulated flameout*]. But, when we tried to put that in the test cards, it got a lot of people excited. SFOs are dangerous! So, we changed the wording to avoid worrying a lot of people about doing that on the first flight.

Still, that was something a pilot needs to know . . . how the airplane will act if the engines are lost. When we did that, we had about a 300-foot-per-minute rate of descent [faster] than we had expected. Again, that was the higher gear drag than we had seen in the simulator. It was good information to have before landing. It also convinced me I didn't want to pull the power off too fast during landing.

* * *

As the bomber approached the two-hour point on its maiden flight, Hinds started a gentle glide from the east shore of the wide Rogers Dry Lake, aiming for Edwards' 15,000-foot concrete runway. It was during this set-up that the only real problem of the flight occurred.

* * *

COL. RICK COUCH:
As we were descending, an alert on the multifunction displays reported a problem with avionics cooling. In an electronic airplane, where even the flight controls can be considered "avionics," that little alert will get your attention right NOW.

My voice must have changed a couple of octaves as I reported this to the control room on the ground. The test controllers seemed a little worried at first, but, after a couple minutes' investigation, they said it was "no sweat." The problem appeared to be with some pressure sensors located in each of the avionics racks. The cooling air was still doing its thing. Bottom line was, "Don't worry about it."

* * *

The rest of the flight was anticlimactic. Even on approach, the aircraft handled almost exactly as the simulator had. The impending landing was cause for some concern, because a number of problems during this phase had been uncovered in ground and airborne simulator work. In flight, though, the aircraft effectively trapped a cushion of air between the big wing and the runway, creating the *ground effect* phenomenon. That cushion allowed the B-2 to settle gently onto the concrete strip, touching down at 8:29 a.m. PDT. Hinds slowly lowered the nose wheel, applied brakes, and the bomber's maiden flight was ended.

(Months later, Hinds admitted that something he had really wanted to do on this flight, but was prevented from doing for safety concerns, was a low approach over the runway prior to landing. Although he fought for it, justifying the low approach from a technical standpoint, it became an impossible political issue. Understandably, there is a lot of superstition and fear in the flight test community that, in essence, says, "If you get it that close to the ground in good shape, go ahead and land it!"

Hinds wanted to get a better understanding of how the aircraft responded and handled in ground effect. Surprisingly, it was about nine months before that particular evaluation was performed. Even then, it was listed as a crosswind controllability test in ground effect. Apparently, an angle of attack error existed in the air data system during the early phases, attributable to the changes that occur in ground effect. In retrospect, it would have been valuable information to learn on the first flight.)

When the B-2 taxied onto the ramp in front of its new home at Edwards, an ecstatic crowd shouted, waved, and waited impatiently for the pilots to shut everything down and climb out. The launch and recovery crew, which had driven to Edwards after seeing the aircraft get airborne in Palmdale, greeted Hinds and Couch with the traditional first-flight drenching.

Many a test pilot, grinning ear-to-ear with the sweet taste of first-flight success in his mouth, has been brought back to earth—so to speak—with a bucket of cold water in the face. It's tradition, though, in the flight test world, and no pilot really wants to be spared the expected drenching.

Dripping but happy, Hinds and Couch were overwhelmed by their reception as returning heroes. High-ranking Air Force and Northrop dignitaries in the welcoming party were as giggly and effusive as the maintenance ground crew. Even Gen. Bernard P. Randolph, chief of the Air Force Systems Command, the organization charged with acquiring the bomber, was as excited as a new father.

After prolific handshakes and pictures, the pilots were taken to a maintenance debriefing to review and write up any problems encountered in flight. Surprisingly, most of the squawks were related to manufacturing items that would have to be completed sooner or later, but none would keep the aircraft on the ground. After refueling, the B-2 would be ready to fly again.

Another odd formality conducted at the debrief was signing paperwork that officially returned the aircraft to Northrop. The Air Force had "taken delivery" of the B-2 before its first flight, then promptly returned it to the contractor after landing. This strange arrangement is a long-enduring twist of new-aircraft program logic that recognizes contractors are better equipped than the services to track engineering and maintenance tasks during the hectic test period when configurations might change daily or even hourly. Consequently, the contractor retains this responsibility during ground operations. This arrangement has been in force on new military aircraft programs for years, so it was nothing out of the ordinary for the B-2.

PRESS CONFERENCE

The next order of business for the two test pilots was preparing for a nationally televised news conference. Few pilots have to undergo such a nerve-racking experience immediately after a first flight, but the B-2's high visibility and the media's extraordinary interest prompted a meeting with the press.

The media event was held in the Air Force Test Pilot School's auditorium, where a special stage and lighting had been set up for the occasion. About 50 reporters from national television networks, local TV stations, large newspapers, and a number of international news magazines assembled there, waiting for the pilots to arrive.

The participants also included Gen. Bernard P. Randolph, Systems Command commander at the time; Brig. Gen. Richard M. Scofield (now Maj. Gen. Scofield), the B-2 program director; and Lt. Col. Jan Dalby, Edwards' public affairs chief. Some kind soul had the foresight to invite the pilots' wives and families, as well.

Gen. Randolph read a statement from the secretary of the Air Force, and hailed July 17 as "an historic day in aviation. We flew the flying wing," he said, hinting that the flight would silence congressional critics and detractors who had claimed the B-2 would never get off the ground. He went on to explain that the aircraft was needed as an efficient leg of the nation's nuclear triad of bombers, submarines, and missiles, costing about 40 percent less than an ICBM to put a weapon on target.

Questions were then taken from the floor, and ranged from very good to embarrassingly naive. The reporters who had followed the B-2 program for years, and had done their homework, asked about the aircraft's composites, fly-by-wire-flight control system, in-flight handling, and methods of control. Bruce Hinds said the B-2 "flies like a real airplane" and "is very nimble." He noted the roll performance was particularly impressive, exhibiting a "very good roll rate for a big airplane." Later, Hinds said the aircraft responded more like a crisp-controlled, agile fighter than a lumbering bomber.

Both pilots said the aircraft's flight characteristics closely matched those they had seen in the simulator, a fact that obviously pleased them immensely. Hinds said the bomber "worked a little better [in ground effect] than the simulation." An Air Force official later confirmed that statement, adding "the only surprise was that there was no surprise" during landing.

The most embarrassing question of the day came from an east coast reporter who, believing she was seizing on a fault of the preflight testing process, only succeeded in displaying a wealth of ignorance. She questioned why nobody had anticipated the clogged filter problem that had caused the first flight to be scrubbed two days earlier.

After the question was patiently answered, she pressed harder, demanding to know "why nobody found this problem during simulation tests." Straight-faced, Scofield explained politely that such off-the-wall anomalies as traces of lint in the fuel system could hardly be anticipated, let alone simulated. She finally let the matter drop, convinced she had demonstrated that neither the Air Force nor a defense contractor could slide anything past a tough-nosed reporter like her! [Moments like that made the rest of us ashamed to be considered part of "The Media."]

The press conference's high point came when another reporter asked if the pilots had found any kinks in the B-2 that would have to be worked out. Couch's face broke into that "I gotcha" Aggie grin and responded, "This is not a kinky airplane." It was classic Couch, completely in character with the wild man his Test Pilot School classmates remembered.

"This is not a kinky airplane" was dubbed the CNN quote of the day and was picked up by newspapers all over the world.

Air Force PAO officials had jokingly warned me to "not ask any hard questions" of Col. Couch, my former USAF Test Pilot School classmate, at the press conference. I said I wouldn't, if I could interview the pilots the next day or so to get some technical details for my *Aviation Week* story. Besides, asking that kind of question only took up valuable conference time and was of little interest to other reporters. The PAO officer in charge agreed to that, so I kept my mouth shut at the media event. As it turned out, the officer disappeared the next day, taking some well-deserved vacation, but leaving me and my story high and dry.

The event ended with a photo session outside, in front of the school building. Couch and Hinds played the role of hero-for-a-day with characteristic professionalism, but were obviously very self-conscious about all the attention. Little did they know this was only a sample of what was to come.

Returning to the test support facility, the test pilots settled down long enough to conduct a detailed engineering debriefing. This was the first time the crew had been able to compare notes with the engineers and ground support team who had monitored the flight carefully from the control rooms. Originally, this debriefing had been scheduled before the press conference, but, in the end, press deadlines and the evening news dictated the final schedule.

The engineers and pilots compared every scrap of data gleaned from their different perspectives, and were delighted with how well everything had worked. The normally staid and emotionless engineers were as giddy as the pilots had been after they landed. Everybody on the test team knew what the flight's success really meant: all the hours spent in simulators and systems laboratories had paid off. Now, the aircraft could be used to validate engineering data, rather than develop them.

This is not an easy point to explain, but it definitely had a significant impact on how the test program would be run. If the aircraft had behaved differently than the simulator, the entire flight test plan would have been changed considerably.

FIRST FLIGHT CELEBRATION!

After the final debriefing, it was time to party. The traditional postfirst-flight party at Edwards AFB is an event to behold. Many first flights had been flown from the remote desert base, and many parties had been thrown to celebrate their success. Traditionally, it was a time to release pent-up frustrations, the stress of long hours, and the conflicts that mark the difficult transition of a complex air machine from concept to flight. And it was true, unabashed celebration.

Organization of the B-2 party was complicated by stringent government regulations established to keep service officials and contractors from getting too cozy on a project. Worried about creating a conflict of interest perception, Northrop, as prime contractor, was reluctant to host the party, as was the tradition. The problem was solved by the CTF taking money from a special fund that had been created through bake sales and other events. Northrop matched those funds and the party was on.

* * *

COL. RICK COUCH:
    Like many parties at the Edwards Officers Club, this one started off slow but started swinging into high gear before long. I was thrown into the

O-Club swimming pool at least three times. Other folks went in more than I did. At one point, I remember seeing a young lady float to the surface, but without her top. She climbed out and jumped back into the pool several times, apparently never noticing or caring that she was topless.

* * *

Rick's wife, Ann, had invited me to the bash, so I attended as a friend, not as a reporter. When I introduced myself to General Scofield, who was looking very tired at that point, he was a bit taken aback, clearly wondering what the hell I was doing there. I explained the connection and congratulated him on a great first flight.

Before we had a chance to talk much, though, several big CTF guys approached and politely asked the general if he would please remove his shoes, wallet, and sunglasses. A few moments later, he was carried feet first out the door and unceremoniously tossed into the pool. Seeing that nobody was being spared, I decided to congratulate Rick and slip out quietly. An *Av Week* reporter would be an excellent target for that crowd!

Shaking Rick's hand, I tapped the B-2 CTF patch on his flight suit shoulder and said, "Rick, one of these days, I have to get one of these." Without a word, he ripped the velcro-mounted patch off and handed it to me.

"Here. Now you have one," he said. I was left holding the slightly damp red, yellow, and black patch as the test pilot/hero-of-the-day was pulled away by a crowd of lady well-wishers.

A few hours later, that patch was in a Federal Express package en route to New York, accompanied by instructions to the *Aviation Week* art department that I would get that patch back, or I'd personally come looking for it. We ran a facsimile of the patch in *Av Week's* B-2 first-flight cover story, although readers were never told of its historic significance.

The two test pilots had carried a number of items on the first B-2 flight that would become historic artifacts. The most significant were two pieces of metal from the original YB-49 that had crashed north of Edwards in 1948, claiming the life of Capt. Glenn Edwards, for whom the test base was named. An engineer at the B-2 CTF had dug the pieces out of the crash site and felt it was appropriate they return to the air aboard the B-2. Couch said the special mementos would be given to the Edwards Historic Museum and the Air Force Museum.

Couch also carried several CTF patches and a U.S. flag for a friend in Washington, D.C.

* * *

COL. RICK COUCH:
The most personal gift, though, was a pair of Texas A&M shorts that I wore for the first flight. Afterwards, the Edwards Flight Test Museum asked if they could have the flight suit I had worn that day. It was a bit too authentic, so I washed it before turning it over to them.

I had a few other requests for that flight suit, but the museum got it.

Later, I even heard rumors that I had been offered money for the suit, but that wasn't true.

* * *

POSTFLIGHT

As high as emotions ran on July 17, there was still no great let down after the first flight. Maintenance and engineering personnel were given some desperately needed time off the next day, but, the day after, everyone was back in place. They were ready to get on with the job of testing their new aircraft.

As part of the postflight assessment process, several reasons for the B-2's successful first test mission were identified. *Full-up* (full-scale) practices of the entire process, with everybody involved, paid off handsomely. This experience helped the key players concentrate on unusual situations, such as the radio problems, while the rest of the team continued with their routines. The pilots were especially cognizant of this aspect.

* * *

COL. RICK COUCH:

Egos and prejudices that are a natural part of a massive undertaking like this program were put aside. Everyone focused on the task at hand and worked together like true professionals. Despite the pressures and fatigue most people felt, there never seemed to be any major disagreements or arguments. Everyone paid attention to the details, and that meant nothing was left to chance.

It's hard to imagine the pressure created by knowing that CNN and half the world is sitting at the end of the runway, waiting for something to happen. It would have been easy to start worrying about that instead of concentrating on getting the B-2 in the air. That didn't happen, though, and it's a tribute to the entire flight test system we have . . . and the people who make it work.

* * *

11

Fame . . .
and a call
from Congress

WHILE THE BOMBER WAS BEING PARKED in its new hangar at Edwards, and the test team was celebrating at the Officers' Club, the press corps was flashing news of the B-2's first flight around the globe. All major television networks carried a short clip of the bomber's takeoff, many as the top news story of the day. Most counterpointed the successful first mission with coverage of the aircraft's more difficult "flight" through the congressional budgeting process. The B-2 had proved it could fly, but, from a fiscal standpoint, its future was still uncertain.

Newspaper headlines the next day reflected the widespread interest the flying-wing bomber had attracted, while underscoring the diversity of opinion about its significance. Any given paper's bias towards defense matters, in general, and an editor's position on the need for a B-2, in particular, were conveyed in the headlines:

"Stealth Bomber Makes Test Flight Without a Mishap"
The New York Times

"Stealth Bomber Takes to the California Skies. B-2 Faces Down-to-Earth Battle"
The Times (London)

"Stealth Flies, But Fate Is Up In Air"
USA Today

"Pilots Love 'Nimble' B-2 In Test Flight"
Shreveport Times

"Costly Stealth Bomber Takes Off Into An Uncertain Future"
The Guardian International (London, Manchester, Frankfurt, Marseilles)

"Stealth Bomber Completes Historic First Flight"
Dallas Times Herald

"Stealth Bomber's First Flight Is Greeted
With Cheers And The National Anthem"
Wall Street Journal

"Stealth Bomber Makes First Flight"
Los Angeles Times

" 'Stealth' Bomber Called Success In First Flight"
Washington Post

"The Flying Bat-Mobile Mission Successful, Reports Project Boss"
Daily Mail (London)

A Saudi Arabian newspaper also carried the first flight story on its front page. However, it distinguished itself by also including detailed instructions, in Arabic, for assembling a paper cutout kit of the bomber.

Hundreds of other news publications, such as the Il Messaggero of Rome, the Turkish Hürriyet and numerous British papers carried front-page stories on the B-2 flight. The unique aircraft and its cost clearly had captured the world's imagination.

This focus caught the Air Force by surprise, relatively unprepared to capitalize on it. Northrop, which had been sweating out Congress' decision on the bomber's fate, though, loved every minute of it.

The two test pilots were totally stunned by all the attention heaped on them. Air Force public affairs officers and security chiefs banned direct interviews with the two pilots over the next few days. They were less successful, though, in deflecting others who were maneuvering to position themselves close to the pilots and capture some of the public attention for their own agendas.

TRIP TO WASHINGTON

The U.S. Senate stepped into the fray and started a tug-of-war with the Air Force over whether the pilots should go to Washington, D.C., and testify before the Senate Armed Services Committee. B-2 supporters in Congress wanted to get all the political mileage they could out of the bomber's first flight. Having the two celebrated pilots there, on camera with the senators, was too much to pass up. Political clout being what it is, the Air Force and Northrop ultimately had very little to say about whether the pilots should testify or not.

Bruce Hinds and Col. Rick Couch had barely finished their debriefings before they were told to head for the nation's capital, but, hold it . . . . Then they were told to wait. This on-again, off-again yo-yo continued for a few days while higher powers debated whether the pilots should be dragged into the B-2 political battles or not.

Finally, the word came down: Go to Washington as soon as possible. By then, getting an airline ticket at a convenient time was impossible, thanks to heavy summer vacation traffic. When Gen. Randolph learned that Hinds and Couch would have to take a red-eye flight—one that arrived in the wee hours of the morning—from Los Angeles to Washington, he was more than a little irritated. He decided it was time to exercise some four-star clout of his own.

Randolph ordered a Military Airlift Command C-21 (Learjet) to pick up the two pilots and bring them to Washington at a more reasonable hour, service usually reserved for generals. This would avoid an all-night trip and further ensure the men were alert enough to answer senators' questions by mitigating the jet lag of a three-hour time zone difference. Bruce Hinds was already in Los Angeles, so he elected to fly the red-eye rather than drive back to Edwards, from where Couch and the C-21 were leaving.

When the two test pilots arrived in Washington, D.C., they were quickly briefed on what they would and would not say at the Senate committee hearing. First stop was a meeting with Jack Welch, the Air Force Deputy Under-Secretary for Acquisition, where technical aspects of the aircraft and first flight were discussed.

Technical questions that had been raised recently by a congressman were studied and direct, but not excessively technical, answers were prepared. It was clear that the congressman was not well-acquainted with some of the B-2's technologies, an observation that would apply equally to most of the committee's senators.

Next came an appointment with General Larry D. Welch, the Air Force Chief of Staff. The general had been under the gun from Congress during the latest funding debates, and made it clear to the pilots that their role was a narrow one. They were told that their job was to talk about flight testing and not about B-2 program requirements. He also made it clear that if Hinds and Couch said anything that could label them as program advocates, their "usefulness as test pilots was over." There was no misunderstanding the career-limiting aspects of that directive.

On July 21, four days after they flew the B-2 on its maiden mission to Edwards AFB, Hinds and Couch spent a memorable day with Congress. The events began at a breakfast meeting with about 30 senators and representatives at the Capitol. Also in attendance was an impressive assemblage of Defense Department brass: the secretary of defense, chairman of the joint chiefs, Air Force chief of staff (Gen. Welch), and commander of the Air Force Strategic Air Command (Gen. John Chain). Feeling humble was no problem, according to Col. Couch.

After breakfast, the pilots were asked to say a few words about the B-2, Gen. Chain discussed the nation's need for the aircraft, then it was time to meet the Senate committee. In the elevator, a staff member wearing a Society of Experimental Test Pilots lapel pin whispered to Couch that he had "planted a few technical questions" with his principal. The staffer was a former Marine Corps test pilot, and part of the brotherhood that binds the profession closely.

Couch and Hinds were somewhat relieved to find there would be a few friends in the caucus room when the hearing started.

The room was dominated by bright lights, television cameras, and photographers, creating a constant sea of confusion. Hinds and Couch were seated as "bookends" at each end of a long table, with Gens. Welch and Chain between them. Under the glare and heat of the lights, the hearing seemed to drag on forever. Questions directed to the two pilots were, for the most part, so broad and general that answering them almost required a preface of "In the beginning, ..." Welch and Chain addressed most of the questions, which centered on the B-2 mission and aspects of the overall program. Clearly, the pilots were there strictly for effect and to draw media attention to the hearing.

Both pilots recalled an interesting moment when the previously planted questions were asked by the appropriate senator. Here was a man who had minimal knowledge of airplanes, asking questions such as, "What can you tell me about the handling qualities of the B-2? How does it feel to fly a neutrally stable, large-winged aircraft?"

Barely able to keep a straight face, Hinds answered, "Well, I can tell you, senator, it felt a lot better sitting in that airplane than it does sitting here!"

The entire hearing smacked of a choreographed event for the television cameras, which Washington insiders said was Congress' normal way of doing business. The hearing room was constantly in motion. Senators would listen for awhile, then leave frequently, reappearing just in time to ask their next question. From the television audience's rectangular perspective, it would seem that the entire panel was present the whole time—intent lions going after the Christians who had been called to testify before the august body. In fact, only two senators were present for the entire hearing, and one of those was the committee chairman who had to be there to run the meeting.

At one point, a distinguished, well-known senator had some trouble making his way to his seat, clearly "under the weather" a bit from an early drink or two. On cue, the chairman asked the new arrival if he had any questions. Of course, he did. He started asking things which seemed to have little relevance to the hearing, then gravitated to topics that had already been covered. He concluded by pontificating mightily about the high cost of modern weapon systems, slurring his words only slightly.

The test pilots and generals politely answered this senator's questions, then endured his cost-related tirade without comment. Fortunately, this marked the hearing's conclusion. As Couch got up to leave, he leaned towards one of the generals and asked if perhaps he should report the good senator for "substance abuse," a topic of much discussion within the Air Force at that time. The only response was a quick half-grin that implied, "We do as they say, not as they do."

After the Senate hearing, the pilots were whisked to a room in the House office building, where they participated in a two-hour forum about the B-2. The discussion was opened by the secretary of the Air Force, who then asked

Hinds and Couch to add their comments about the first flight and planned test program.

During the somewhat informal session, several congressmen subsequently approached the pilots and talked briefly. Representative Beverly Byron (D-Md.) confided that she had a son in the Strategic Air Command and expressed hope that he would have a chance to fly the B-2 sometime during his career. Her comment was a welcome, friendly gesture that served to humanize the day's activities somewhat.

While the entire trip to Washington was a blatantly orchestrated effort by certain congressmen and the Air Force to capitalize on the B-2's first flight, it probably paid dividends. It might have helped drum up additional support for the program, and it allayed a few nagging fears and suspicions about the aircraft itself. Some elected officials had expressed doubts about the bomber, based on dire predictions from several engineers concerning a flying wing's inherent instability and, of course, its heady cost.

Hinds and Couch provided a comforting assurance that, yes, the strange-looking bird really could be flown safely. They were credible sources, ones with direct, first-hand experience. Their on-site technical expertise might have helped dissipate a plethora of B-2 misstatements that had been floating around the halls of Congress for months, adding a welcome dose of accuracy that, coming from other quarters, might have been suspect. Test pilots who had actually flown the B-2 were more credible than a biased messenger from the Pentagon, at least to some skeptical members of Congress.

Fortunately, the pilots' Washington trip really did not interrupt the B-2 test program, either. As Bruce Hinds said, "I had already written my [flight] reports, and was able to work on some deficiency reports on the airplane going to and from Washington. I don't think the trip impacted the program much, and it may even have done some good."

TEST PILOT HEROES

Hinds and Couch were completely unprepared for the hero treatment they received after the first B-2 flight. Public and media attention heaped upon them was "absolutely beyond my wildest thought," Hinds said. "I never dreamed it [the flight] would get that much attention." Cards and letters from both unknown well-wishers and friends found their way to the stunned test pilots. Many were accompanied by requests for signed pictures and speaking engagements.

Media attention covered the spectrum from highly complimentary to sarcastic. Most of the latter centered on cost, a message often conveyed via innovative and humorous vehicles. For example, a creative San Diego, Calif., radio station disc jockey sent Couch a letter and tape of a simulated advertising spot that offered "B-2 Day Care Centers." In essence, the spot suggested that a pay-as-you-go mission for the B-2 might be baby-sitting children aboard the B-2 at

35,000 feet. Air Force officers privately responded, tongue-in-cheek, that the concept would complicate the flight test program a bit, but might help pay for it.

Not all of the hype was welcome, or accurate. Col. Couch's wife, Ann, was extremely embarrassed when a reporter for a quasimilitary newspaper interviewed, then misquoted her. Although probably not done maliciously, the East coast-based reporter apparently misunderstood Ann's strong Texas accent and wrote not what Ann actually said, but how the reporter understood it. Unfortunately, the way the article was written gave the totally erroneous impression that Ann was either a terribly insensitive woman or a complete idiot. Neither described the gracious southern lady that is Ann Couch.

As a result of Ann's experience, both pilots, as well as their families and colleagues, became very cautious in dealing with the press. "Despite this, it didn't seem to really matter what we said," Col. Couch observed. "Our comments were still reported in whatever context fit the story being told, regardless of how they were meant in the first place."

* * *

BRUCE HINDS:
The media had more of an effect on the program than on me. Some [reporters] were very fair, and some were quite unfair . . . we got the full range of them. [Their articles] were based on a reporter's or publication's bias, it seemed, and some hurt the program, I think.

The press tends to jump on a bad-news bandwagon, because bad news is more salable. So, they jump on any problems [with the aircraft] that surface. It's just a way to needle the defense and military-related industries.

* * *

IN DEMAND

Except for an occasional negative brush with reporters, such as the Couch family experienced, the two pilots were very well-received by the diverse groups that swamped Northrop and CTF offices with speaking requests. Couch, the more gregarious of the two pilots, rarely turned any of them down if it was possible to fit a request into his hectic schedule. He traveled throughout the nation, speaking to Air Force ROTC units at colleges, Rotary clubs, and professional aerospace organizations.

Hinds was more selective, limiting speeches to technical organizations, Air Force Association or other military-oriented groups, and B-2 subcontractor management clubs or employee get-togethers. These groups typically were most interested in the bomber's mission and its technical aspects.

A year after the historic flight, Northrop test pilots who routinely flew the B-2 shared the speaking load, giving roughly five or six presentations per month. Hinds limits his engagements to approximately two or three per month, while the remainder are given by the other contractor pilots.

For months, Couch's time was dominated by speaking tours. He felt obligated to spread the word about the B-2, at least in a technical sense, to increase public awareness of the program beyond what most citizens could glean from news sources.

* * *

COL. RICK COUCH:

Even though the audiences varied from Rotary Clubs to all-Air Force groups, the questions asked after the main presentation were pretty much the same. Initially, some of the more "feeling" type of questions caught me off guard, but, after they started repeating themselves all the time, it was easy to give a decent answer or two.

Probably the question asked most often was: "What did it feel like to fly the B-2?" There's really no easy answer to that. On the first flight, we were so busy that there really wasn't much time to think about feelings. We were concentrating on what was happening in the airplane, not the more esoteric things going on around us. A person tends to focus on the most important tasks and ignore what isn't essential.

After the flight, I do remember being amazed at how smoothly everything had gone. But that was no accident. All of us had devoted a lot of time practicing for the first flight. That preparedness kept us from being distracted when we saw some of the same problems we had worked on in practice sessions.

The next most-asked question was: "How did it fly?" That one was easy to answer . . . it flew great. The computerized flight control system had been tailored to provide good flying qualities throughout the entire aircraft flight envelope. While that may be quick to say, believe me, the flight control mechanization is extremely complex and getting it to act that way was no easy job.

Hour after hour had been spent in the labs and mission simulator, testing that control system at every possible flight condition. When some things didn't look so good at first, engineers would play around with the control laws and we'd try it again until the system flew well.

The real question during first flight was "Did the airplane fly like the simulator?" It did, and that indicated the simulator was probably a good representation of how the B-2 would fly at other speeds and altitudes throughout the flight envelope.

* * *

Both pilots were challenged by trying to explain to a lay audience how the fly-by-wire flight control system worked. Visualizing this is difficult, and there are few good analogies that aid understanding. Couch developed a workable description for his audiences, but was occasionally surprised by unexpected questions the explanation triggered.

* * *

COL. RICK COUCH:

The pilot, when he moves the control stick, is actually telling a computer what he wants the airplane to do; he pulls back, and that means he wants the B-2's nose to come up. The computer then tells the big control surfaces on the aft edge of the wing what position they should be in to provide the aircraft response the pilot is commanding. Multiple paths are built into the system, so it is almost impossible for the computer to become disconnected from the pilot or the flight control surfaces.

After giving this explanation one time, and relating that the B-2's control system uses many of the same electronic techniques the F-16 does, someone asked how I could fly the F-16 when I was left-handed. He knew the stick in an F-16 cockpit was on the right side, making it more comfortable for a right-handed pilot. I had never thought about it. Pilots just get in and fly without ever thinking about what side the stick, or wheel, is on and which hand you have to use.

Later, after thinking about it for awhile, I decided the man's question was like asking a golfer if he inhales or exhales during his back swing. You never think about those things . . . if you do, especially while trying to swing a golf club, or fly, it'll probably screw you up royally!

* * *

Questions invariably worked their way around to the B-2's cost. Naturally, people have a hard time understanding how any one airplane can cost hundreds of millions of dollars. They also wanted to know how it felt to fly such airborne wealth. The answer was simple: Pilots never really worry about how much their airplane costs. Whether flying a B-2 or a Cessna 152, the primary job at hand is to keep one's pink body safe by preventing it and the airplane from hitting the ground. Cost of the vehicle is a distant secondary issue.

Explaining the B-2's cost was never easy, because *cost* is such a nebulous term that is subject to many definitions. Are we talking about cost to build the airplane, or its life-cycle cost (the price of long-term ownership)? Should we add in the cost of research and development, spare parts, nonrecurring engineering, and dozens of other things? Then the "dollar years" have to be agreed upon in order to compare the B-2's cost to that of some other weapon system.

Comparing the cost of an aircraft calculated in 1980 dollars to one based on 1990 dollars is a real apples-to-oranges situation. The value of a dollar from one year to the next varies substantially. In other words, discussing the cost of a B-2 usually degenerates into an exercise in definitions. Like statistics, the numbers a person decides to use depends upon what he is trying to prove.

In the end, though, cost must be balanced against need. If the United States truly needs the B-2, and there are no viable alternatives, cost should be a secondary issue.

The B-2's mission also was a topic of interest to most audiences. While the Strategic Air Command sets the requirements for an aircraft like the B-2, not the test team that Hinds and Couch represented, the pilots typically gave a standard, USAF- approved answer: The B-2 really has two missions.

The primary one is to provide strategic deterrence into the twenty-first century. In other words, just having the B-2 should be enough to discourage the

Soviets or some other potential aggressor from starting a nuclear conflict. If the policy of deterrence ever fails, the bomber must then be capable of retaliating with awesome force.

Secondly, the new bomber also has a conventional warfare mission: dropping nonnuclear weapons on military targets in a regional conflict fought with guns, tanks, and fighter aircraft. The B-1B and B-52 bombers already have this mission, and the B-2 must assume at least part of it into the next century.

Everybody the pilots addressed wanted to know about the materials used in the B-2. Quite simply, the bomber is made of the same materials used in most other aircraft, just in different proportions of each. It contains steel, aluminum, titanium, and plastic, but the percentages of each vary significantly from those of most other aircraft today. About 60 percent of the B-2 is made of composite materials, which are plastic-like materials that can be as strong as steel, but weigh a lot less.

A FORMER PRESIDENT VISITS

Several months after the B-2's initial flight, former President Ronald Reagan asked if he could visit Edwards AFB, see the aircraft, and meet some of the people who worked on the bomber. The B-2 had been a central element of the strategic arms buildup during the Reagan administration, and the former president was anxious to see the actual vehicle.

Air Force public affairs personnel handled most of the arrangements, but contractor officials also participated. As part of the preliminary arrangements, Col. Couch was asked to brief Mr. Reagan about what to expect during his visit to the desert base. As B-2 CTF Director, Couch and Maj. Gen. John Schoeppner, commander of the Air Force Flight Test Center at Edwards, provided the requested briefing at the former president's offices, located on the top floor of a high-rise building in the Century City section of Los Angeles. The offices commanded a terrific view of Beverly Hills, Santa Monica, and, on a clear day, the Pacific Ocean.

Security was extremely tight, reflecting Reagan's status as a former president, but was not intrusive. Couch and Schoeppner met with Reagan for about 30 minutes, discussing the CTF and the bomber test program. Ever the charismatic gentleman, the former president insisted the upcoming visit should remain simple with no pomp and circumstance.

Consequently, to keep costs to a minimum, the CTF suggested serving hamburgers and hot dogs. Reagan's staff said that's exactly what he preferred. Maintenance personnel at the CTF planned a stereotypical American cookout: grilled hamburgers and hot dogs, potato salad, and soft drinks. Cost would be $3 per person.

Feeding the entire 1,200-person B-2 organization at Edwards would not be possible, so about 300 lunch tickets were distributed evenly to all the different CTF units. In keeping with Reagan's wishes, seven working-level people were selected to sit at the former president's table. An Air Force lieutenant, two enlisted people, a young civilian engineer, a secretary, one of the building custodians, and the oldest engineer in Northrop's Edwards contingent had the honor of meeting and sharing lunch with the two-term president that had shepherded the B-2 bomber to its current status.

* * *

COL. RICK COUCH:

The lunch was a huge success. The president would have stayed all day talking to our folks if he could have. He was one of the most friendly, outgoing persons I have ever seen when dealing with "real" people. His visit meant an awful lot to our workforce.

At one point, we presented Mr. Reagan with a hand-carved plaque made by one of our talented maintenance men and a picture of the B-2 on its maiden flight. The day's only screw-up came at that point, when I forgot to ask Bruce Hinds to help me present the B-2 picture.

* * *

During a tour of the CTF's mission control rooms and the B-2 test aircraft, Reagan stopped frequently to shake hands and allow his picture to be taken with several groups of people. The politician in him was evident as he very graciously handled all requests for pictures.

At one point, after Couch was briefing him in the B-2 cockpit, Reagan pulled a comb out and ran it through his thick hair. His timing was excellent. A photographer snapped his and Couch's picture a moment later, and the photo later appeared in several local newspapers.

Just before entering the main hangar for lunch, the ex-president again whipped out the comb and adjusted his hair. At that point, Couch, who has lamented his own hair loss in recent years, asked Reagan to stop doing that. A startled look flashed across the former Commander-in-Chief's face and he demanded, "Why?"

"Because you're making me jealous, that's why," Couch deadpanned.

Reagan cracked up.

Later in the day, after the president had left, one of his Secret Service men cornered Couch and told him he had some real nerve telling Reagan to stop combing his hair, then smiled and walked away. Couch had the feeling that maybe the slightly balding Secret Service agent had wanted to do the same thing for some time.

12

Expanding
the envelope

POSTFLIGHT INSPECTIONS OF THE B-2 CONFIRMED the new aircraft had weathered its first test mission extremely well. The flight and ground crews reported very few *squawks*, which are discrepancies that had to be fixed before the next flight. In fact, Col. Couch said the aircraft was in such good condition that "it could have been refueled and flown again right away."

However, several important ground tests that had been deferred until after Flight No. 1 were to be completed before the bomber could fly again. A number of these would normally have been accomplished before the all-important first flight, but pressures to get the bird airborne dictated their delay.

Only those tests that would not be flight safety problems, though, were deferred. For example, landing gear ground tests could be done later if everybody agreed that it would be safe to fly the B-2 with its undercarriage locked in the down position.

Although the landing gear's operation had been checked thoroughly, it still had not passed the installation test procedure. Rigging problems and minor engineering adjustments were needed before it could pass the test. This fine tuning of the landing gear was time consuming, requiring repeated jacking, hooking up external hydraulic and electrical power, then cycling the gear. Consequently, the final tests were deferred until the aircraft arrived at Edwards.

Bruce Hinds had not been wildly enthusiastic about the idea, but agreed to a gear-down first flight as a means of getting the bomber airborne as soon as possible. But that also meant the gear tests would have to be completed before the second flight.

Performing landing gear, cabin pressurization, and emergency power system tests at Edwards instead of Palmdale, as originally planned, presented organizational and equipment problems, and might have delayed the second flight. Bruce Hinds had strongly advocated doing the gear tests before first flight, because he was concerned the overall program would suffer by delaying them.

* * *

BRUCE HINDS:

I really wanted to have the gear swung as a ground test, so we would at least have the capability to raise it if we had to [on the first flight]. As it turned out, we didn't have that option. We flew with the gear pinned and couldn't have raised it. That was the only thing I disagreed with [before okaying the first flight].

I also thought it would take about two weeks to swing the gear at Edwards, versus taking one week at Palmdale. We had all the people and equipment to do it at Palmdale, and would have to move them to the base.

I always tried to think about how a decision . . . like swinging the gear . . . would affect us downstream. I tried to ask: Was expediting in the near term going to hurt us later?

* * *

Clearly, landing gear checkout was one of the most immediate tasks to get out of the way before the second flight. Because proper operation of the gear is so critical, the ground test plan called for jacking the aircraft up, then *swinging* (retracting and extending) the gear 24 times in the normal mode and another 24 times in emergency backup modes without a single problem showing up. If it could pass this confidence test, the B-2's landing gear had a high probability of working correctly in the air.

Fortunately, the tests proceeded without a hitch and were completed within a week, thanks to the care and attention to detail the manufacturing team at Palmdale had put into the entire gear system.

Cabin pressure tests required clearing most people away from the aircraft, pumping air into the cockpit area, and checking its ability to hold pressure. This capability was particularly important for pilot comfort on long test flights at high altitude. Flying an unpressurized airplane can become quite fatiguing because pilots must then rely on oxygen masks throughout the flight, and any trapped air in the body, such as under dental fillings or in sinuses, expands as the surrounding air pressure decreases at high altitude.

Besides causing general discomfort and even pain, at times, flying unpressurized for a long period simply causes the whole body to work harder. It also increases the risk of a pilot getting decompression sickness after the mission, and that can be life-threatening. Safety and good sense dictated getting the pressurization system working as soon as possible.

Once the B-2 fuselage was pumped up to a certain pressure, maintenance technicians carefully inspected the skin and internal structure, looking for areas where air was escaping. Leaks were found primarily in an aft bulkhead directly behind the cockpit and in the nosewheel area, beneath the crew compartment floor. The aft bulkhead, fortunately, was accessible through the bomber's weapons bay.

Later, each of the identified leak points was sealed and the whole process repeated until engineers were satisfied the cabin would maintain a desired inside-to-outside pressure differential. The ground test was a slow, painstaking process, but a necessary one.

GROUND TEST SCARE

Next came the *emergency power system* (EPS) ground checkouts, which surely will rank among the most frightening moments of a certain young engineer's life. The B-2 is equipped with two *emergency power units* (EPUs) originally designed for use on the F-16 fighter. The two fighter systems were hooked together to provide emergency hydraulic and electrical power, mainly to the flight control system, in the event of a four-engine flameout or the loss of all four electrical generators on the B-2.

The advent of modern aircraft that rely on fly-by-wire flight controls brought with it the need to ensure a reliable source of electrical and hydraulic power. In the days of mechanical flight controls, losing generators and hydraulic pumps or even experiencing a fire that disabled the whole electrical system was an emergency situation, but at least a pilot could continue flying the airplane. He was still hooked directly to the control surfaces by pushrods and cables.

That all changed when the only thing between a pilot's stick and the airplane's elevons, rudder, and other control surfaces became a bundle of wires, a computer, and hydraulic components. Pull the electrical plug on a fly-by-wire aircraft and that all-important link between pilot and flight controls is broken; they no longer communicate.

Consequently, F-16 designers—the first to face this critical need for emergency power—came up with redundant systems to ensure an uninterrupted power supply. If the F-16's only powerplant is disabled or the engine-driven generators and pumps cease to function, an ingenious system, the emergency power unit, or EPU, kicks in automatically.

The EPU is a small, self-contained gas turbine powered by hydrazine, a chemical that, when activated by a catalyst, rapidly converts liquid to gas. The expanding gas drives the turbine, which, in turn, drives an electrical generator and hydraulic pump. This keeps the flight control system powered, ensuring the pilot can land safely.

The EPU's most critical function is providing hydraulic power for the flight controls because backup permanent magnet generators and batteries will still supply the F-16's flight control computer. But, if the EPU fails, or when its hydrazine is exhausted, only the pressure in hydraulic accumulators will keep the flight controls working awhile longer. At that point, the pilot had better be close to landing, because all his options are disappearing rapidly.

Because the F-16's EPU has proven to be a dependable backup power source, B-2 designers adapted two of the units for use on the bomber. For all its great features, though, the EPU has one drawback, its hydrazine fuel supply.

Unfortunately, hydrazine, in the form used by these aircraft, is incredibly toxic to humans. A few parts per million will kill a person in short order. That means the Air Force and its subcontractors go to great lengths to make sure that hydrazine does not escape from emergency power systems, and, if it does, that people are well clear of it.

Even though people who work in the aerospace industry are very leery of hydrazine's dangers, it should be noted that the chemical is not an inherent killer. Hydrazine is an important compound used in jet and rocket fuels, as well as in agricultural chemicals that regulate plant growth. But because it is a colorless, fuming corrosive, aerospace workers have learned to give it a wide berth, just to be on the safe side. And that brings us to the B-2's EPS ground tests.

Test engineers and managers had gone to great lengths to make sure the EPS tests were carefully designed and controlled, to ensure that any inadvertent escape of hydrazine wouldn't harm any workers in the area. Here, too, extreme safety precautions were better than not enough.

Before running the test with hydrazine, engineers had already demonstrated the system's basic integrity by operating it with pressurized nitrogen prior to the first B-2 flight. That led to a strong confidence that the system would work correctly with the more hazardous hydrazine fuel.

A young test engineer had carefully planned the EPS checkout and had everything in place for the first critical test. On the designated night, the system was charged with hydrazine, a flight crew was seated in the cockpit and about 20 maintenance technicians were positioned around the aircraft to monitor the test's progress and report their observations. The test engineer assured everybody involved that the natural byproducts of hydrazine were nontoxic, so, if everything went as planned, there was nothing to worry about.

All four aircraft engines were started and, thanks to a few computer commands, the B-2 was tricked into thinking it was flying. Moments later, a command was given that simulated loss of electrical power, signaling the EPS to automatically start up. The system functioned as advertised and everything looked good, according to the maintenance observers.

A few minutes later, though, the ground crew reported a leak under the hydrazine tanks and that they were evacuating the area. What they did not say was that they were leaving their two-way radios behind and simply "getting the hell out of Dodge." However, from her control room position, the test engineer could not see the aircraft or ground crew. As soon as the report of a leak came in, she immediately directed the cockpit crew to shut down the EPS.

The pilots promptly moved the switch to OFF, but the EPS continued to run. Nothing the crew did would shut the persistent system down. It was an emergency system designed to perform under critical conditions, and it seemed determined to run until the entire hydrazine supply was gone. The system shut down only after all the hydrazine was depleted.

Suddenly, the test engineer turned as white as a ghost, seemed to shrink away, and started mumbling incoherently. Others in the control room came to her aid, trying to ascertain what was wrong. She managed to whisper something about "killing all the maintenance guys."

In her mind's visualization of the scene, something had gone terribly wrong. Hydrazine had escaped and there were about 20 bodies now lying around the airplane while the EPS continued to run out of control, she thought. After all, her repeated radio calls to the ground crew elicited no response. A test engineer's worst nightmare had just come true.

It took awhile, but her control room colleagues convinced her that everybody down there was alive and well. The maintenance team had simply abandoned its communications equipment as soon as people saw what they thought was hydrazine escaping. Subsequent inspection proved that the leak was nothing more exotic than water condensation dripping from the suddenly cooled hydrazine tanks. Nobody was ever in danger of being poisoned or dying.

BACK IN THE AIR

With top-priority ground tests out of the way, the B-2 was prepared for its second mission. Col. Couch would fly this one from the left seat and Bruce Hinds would serve as his copilot, an arrangement typical of modern combined Air Force/contractor test programs.

Public interest in the B-2 still ran high, so the Air Force had conceded that reporters would be allowed to cover the second B-2 takeoff and landing, stationed near the main Edwards runway. Reminiscent of the first flight, the second sortie was delayed, then rescheduled for the next day when several last-minute problems cropped up during preflight preparations. That meant the aircraft would not have been ready to fly until late in the day, when both the flight and ground crews were fatigued. They had been on duty for more than 12 hours, and everybody's effectiveness was flagging.

Some of the visiting press had trouble understanding that such delays are a matter of course in the flight test business, and assumed that there must be something drastically wrong with the new bomber. So many things must be ready and working exactly right on any test aircraft that the chances for a glitch causing a postponement are quite high. Consequently, adhering to a takeoff schedule with a brand new flight test aircraft is unlikely, at best.

The next day, the big bat-winged aircraft took to the skies for a second time. Takeoff and climbout were uneventful, and the pilots moved directly into the first test point. Flight No. 2 was devoted to *expanding the flight envelope*, a test term that basically means flying the aircraft at speeds and altitudes more critical than what had been done previously. Of course, a primary test was to retract the landing gear for the first time in flight.

For a flight crew, the first gear retraction is a traumatic event, simply because a failure to work right could turn the mission into an immediate, very serious airborne emergency. If the gear only retracted part way, or later failed to extend and lock in the DOWN position properly, Couch and Hinds would add another first to their logbooks—the first pilots to belly-land a B-2.

At a predetermined airspeed and altitude, Couch raised the gear handle while a couple of dozen engineers on the ground stared at critical parameters moving across their computer screens. A few seconds later, the gear doors swung shut, enclosing the big wheels. The gear had retracted without a hitch.

After accelerating approximately 30 knots above gear operating speed, then slowing again, the pilots lowered the gear handle and waited, listening intently. The gear dropped and locked. The crew reported "three green" to the test controller and everybody started breathing again.

The gear system worked.

Couch raised the gear handle one more time, tucking the gear inside the bomber's belly. Then he started setting up for the next test point.

The test conductor called about an hour into the flight and reported, "We're seeing some indications of an oil pressure drop on the No. 2 AMAD." That particular airframe mounted accessory drive (AMAD) connected engine No. 2 to its respective generator, hydraulic pumps, and engine starter. Although the AMAD could be disconnected in flight, it could not be reengaged.

There were no indications in the cockpit that anything was amiss, but the pilots were advised to slow down, extend the gear, and land as soon as possible. During the approach to Edwards' 15,000-foot main runway, a warning started flashing on one of the multifunction displays in the cockpit, indicating the No. 2 AMAD was sick. The landing was uneventful, but the planned long flight had been curtailed by several hours.

Couch and Hinds shut down the No. 2 engine after they were clear of the runway and taxied to the B-2 facility as reporters filmed their progress. A quick inspection showed that the No. 2 engine bay was full of oil, due to a cracked AMAD housing. In retrospect, electing to end the flight as soon as the problem appeared was a smart decision.

The AMAD failure was caused by a crack in the housing, a problem area that had been identified two years earlier. Ground tests of the AMAD system in Northrop's Auxiliary Power Integration Test Laboratory—built at Edwards specifically to support the B-2 program—had uncovered a manufacturing problem, triggering a redesign effort to correct the deficiency.

Even though new AMADs had been built and tested, flight-quality units had not been delivered prior to the B-2's first flight. Engineers had calculated that the AMADs already installed were safe for about 70 flight hours before they had to be replaced with the new, redesigned units. Their estimates were considerably optimistic.

As luck would have it, the first two redesigned AMADs were delivered on the same day as the B-2's second flight. Both new units were installed immediately, prior to the third flight. Although consideration was given to simply waiting until all four AMADs could be replaced before resuming flight tests, it was decided that the risk of putting new equipment on all four engines at the same time was higher than the risk of having one—or both—of the old AMADs fail in flight.

Such is the norm in a flight test program: assessing all the potential hazards and deciding how much risk is warranted, balancing that against the potential payoff of taking the risk.

* * *

COL. RICK COUCH:
   There was some good news out of the whole AMAD episode, though. We gained a lot of confidence in the effectiveness of our real-time data system, in our method of using engineers in ground control rooms to monitor a wealth of TM'ed [telemetered] data, and in our ability to make rational, on-the-spot decisions based on the information these resources could provide.
   It also proved the value of our laboratory support system. The lab had found the AMAD problem about two years before we saw it in flight, and a fix was already in hand. Had we first discovered the problem on the airplane's second flight, then had to go back and redesign the AMAD, especially after many had already been built for production aircraft, it would have impacted the program tremendously. We would probably have had to ground the aircraft or come up with some kind of a work-around fix until a redesigned AMAD could be obtained. The financial cost of doing that in a hurry . . . to say nothing of the time lost and the cost to rework existing AMAD units . . . would have been staggering.

* * *

A footnote to the AMAD problem is that, on the B-2's fourth flight, the other two older AMADs started leaking. The aircraft again had to land early, for precisely the same reason it had landed on the second mission.

TESTING ROUTINE

The B-2 test program started settling into a routine after the second flight, and the CTF buckled down to the job of evaluating its new bird. All the hype and attention the media had accorded the B-2 program over the previous few years rapidly dissipated at about this time. Aside from occasionally lambasting it over cost issues, all but the aerospace industry trade press quickly seemed to lose interest in the B-2. *Aviation Week* continued to report the occurrence of each flight: date, how long it was, who flew it, and any information released about tests completed. A few other national publications and local newspapers in southern California comprised the primary press following.

   Most of the CTF's efforts between flights were devoted to fixing any maintenance or design problems that were uncovered on a test mission. Instrumentation and other tasks related to specific test objectives also required considerable attention. Flight crews and test engineers were continually balancing demands for new data on the next flight and the need to follow a logical, build-up sequence based on the aircraft's evolving configuration.

   This has always been a frustration of flight testing and always will be. Despite the most detailed, well thought-out planning an engineer has done, he or she can be sure of only one thing: The plan will have to change once the flying starts. The aircraft is never built quite the way it was supposed to be, or something has broken and parts are coming.

That means a planned test of a "whatzit" can't be done, because the whatzit needs a "smoke grinder," a "rebarsak" or a "howzit" to operate properly; all the howzits are being delivered late, so they didn't get installed before first flight; the aircraft can still fly, but we can't operate the whatzit until we get the new howzits. Consequently, the engineer shelves that test and looks for one that can be done in the configuration available. The B-2 was no exception.

Tests advanced cautiously into new regions of the flight envelope each time the aircraft flew, following a rigorous build-up strategy that demanded each condition be well understood before progressing to a more demanding one. This "engineering clearance" often took place after each test point, before the pilots were allowed to go to the next test.

Engineers on the ground monitored the computer-processed output from billions of data bits transmitted by the airborne B-2 over real-time telemetry links. They compared data from a test point completed a few seconds earlier to projections made before the flight. If actual data matched the expectations, the test controller gave the go-ahead for the next point. Postflight data reviews involved a more detailed analysis of each test point's results, confirming the aircraft was performing as designed.

Of course, a major concern in the early days of the B-2, or any other aircraft, flight test program was making sure unwanted "airframe dynamic flutter" never occurred. That is the trickiest part of any flight envelope expansion program: safely testing the aircraft in airspeed/altitude regimes it has not been in before without inadvertently triggering the dreaded "flutter" problem.

Flutter is one of the nastiest phenomenons in aerodynamics. In its worst form, flutter means that some part of an aircraft starts vibrating or flexing in an uncontrollable fashion. This can be caused by something as simple as the air flowing over a surface at the correct speed and pressure, and can be triggered by turbulence or a rapid control input.

If the response, or flutter, is divergent, the flexing or amplitude of vibrations gets larger as time goes on. Eventually, the entire aircraft can disintegrate if the flutter mode is severe enough and cannot be arrested. Worse, it can happen in a matter of seconds. This has occurred any number of times in the past, and numerous test pilots and flight test engineers have died when their aircraft literally came apart around them.

Engineers worry a great deal about flutter and design the aircraft to avoid any possibility of it happening. They run computer simulations and other tests to minimize the possibility of flutter. But, regardless of what the experts claim, flutter still remains mostly science with a dash of black magic thrown in, just to keep the mystique of flight alive.

The ultimate proof of an aircraft's flutter tendencies still must be determined in flight. And, until test pilots carefully fly their aircraft into all areas of the defined flight envelope, the possibility exists that a flutter response can be triggered unexpectedly.

Northrop

Test pilots Bruce Hinds and Col. Rick Couch force a smile at the end of a long and frustrating day. High-speed taxi tests had ended on a dim note when the B-2 had become stuck in a sun-softened asphalt runway overrun area.

Calspan

The Calspan Total In-Flight Simulator (TIFS) NC-131H was flown by B-2 test pilots to evaluate bomber handling characteristics, particularly during landing. The flying simulator includes an extra cockpit grafted on the C-131 nose, direct-lift flaps, side-force surfaces on the wing, and sophisticated systems.

Three ejection seats blast free of a simulated B-2 cockpit during high-speed rocket sled tests at Holloman AFB, New Mexico. Although the bomber will only have two seats, provisions for a third crew position have been incorporated for possible future needs.

The Flight Controls and Hydraulic Integration Laboratory (FCHIL) was a full reproduction of the B-2 control system. A rudimentary cockpit allowed pilots to "fly" the "Iron Bird" on the ground.

A mockup of the B-2's cockpit was used in the Northrop Environmental Control System Laboratory for development of crew and avionics air conditioning.

This cutaway drawing details the B-2 Engine Run Dock (ERD) at Northrop's Site 4. Final assembly of AV-1 was performed in this facility, which is designed to muffle noise produced by bombers operating their engines at high power settings during preflight checkouts.

A highly modified KC-135A was used for several years as a flying avionics testbed laboratory, which permitted detailed development of the B-2's radar and other electronic systems in an airborne environment.

Soaked but happy, Bruce Hinds is congratulated by Northrop CEO T.V. Jones. Gen. Bernard Randolph, Air Force Systems Command chief, and Col. Claude Bolton, B-2 deputy program director, look on.

After the traditional first-flight hose-down from B-2 ground crews, a slightly wet Col. Rick Couch is congratulated by Gen. Bernard Randolph, Air Force Systems Command chief; then-Brig. Gen. Richard Scofield, B-2 program director; and a video team.

A few days after AV-1 became stuck in soft overrun asphalt, the two pilots (Hinds, left, and Couch) are ready to fly and confident they will get airborne.

John "BJ" MacWhirter keeps a sharp eye on aircraft flights at the Palmdale Regional Airport/Air Force Plant 42. BJ can usually be found in his personal "control center," a canary yellow step-van parked on the corner of Sierra Highway and Avenue N. John's Corner was a frequent gathering spot for hundreds of aviation enthusiasts hoping to see the B-2 during taxi tests and first flight.

Reflecting its test focus, the two-pilot cockpit of B-2 No. 1 includes displays and controls unique to testing. Orange-colored or outlined panels identify this nonstandard equipment, some of which has displaced operational items. (See color section.)

For example, instead of a standard configuration with four multifunction displays (MFD) in front of each pilot, flight test panels have been substituted for the inboard MFDs on each side.

The pilot's inboard MFD (A) was replaced by four mechanical instruments.

Above the glareshield, pilot-selected data parameters such as brake temperatures are presented digitally on the liquid-crystal test parameters display *(B).*

An instrumentation master power switch (C), which controls electrical power for all aircraft data acquisition equipment, is directly above a guarded emergency landing gear reset switch.

The right-seat pilot's inboard MFD position is dedicated to the bomber's flutter system control panel *(D), which will activate predetermined cyclic vibrations.*

The flight test pilot's display keyboard *(E) allows the copilot to call up specific test-related graphic presentations on an MFD. These displays were developed as a test pilot aid for flying specific precision maneuvers.*

Data entry panels and scratchpad displays are to the right of each pilot (F), the crew's primary interface with weapons and satellite communication systems.

Although production B-2 fuel systems normally will be controlled automatically, either pilot can intervene through the manual fuel control panel *(G) just above the center console on aircraft No. 1. Similarly, test pilots can alter the flight control system's sensitivity through an orange-bordered* flight control gain panel *(H) forward of the copilot's throttle quadrant. Aft of the throttles, another test panel controls video recorders (I) that document panel readings and crew actions.*

Standard B-2 features include a flight data control panel *(J) at the lower left of each pilot's instrument panel. The landing gear handle (K) is at the far left and is accessible only to the pilot.*

*Principal B-2 designers John Cashen (left) and Irv Waaland at the rollout cere-
mony. Cashen approached the design from a stealthy, low observables orientation,
while Waaland focused on aerodynamic performance requirements. Independ-
ently, they each came up with a flying wing design in order to meet Air Force
criteria for the new bomber.*

*A quiet groundbreaking ceremony at Edwards AFB in early 1985 launched con-
struction of the B-2 Test Support Facility (TSF): (from left) Dick Hildebrand,
First B-2 CTF director (then 6520th Test Group technical director); Stassi
Cramm, chief, Technical Support Engineering; Dennis O'Keefe, chief, Technical
Support; Charlie Van Norman, B-2 CTF director at that time; "Smokey" Myers,
chief, Northrop facilities at Edwards.*

Generals Randolph and Scofield gather their thoughts before the postfirst-flight press conference begins, while the obviously happy pilots, Hinds and Couch, trade one-liners with two Aviation Week & Space Technology *editors.*

With drag rudders opened for better slow-speed control, the B-2 prepares for its first landing. Gear-down drag was higher than anticipated, prompting Hinds to carry a bit more power than originally planned.

First hookup to the KC-10. Pilots Hinds and Couch said the B-2 was very stable behind the tanker.

The B-2 landing gear test stand at Boeing's Seattle facility permitted thorough checks of the bomber's gear mechanism, wheels, and brake systems.

Northrop

A comprehensive real-time data system that allows ground-bound engineers to closely monitor an aircraft's structural response at any time has become a key weapon in the flight test arsenal against flutter. Studying the vibrations caused by a series of specific tests, engineers can spot any trends that might lead to trouble at higher speeds and different altitudes. Consequently, their judgment is held in high regard by pilots, who are more than willing to wait patiently, boring holes in the sky, while the engineering team decides whether it is safe to go on to the next test condition.

The third and fourth B-2 flights included a number of key events that were vital to the rest of the test program, but did not qualify strictly as envelope expansion in the purest sense. Hinds and Couch flew the big bomber behind a KC-10 air refueling tanker to evaluate its handling qualities when subjected to the other aircraft's influence. Downwash from the KC-10 wing, as well as turbulence caused by the engines and fuselage could make refueling the B-2 a real problem. Fortunately, these *proximity tests* proved the B-2 is as "stable as a rock," the pilots said. Refueling behind the big tanker, which is adapted from the DC-10 commercial airliner design, should be easy, they reported.

This was another good break for the stealth bomber. Other large aircraft, such as the monstrous B-52, are a bear to refuel behind a KC-135 tanker (adapted from a Boeing 707-type airliner), requiring plenty of pilot skill and substantial practice to do it correctly. It is also a fatiguing, high-workload task that usually leaves pilots drenched in their own perspiration.

Subsequent flights confirmed the B-2 could connect to the KC-10's refueling boom and receive fuel in flight. With that point completed, the bomber could start extending the length of its test missions by refueling several times, greatly enhancing the efficiency of each flight.

A maxim of flight testing is: "Airplanes are meant to fly. Once you get one into the air, keep it there as long as possible and you can accomplish a lot. Airplanes on the ground tend to break, so avoid down time by avoiding ground time." Proving it could be refueled readily, the B-2 passed a critical milestone, not only for testing purposes, but also for its ultimate, operational role as the Air Force's premier long-range bomber.

By the fifth flight, the Hinds/Couch pilot team that had brought the bomber to its current point in the program was expanded to include Lt. Col. John Small, an Air Force test pilot assigned to the B-2 CTF. Hinds flew with Small to check out the new pilot in the aircraft. Such flights are required for any pilot, especially a test pilot, starting to fly an airplane that is new to him.

Col. Couch stayed close to the operation, however, by flying one of the F-16s chasing the B-2 on its fifth mission. Couch was supposed to make a *rolling pick up*, a maneuver that tests a pilot's sense of timing to the utmost. As the B-2 started its takeoff roll, accelerating down the Edwards runway, Couch dived his already-airborne F-16 on a course that would put the chase aircraft abeam the B-2 just as the bomber became airborne. A photographer in Couch's back seat was charged with filming the takeoff.

A rolling pick up is not easy, no matter how experienced the pilot. He must continually judge where to position his chase aircraft as it overtakes the other vehicle, while the latter is accelerating on the ground. Many a student test pilot, trying a pick up for the first time, has been severely humbled by either being too slow or too fast, putting him totally out of position at the crucial moment of lift-off. Pick up maneuvers are unique to flight testing, and are a challenge to even seasoned fighter pilots who pride themselves on being able to fly tightly controlled intercepts with a target and joining up with a wingman.

* * *

COL. RICK COUCH:

At the start of the B-2's takeoff roll, everything looked good. I was in position, descending in the F-16 at exactly the right speed . . . or so I thought. A moment later, as the B-2 accelerated, I decided I was too slow . . . I would be too far behind when he lifted off. I pushed the throttle up and the lightweight F-16 responded instantly. Before I knew it, I blew right past the B-2. With all my friends and coworkers watching, I struggled for about three miles to get that damned fighter back in position abreast of the B-2. It seemed to take forever.

The photog [in the back seat] didn't help any. He was laughing so hard at my frantic efforts that it made getting set up right even more difficult.

After that flight, I took a lot of grief for weeks about my flying skills. About the time I thought it had run its course, some character brought it up again at my going away party.

* * *

As happens on every flight test program, a number of problems surfaced along the way. None of them, so far, indicated that the basic B-2 design was faulty, but were the result of how something was mechanized or built. These discoveries are not unexpected, and, in fact, are exactly why a new aircraft is so thoroughly tested. A comprehensive flight test program will uncover any number of things that must be corrected before the aircraft is turned over to the Air Force's operational users.

The AMAD problem was the first to surface, but it was quickly solved and has since become history. Another, more knotty anomaly that appeared early in the flight program was the "T bus" problem. On the third test flight, while conducting evaluations at 25,000 feet, several components attached to one of four flight control busses failed.

A *bus* can be thought of as a long electrical wire having several remote terminals where other equipment or systems can be hooked to it, enabling communication between the devices. However, they are hooked to the bus in such a way that the systems plugged into it can be affected by what happens on the bus upstream of them. The B-2's problem seemed to be related to a terminal, or attachment point on this type of bus.

Yet, when it was back on the ground, the aircraft seemed to work perfectly. Troubleshooting engineers decided the intermittent problem must be related to a heating or overcooling situation. They launched an aggressive hunt for the weak culprit by crawling all over the aircraft, armed with ordinary hair dryers and cans of freon; if cooling a component on the T-bus with freon had no reaction, they would try heating it with the hair dryer.

After checking 25 or so remote terminals on the T-bus, which ran from the cockpit to the big wing's trailing edges, with zero results, frustration levels were running high. Just getting to the terminals was a test of the human body's flexibility, not unlike crawling under the dashboard of a small car. Likely suspects were found and fixed several times, but subsequent flights invariably showed the problem still existed.

As often happens in dealing with the perversity of inanimate objects, luck solved the problem where science and logic had failed. A technician was leaning over an avionics rack in the aircraft one afternoon and—YAHOO!—the T-bus failed. One of the terminals or couplers had been installed in an area that had been stressed over and over by technicians having to reach across the rack to service another piece of equipment.

The coupler had been damaged in such a way that it could not be detected easily. On the ground, it made connection, but in flight there was enough vibration and flexing to cause the device to fail intermittently. Replacing the broken part, and altering subsequent maintenance practices, solved the problem. The T-bus was not a particularly exciting, critical problem, but was typical of the many mundane problems that have to be wrung out of any new military aircraft before it goes to the field.

Exciting, though, is an understatement for another anomaly the pilots discovered upon landing a few times. Just after the B-2's nosewheel touched the ground, the big aircraft occasionally wanted to swerve off to the left, requiring some deft footwork to keep it on the runway. This tendency first showed up during taxi tests at Palmdale, and complicated Bruce Hinds' attempts to bring the big bomber to a halt on the runway.

Later, the pilots theorized it must be either a gust of crosswind or a tendency for the tires or brakes on one side to grab more than on the other side. The problem had been seen a few times after taxi tests at Palmdale, but seemed to come and go at random. Later, there was some discussion about whether the aircraft was "built crooked" or not.

* * *

COL. RICK COUCH:

After the fourth flight, just as I landed and was starting to say "I think we've got the problem fixed," the aircraft tried to make a 90-degree left turn into the weeds. That was the clincher . . . we decided then and there that something was definitely squirrely about this airplane.

* * *

The flight controls and landing gear engineers, while busily troubleshooting the problem, were also trying to prove it wasn't their system at fault. After considerable investigation, flight control mechanization turned out to be the culprit.

It seems the B-2's designers decided that the miracle of computers could help the pilot by automatically providing some compensation for crosswinds. Crosswinds can complicate a touchdown, so this feature should have simplified landing in any weather; the flight controls were mechanized to do just that.

Pilots evaluated the feature in the flight simulators and decided the automatic compensation was acceptable. However, in the aircraft, the large control surfaces, deflected automatically by the crosswind compensation feature, turned out to provide more help than pilots could tolerate! Simply removing the crosswind compensation software feature immediately solved the left-swerve problem.

Other flight control features that looked good in the simulator have proven otherwise during actual flight testing and were modified early in the program. During the first planned downtime, several flight control system software changes were made to improve overall B-2 handling characteristics.

For example, initially, all the big, barndoor-size control surfaces automatically drooped from the wing's trailing edges while the aircraft was on the ground. Pilots had no control over them, no capability to raise or lower the surfaces. Even though they look like big flaps, they can not be set to a desired position like traditional flaps.

At 65 knots during takeoff roll, the surfaces slowly retracted to a faired position. Bruce Hinds foresaw a number of operational disadvantages to this design. From his standpoint, this feature meant the pilot had to glance down into the cockpit at around 65 knots to verify the surface positions were, indeed, retracting properly.

* * *

BRUCE HINDS:
Looking inside at a critical point in the takeoff isn't a good idea. You like to keep your eyes outside while you're accelerating for takeoff.

Having those huge surfaces drooped could cause operational problems, too. Any rocks and debris kicked up could damage [the controls]. Taxiing at Minot [North Dakota] in the winter could cause the surfaces to drag in snow banks beside the taxiways. Just not a good deal.

Once we got a little experience with them, we convinced everybody that we should keep the surfaces up while on the ground. That's the way they're mechanized now.

* * *

This particular feature is a good example of how flight testing can change a designer's views on what is good and not so good about a particular idea or feature. The B-2's elevons and drag rudders were designed to droop in the first place because there were no *snubbers* in the hydraulic system. Typically, an aircraft's hydraulic actuators would have snubber devices to cushion the shock of surfaces falling to their neutral or resting position when pressure was removed at engine shutdown, for instance.

The B-2, however, has very fast-acting control surfaces, driven by a 4,000 psi hydraulic system. Putting snubbers in the actuators, which have to move the big surfaces as much as 100 degrees per second, could add too much internal impedance to the devices and slow them down excessively. Consequently, without these snubbers, the big surfaces would fall as soon as hydraulic pressure was removed. Engineers were worried about cracking brackets and other structural components when the heavy surfaces banged against their stops.

At the time, it seemed their concerns could be alleviated by simply drooping the surfaces to a safe position as long as the aircraft was sensing negligible airspeed.

As a result of flight testing, though, a more acceptable configuration was devised. When the pilots set their onboard gyroscope, which controls aircraft pitch and rate sensors, to the ALIGN position, the hydraulic system is alerted that the aircraft is stopped, and engine shutdown is imminent. That causes the flight controls to droop slowly, eliminating any possibility of falling and causing damage to aircraft structure when hydraulic pressure is removed.

Other "pilot-proof" methods of doing the same thing were being investigated as of this writing. Bruce Hinds said Northrop and the Air Force were considering use of the parking brake or a wheel speed sensor as a signal for drooping the control surfaces. Once the parking brake is set, the controls would slowly droop.

SOFTWARE—A NEW "FOUR-LETTER WORD"

Several problems that arose during the early days of testing were unique to a highly computerized airplane. In the past, designers and test engineers never had to worry about software glitches because their aircraft never had any computers or software. Those days are long gone. Fly-by-wire aircraft are the norm today, and many onboard systems are computer-controlled. Millions of lines of software code, the computer programs that tell the hardware what to do and when, are required to keep the computers doing their jobs.

Computers are nothing more than very diligent laborers that work extremely fast, but are inherently dumb. They must be given very explicit instructions, via software, or they will not perform. Consequently, software has become a two-edged sword to the aircraft designer of today: both magic wand and time bomb. Today, when something on the aircraft performs in an unexplainable way during a test, the conclusion most often heard from pilots, engineers, and maintenance technicians is: "Must be software." And they are usually right.

Software experts are today's super-sleuths of flight testing—they look at inputs and outputs, then determine how the software might have caused what happened in between. An interesting software-related glitch that showed up early on the B-2 was a sensitivity to the sequence in which various avionics systems were switched on. Similar to a home computer, where certain programs must be run in a predetermined sequence to work correctly, the B-2's black boxes were stubbornly resistant to anything but the right turn-on sequence.

Engineers explained that the software was sensitive to *initialization se-quences,* which are start-up commands that the computer follows. Pilots, though, are adaptive creatures accustomed to working through a problem [commonly called *work around* by flight test pilots and engineers] in order to get a job done. They discovered long ago that, if a computer is acting squirrely, turn the thing off, let it rest awhile, then turn it back on. This restarting proce-dure has cured more than a few software initialization problems on the F-16 over the years, and seemed to be the most expeditious way to fix B-2 avionics glitches.

But not over the long term. Turn-on sequence and software initialization peculiarities cannot be tolerated in a strategic weapon system sitting on alert with a load of live nuclear weapons onboard. Therefore, contractor engineers are chasing down each software "funny" that arises during the B-2 test pro-gram, and will ensure it is resolved before the aircraft transitions to the Strate-gic Air Command.

Changes to the B-2 will be a continuing process throughout the bomber's useful lifetime. Most of them will have their genesis during the flight test pro-gram, as the test team evaluates how the aircraft and its myriad systems oper-ate. Although deficiencies will be found that must be corrected, many of the changes will evolve from a better understanding of what is really needed or desired. Others will be instituted because they improve handling qualities, per-formance or simplify maintenance in the field.

After almost two years of testing, with more than 177 flight hours on the B-2s, a number of changes have been incorporated already:

- Pilots' controls have been altered to improve pitch sensitivity and feel. Originally, the control stick could be moved a total distance of 4 inches to command maximum pitch control, compared to only 3 inches total in the roll direction. After the first set of eight flights, full-throw pitch deflection was changed to 3 inches, which is better "harmonized" with the 3-inch roll control deflection.
- The amount of stick force needed to command a particular maneuver in the pitch direction was decreased from an initial setting of about 25-30 pounds for takeoff to about 15 pounds. "There really was no need to work that hard on takeoff," Bruce Hinds said. "It was also hard to make small pitch changes when you're pulling that hard. It's easier to modu-late pitch when you're dealing with less force. We changed the pitch set-ting to 12 pounds per inch [of stick deflection] and roll has always been at about five pounds per inch. Now, our pitch feel is about the same as the B-1B's." Although 12 pounds per inch is on the low side for this class of aircraft, it is still within military specifications. (Actually, the *mil spec* was designed to ensure that 1950-era aircraft handled properly. It is out-dated and is not totally relevant to modern fly-by-wire aircraft.)
- The software that controls the large flight control surfaces has been *rescheduled* (reprogrammed) to make better use of the drag rudders for

pitch control. Initially, the huge outboard surfaces were not used for nose-up/down pitch control. After the first set of flights, the upper drag rudder was reprogrammed to deflect upward a bit more when the pilot pulled back on the control stick, somewhat improving the B-2's pitch rate and takeoff performance.

- Braking systems have been adjusted to require less pressure for a given deceleration rate, especially during landing rollouts.
- Air data system software has been changed to get rid of a six- to nine-second delay in airspeed readout. This was done by altering the software smoothing function discussed earlier.
- The communication antenna selection software is being changed to allow manual control rather than automatic. This should preclude communications dropouts right after takeoff, such as those experienced on the first flight.
- Although changes are not yet fully defined, the *angle of attack* (AOA) sensing system will have to be incrementally adjusted to remove AOA errors that show up when the aircraft is in ground effect. This error is fed into the flight control system, and was responsible for the aircraft becoming airborne during high-speed taxi tests in early 1990, after the first planned maintenance downtime. Engineers are still learning a great deal about the B-2's advanced, stealthy flush-air data system's performance, and additional changes will have to be made in the future.

SUCCESSES

The natural tendency of a flight test program is to focus on the problems uncovered because that is the intent of such an effort: to find discrepancies and correct them. However, the B-2 has seen a lot of successes, as well. After the first 16 flights and about 61 flight hours, the test team at Edwards gave high marks to the General Electric F118 engines. These powerplants are based on the same engines used in the B-1B bomber, which reduced the risk that would have been inherent in a totally new engine. Still, in the early days of any new aircraft test program, there is significant concern about engine/airframe compatibility.

On the B-2, which has its engines buried deep in the wings, there was more than a little concern about how well the new powerplants would perform. Ground tests showed there was nothing to worry about, and flight tests have confirmed those early assessments. "The engines have done a superb job," Couch said.

Historically, hydraulic systems also have been notorious problem areas, particularly with leaks caused by aircraft flexing in flight. The B-2, though, has had minimal hydraulic troubles, despite its complex system of long tubing runs throughout the aircraft. A thorough wring out of the system on the FCHIL [Flight Controls and Hydraulic Integration Laboratory] was credited for hydraulic successes experienced so far.

Aside from early braking problems, the landing gear, brakes, and antiskid systems also operated extremely well during the first few rounds of flight tests. Again, the laboratories were credited with eliminating many potential problem areas long before these systems reached the first aircraft. Logistics testing— an area that received considerable Air Force attention during the planning phases—has been a success, as well. For once, up-front attention is being given to issues that will affect the maintenance man's job throughout the B-2's life.

So far, logistics testing is being accomplished during periods when the aircraft is down for either extended maintenance or planned modifications. This process was well underway even before the first flight, and has continued unabated. In fact, all the technical data required for engine tear down and repair was verified and accepted by the Air Force prior to first flight—the first time that had ever been done on a new USAF aircraft, according to service officials.

Having Air Force technicians working side-by-side with their contractor counterparts since the first aircraft started coming together in Palmdale also has contributed greatly to meeting logistics test goals. USAF ground crews helped launch many of the very early flights, and an all-Air Force crew performed ALL recovery functions on the third test mission. For the first time ever, Air Force maintenance crews already have a pretty fair understanding of the aircraft they will have to take care of in the field. That, alone, will be a considerable asset to the Air Force in setting up an in-house maintenance capability for the aircraft when it becomes operational.

CHANGE OF COMMAND AT THE CTF

A major change in one corner of the B-2 program's life occurred on October 13, 1989. That was the day Col. Rick Couch traded his job as the Air Force's chief B-2 test pilot and Combined Test Force director for a new position at Edwards, vice commander of the 6510th Test Wing. Assisting his boss, the wing commander, Couch was then responsible for overseeing key Air Force test programs and combined test forces on the sprawling desert base.

Couch turned the reins of the B-2 CTF over to Col. Frank Birk, an accomplished test pilot who had served a few years earlier as an operations officer and deputy for test on the B-1B test program. Birk also had spent a tour at Strategic Air Command headquarters before getting the nod to take over the B-2 bomber test program.

Couch was later scheduled to fly the B-2 on a couple of test flights, but hardware and maintenance problems prevented his doing so. He managed to fly one more chase flight in the F-16, but a seat on the B-2 eluded him after leaving the CTF.

The test pilot still was considered an on-base consultant, in essence, available for B-2 safety reviews and advice. Unknown to him at the time, though, he had flown his last flight as a test pilot on the big bomber.

* * *

COL. RICK COUCH:
   I officially left the B-2 test force during a change of command cere-

mony on 13 October 1989. That was not a fun day for me. The CTF, which had grown from about 40 people when I joined it to over 1,100, was like family. But leaving was inevitable.

The work that this group had accomplished during the four years we had been together was nothing less than incredible. I was extremely proud to have had the honor of serving with these professionals.

During the ceremony that day, I used a quote from Gen. Dwight D. Eisenhower: "Humility must always be the portion of any man who receives acclaim earned in the blood of his followers and the sacrifices of his friends."

That seemed especially appropriate for this occasion. It acknowledged what all the members of our B-2 team had accomplished while I was part of it.

* * *

Six months later, the Air Force sent Couch back to Washington, D.C., this time as a student at the Defense Systems Management College. The three-month course prepared the young colonel for his next assignment as deputy program manager of a system program office at Wright-Patterson AFB, Ohio.

MORE B-2s

Under Col. Birk's command, the B-2 test program continued to progress rapidly. In the spring of 1990, Birk flew AV-1 back to Northrop's Site 4 facility at Palmdale for several months of detailed "surface preparation" prior to starting an intensive period of low observables testing that fall. These highly-classified evaluations, which will determine exactly how effective the B-2's "stealth" technologies really are, were dominating AV-1's schedule during the early months of 1991.

Another B-2 first flight occurred on October 19, 1990, although it was significantly less spectacular an occasion than that of AV-1 in the summer of 1989. Only a few local Antelope Valley residents braved a chilly fall wind to watch B-2 No. 2 make its maiden flight early that morning.

Northrop test pilot Leroy Schroeder and USAF Lt. Col. John Small surprised most of the "watchers" by pointing AV-2 west and taking off on Plant 42's Runway 25. Although it was the logical choice, given the westerly wind direction, the takeoff flight path placed the bomber over lightly populated areas of Palmdale.

Most first flights from that airport takeoff to the east or northeast to avoid overflying houses and businesses with an unproven aircraft. However, that decision for AV-2's initial test mission was indicative of the confidence B-2 pilots have in their aircraft as it matures.

On that first 2.6-hour test sortie, AV-2 reached 325 knots and 10,000 feet before the flight ended at Edwards AFB. Winds that almost scrubbed the day's flight at Palmdale were later gusting to 19 knots at Edwards, prompting a decision to land earlier than had been planned. Program officials said the winds also were approaching crosswind limits in effect at that stage of testing.

The highly instrumented No. 2 aircraft is not configured with a production-level low observable exterior because it will remain a test bird throughout its life. AV-2 was well into its planned structural testing program as of this writing.

13

Superstars

MORE THAN 15,000 PEOPLE, scattered throughout the United States, worked on the B-2 program during the early phases that encompassed initial flight tests. Thousands more provided indirect support in one way or another.

Of course, getting that many individuals, each with his own unique personality, pointed in the same direction, working towards a common goal, was often a real challenge for program leaders. But leaders, often as not, are guides; they did not really make the B-2 happen. The skills and dedication of thousands of everyday people are what made the B-2 program, like any other major endeavor, actually work.

Even though it looks radically different and might have unique stealth characteristics, the B-2 boiled down to just another big project, similar in many ways to large undertakings in other fields. Not unlike building a super-highway or developing a new computer chip, the B-2 program had its problems and successes, its depressing setbacks as well as quantum leaps forward, and, of course, a full range of personalities. But it also had more than its share of superstars, those people who rose above the expertise and skills and dedication of those around them to shine just a bit brighter than the rest.

Extra doses of drive, dedication and unwavering positive attitudes were common ingredients shared by the superstars. They kept the home fires stoked, persevered, led their respective groups, argued their cases with cost- and schedule-conscious senior managers, and overcame awesome odds to accomplish what they felt was vital to the B-2's successful development.

Rarely were the superstars recognized for their contributions, but their efforts were truly meaningful and their accomplishments tangible. Col. Couch, like many other senior program officials, felt very strongly that these superstars definitely made a positive difference.

* * *

COL. RICK COUCH:
    When asked who the superstars were in the B-2 process, I'm reluctant

to give examples. But, then again, this story wouldn't be complete without some examples of those who stood out from the crowd.

A lot of these heroes were directly responsible for getting the B-2 into the air, and, in many cases, making sure the first flights were conducted safely. The B-2 [program] will be eternally indebted to them.

Not many of these people are pilots that fly airplanes into the sky, but each one definitely has the "right stuff," that something special that sets them apart from others.

* * *

The task of trying to identify a few B-2 superstars is fraught with risk. How does one identify individuals who made significant contributions without slighting the thousands of others who also have played important roles in the program? They were no less important, to be sure.

There was some debate about whether to even attempt to pick out superstars for acknowledgment here. Criticism and possible hard feelings could be avoided by just skipping it altogether.

Still, it seemed important to convey how much the extra efforts of the superstars, as well as the thousands that they represent, are appreciated by their contemporaries, colleagues, and nation.

"These folks are individuals or groups of people who remind us that human beings make the difference in a program like this," Couch said. "Technology is nothing without the people who bring it all together and make it work."

Because they are representative of the multitudes that make a company, a military service, or an entire nation function well, the B-2 superstars, with two exceptions, are not identified by name here. Most seem to prefer it that way. They were there to do a job and they did it, accepting responsibilities as they defined them. After all, anonymity has its own benefits and rewards, although larger egos might never quite understand why that is so.

WIVES AND HUSBANDS

The superstar list is topped by the wives and husbands of the B-2 team members. They never knew what their spouses were doing a good bit of the time, and they often had to take over when B-2 work called a husband or wife away from home for long hours, days, and weeks. Some never quite understood or accepted the lifestyle they had been forced to adopt when their significant other signed on with the B-2 team, but most did. They rose to the challenges imposed and made do.

* * *

COL. RICK COUCH:

My wife made sure that I was able to commit myself to this project, while helping me keep life's priorities in order. That meant I was able to focus on the B-2, yet rarely missed the special moments: birthdays, Christmas and the kids' school activities.

For two years preceding the B-2's first flight, we couldn't get away for a vacation, go skiing, or make long term plans. Everything was in limbo, because the B-2 was dominating my life.

Typical of what I'm talking about here was the time my wife had planned a dinner party for Saturday night. Eight people were invited and everything looked good, until the last minute. That night, I walked into the house at about 6 o'clock and told her I had to go to Palmdale for a test being conducted that night. I had to be there; I had no choice in the matter.

She didn't scream and yell and throw a fit, which she probably had every right to do. She just said, "Be careful and get home as soon as you can." I didn't get home until about 1 o'clock the next morning.

Of course, this happened more than once. I missed a lot of parties, dinners, and too many other events to even count. Through all of this, I knew I had a rock at home that I could depend on without having to take a lot of grief in the process.

When we were in the middle of engine checkouts, I was home for only short periods of time, usually during the day, and rarely at night. My wife once asked me during that time whether we really were divorced and I had just forgotten to tell her! I'm sure it seemed that way to her.

* * *

As can be imagined, the development of a brand new aircraft like the B-2 has more than its shares of ups and downs. Everything is roses one day, then, the next day, everybody is worried that the program is going to be canceled or the airplane will never fly.

Like every other worker in the world, the baggage of the day went home with B-2 people, too—but with a major difference. The day's problems and triumphs could not be discussed in detail with spouses or best friends, thanks to security restrictions during the program's early years. For example, although he had been hired as Northrop's chief test pilot for the next generation U.S. nuclear bomber, Bruce Hinds couldn't even tell his family or friends who his employer was for approximately one year, let alone what he was doing.

* * *

COL. RICK COUCH:

It was frustrating, not being able to talk to my wife about things that bugged me at work. But, throughout all of this, she was patience personified. She was a great help, tempering her own problems and those of the family so I could keep my mind on B-2 work.

My family situation was no different than that of thousands of others working on the program, though. When I started feeling down because I was spending an inordinate amount of time away from home, all I had to do was think about the B-2 program manager. He must have spent twice as much time on the road.

We weren't exactly traveling salesmen, but we sure lived like them— we were always away from home. The patience, caring, and understanding that all of our spouses showed deserves a huge "Thanks!"

* * *

B-2 PROGRAM DIRECTOR
—MAJ. GEN. RICHARD M. SCOFIELD

Management and leadership are the secrets to keeping the 15,000 individuals working on the B-2 going in the same direction. At all levels of the program, managers are held responsible for making the critical decisions that shape this effort. They determine, then balance costs, schedules, and risks while orchestrating the countless activities required to execute such a massive undertaking.

When considering the tens of thousands of program elements—designing every bit and piece of a 350,000-pound aircraft; then building, integrating and testing it; keeping track of all the drawings, software and data—one wonders how everything could possibly be controlled by managers. Then, throw in the unpredictable external influences of Congress, a shifting world order, the media, and final users of the aircraft, one begins to appreciate the magnitude of the management task.

In the U.S. Air Force, one person was given overall, total responsibility for creating and delivering operational B-2 bombers—the program director. That person has the task of being "Master Juggler," the one who handles both internal and external matters.

The program director must be incredibly skilled at cutting through smokescreens and the clutter of detail, focusing on what is important, and deciding what must get accomplished to meet the ultimate program goals. He must have a sense for detail because he must answer to higher authorities for problems that arise, while maintaining a global perspective, the big picture.

Thousands of people outside the program's processes will invariably surface as self-acclaimed experts and critics who are convinced they know more about what must be done than the director does. These also are the first to blame him when something out of the ordinary happens, whether or not he had any control over the incident.

For example, when administration and congressional budget cuts started reducing the number of B-2s that would be produced and delivered to SAC, the cost-per-aircraft went up accordingly. There were fewer bombers to absorb total program costs. That cause-and-effect relationship is a basic law of program and cost control, and has nothing to do with poor management.

Yet, critics are quick to wail: "The program is out of control! Aircraft costs are skyrocketing!" The accusations, either veiled or direct, are often aimed at the program director, although he has no control over how many aircraft the government decides to buy.

* * *

COL. RICK COUCH:

Maj. Gen. Dick Scofield was the B-2 program director while I was the CTF director at Edwards. I had known him since he was a lieutenant colonel, working in Systems Command headquarters at Andrews AFB [Maryland].

He is a professional with the patience of Job, the strength of Hercules, and the wisdom of Solomon. He's also a genius. That's the only way to explain how he could keep program specifics and the world around him in proper perspective.

I'll guarantee the Air Force and this country don't pay him enough for all he does. The hours he devotes to his work are endless. And his program is constantly harassed by the media. All this would be enough to make most of us give up and just quit.

I have the utmost respect for this officer. His balancing act is remarkable and his stamina is unbelievable.

* * *

BRUCE J. HINDS, Jr.
—NORTHROP CHIEF B-2 TEST PILOT

Another superstar nominated immediately when the subject comes up within the flight test community is Bruce Hinds. He has been called "one of Northrop's most dedicated and skilled people on the program," according to Air Force officials.

Hinds had only recently retired from the Air Force as a test pilot when he joined Northrop. Consequently, he immediately had a clear understanding of what had to be done during the B-2 flight test program, as well as a pretty fair idea of what the Air Force wanted in its new bomber. As a senior manager charged with testing the B-2, he transmitted that understanding throughout the B-2 Division. He fought any number of internal battles to secure the best possible company resources for the flight test unit.

Throughout the aircraft's development, Hinds drew heavily on his extensive flying experience, insisting on design changes simply because they made good sense from the operator's viewpoint. He was unforgiving when engineers suggested that a pilot could adapt to any feature or operational situation, no matter how bad it was for the crew. He demanded that a component or system be designed to make flying or maintaining the aircraft easier, even if it meant more time and work for the development team. Then, he insisted hardware be built to the design and that it operate correctly. If it did not, he made sure those responsible went back and fixed it. In the end, his input and diligence will pay off handsomely for both the Air Force and his own company, Northrop.

Understand, now, that Bruce Hinds really did not have to go to all that trouble. He could have relaxed in his chief test pilot role and taken a more passive approach. Because Hinds has an easy-going demeanor that can be mistaken for softness or someone easily influenced, a few mistakenly thought he was passive. They were mistaken, though, and quickly learned that nobody could "shine it on" with Bruce Hinds. Not only is he an excellent pilot, dedicated to delivering a good product to the Air Force, he can hold his own as an engineer.

* * *

COL. RICK COUCH:
As an engineer, few were equal to Bruce. Without a doubt, he is one of

the smartest individuals I have ever met. And he used his talents with great skill in reviewing the flood of engineering documents and information generated by the design groups.

I think Bruce knew as much or more about the complete aircraft than any other single person on the program. If he didn't know the answer to a question right off the top of his head, he always knew exactly who to ask. His knowledge proved especially valuable during development of the B-2's emergency procedures as we went into the systems checkout phase.

During those ground tests, Bruce and I took the 6 p.m. to 6 a.m. shift, sitting in the cockpit and operating systems as necessary. I had a chance to witness Bruce's knowledge and expertise firsthand during this time, since he and I were seeing more of each other than we were of our wives!

Just the hours Bruce was putting in were an indication of his commitment . . . 12-to-16 per day during checkout. Through it all, Bruce seemed to stay on a higher plane than most of us, somehow. At times, he literally forced the aircraft and the people working on it through this checkout period by setting a positive, determined example.

Everything I had seen in Bruce over several years was brought together on the first flight, though. I can't think of anyone more qualified and competent to fly the B-2 for the first time than Bruce. His skills and experience all came together that day . . . and they were unmatched.

* * *

SYSTEMS SAFETY

The B-2's initial ground and flight testing phases were considered very successful, thanks in large part to the Six Million Dollar man and a lot of competent people in his group.

Not the actor who made the television show of the same name so popular in the 1970s, but the real one, a now-retired NASA test pilot who was flying the M2F2 lifting body that tumbled across TV screens at the start of that show. The pilot of that experimental aircraft suffered very serious injuries, including the loss of one eye. He laughs when he says, "it probably took something close to $6 million to put me back together, but I didn't get any bionics!"

Today, he is a Northrop systems safety specialist, part of a group of safety experts that are heavily involved in all aspects of the B-2, from engineering and manufacturing through test planning and flight phases. From the start, their contributions have been invaluable, assessing the safety implications of the nuts and bolts of program activities, but from a very practical perspective.

When they foresaw the potential for problems on the aircraft, the systems safety group led the fight (and there were some major ones) with the engineering design teams in charge of making necessary changes. Many disagreed with the need for such changes, threatening that the cost and time, in some cases, outweighed potential benefits. However, the safety experts had a high success rate in pushing through changes they saw as necessary for one important reason: they did their homework before raising a particular issue.

The Six Million Dollar Man—the real one—was literally on the leading edge of every one of these battles, addressing practical points that could affect the aircraft, pilots, and ground crews. His driving concern was always for the machine's safety, as well as that of its operators.

He was a leading figure in the safety unit at Northrop's Palmdale final assembly site, but a sister group provided the same function at the Pico Rivera facility. Both groups coordinated their efforts well, and, together, had a tremendously positive influence on the B-2.

The safety group's task was never easy. These experts walked a fine line between ensuring safety and being an encumbrance, an obstacle to getting a job done. By all accounts, though, they never crossed that line. They fully realized that, as important as safety was, if it was allowed to dominate other activities, the aircraft would never fly. They knew that the only way to guarantee aircraft and pilot safety was to lock the bird in a hangar and forget about flying it. Risk always has been and always will be a part of flight; one can only minimize risk within practical limits.

MAINTENANCE OFFICER

Ask any seasoned test pilot who the most important people are in his professional life, and, chances are, terms like "crew chief" and "maintenance officer" will be high on the list. Next to a great wife or husband, a top-notch maintenance officer comes closer to determining the well-being of a test pilot than any other individual.

The B-2 CTF's maintenance chief is responsible for about 75 percent of the people comprising the huge testing organization. And their health and well-being are directly related to how well the CTF's aircraft operate.

* * *

COL. RICK COUCH:

Maintenance is one of the most critical elements of any safely run flight test program. If it is not done properly, maintenance can cause more grief, and even tragedy, than almost anything else, except maybe a stupid pilot.

The B-2 CTF had the best maintenance officer I have ever known. He knew more about maintaining airplanes than most people in the Air Force, and well he should. He has a varied background and experience covering about every possible aircraft category . . . strategic, training, tactical, you name it. Granted, he and I have significantly different views of the world. But then, I've never had to worry about generating sorties in support of an operational readiness inspection or an alert.

Since the B-2 will be stationed in places where the summers and winters can get a little rough, we have to be able to perform maintenance on the aircraft in almost any kind of situation. This guy understood that; he had a very good appreciation for the job troops in the field will have to do and the conditions they'll work under. So, he saw to it that Northrop understood what bad weather and tough maintenance conditions really meant and how that translated to the B-2's design features.

Without question, his tenacious hammering away at issues related to supportability, maintainability, and reliability will pay big dividends for the Air Force over the airplane's life.

* * *

Mr. Maintenance was also charged with creating an organization that could perform all the B-2 logistics testing needed. He had spent his career in traditional Air Force maintenance units and knew standard procedures backwards and forwards. At the B-2 CTF, though, he was introduced to "testing," a foreign word to him in many ways.

He quickly learned that, for a brand new aircraft, there are no standard maintenance procedures; they must be developed. And testing, which is part of that development process, requires a significantly different approach than approved USAF by-the-book maintenance methods do. True to form, though, this professional maintainer quickly adapted to his new environment. He then led a crack team in developing an effective maintenance/logistics test program for the B-2. It seems to be working so well that some officials expect the Air Force will adopt the program for future aircraft acquisitions.

ILS SENIOR MANAGER

Another superstar qualifier was not always a very popular person around some corners of the B-2 organization, but he did a terrific job: the Integrated Logistics Support (ILS) senior manager. This individual obviously had a special place in his heart for the Air Force maintenance man and he appreciated the problems associated with supporting a new, complex aircraft after delivery to operational units in the field.

The military services have traditionally placed logistics at the end of the line when competing for resources, especially time on the aircraft during a development program. During the hectic days of building, testing, and delivering a new weapon system, logistics' concerns tend to be brushed aside in favor of more important things, like getting ready to fly, flying, and recovering from a flight so the airplane can fly again.

Consequently, in the past, the first batch of a new aircraft type has been delivered to operational units without spare parts, technical data needed by technicians to fix the bird, and even the correct ladders, stands, and tools. Those items were either overlooked or deferred in favor of more pressing issues. They ultimately arrived, but long after the aircraft should have been declared "mission ready."

One systems manager in the Air Force Logistics Command—an overall support agency that assumes responsibility for the life-long care of an aircraft after Systems Command completes the acquisition process—posted a cartoon over his desk that graphically depicted the logisticians' plight. A takeoff from the 1970s movie *Jeremiah Johnson*, the cartoon shows a buckskin-clad mountain man (labeled Systems Command) running through a log cabin with a mean-looking grizzly bear (labeled New Airplane) in hot pursuit. As the pursued races past his startled roommate (labeled Logistics Command), who is eating at a split-log table, the runner shouts, "Jake, you skin this one while I go get another one!"

Program managers on the B-2, however, decided very early that this aircraft would not repeat the logistics errors of its predecessors. They decided the bear would be skinned and packaged before it arrived at Strategic Air Command bases. They picked an effective manager and told him to make sure logistics received its fair share of emphasis during the test phase.

Mr. Logistics took his job seriously, periodically standing toe-to-toe with those who felt *log testing* (logistics testing) should wait. No way. He was determined that SAC maintenance technicians would receive an aircraft that was as easy for them to maintain as it was for pilots to fly. Consequently, he probably irritated hundreds of people on both sides of the Air Force/contractor fence, but he moved the ILS program steadily forward.

Even political adversaries now admit his efforts will pay off for both the Air Force and Northrop, because the service will receive a complete fighting system that will be ready to start flying missions shortly after delivery to SAC units. It has not been easy, but the ILS senior manager has made logistics an integral part of the entire B-2 acquisition process and he deserves a hearty "Thank You."

TEST CONDUCTORS/DIRECTORS

These are the referees—a small group of testing professionals who serve as the interface between a control room full of engineering experts and a flight crew trying to perform difficult tasks—either in the air or on the ground. They are the men and women wearing a headset and microphone, listening with one ear to engineers' suggestions and requests, and the other tuned to sometimes-weary pilots who just want to get the damned test completed as quickly and painlessly as possible.

The TC/TDs set the pace for the entire operation. They must think on their feet, making real-time decisions about whether to continue a particular path of testing, repeat a maneuver, or call a halt to the whole mission. They are a combination of field general and symphony conductor, balancing acceptable risk against safety, real progress with low-payoff "interesting" data, and a host of strong personalities on both ends of the communications link.

For example, assume a pilot is in the middle of an engine test and a ground-based engineer (who is watching telemetry data squiggles on a television screen in the control room) starts reporting problems that look like data acquisition instrumentation is going haywire. He advises that the test be terminated. The TC/TD must decide, on the spot, whether to cut the test off or continue with it. In a couple of moments, he must assess whether the test can be continued safely or not. If something hiccups in the engines, will the onboard data system capture the necessary data? Is the data problem in the telemetry link or on the aircraft? Are the data valid or not?

Real-time decisions mean "decide right now, not a few minutes from now."

TC/TDs can't consult every engineer in the room or mull a problem over for long. Every minute a four-engine bomber drones around in circles, waiting for a decision, it is burning several hundred pounds of fuel. Wasted fuel also translates to lost time in the air and other tests not completed.

In other words, the TC/TDs have to act quickly and correctly. Overriding knowledgeable, persistent engineers, who have their own very-valid agendas, can get dicey. The TC/TD better have a good reason for doing it because he most definitely will have to defend the decision. On the other hand, assessing the implications of a potentially hazardous situation, taking into account hundreds of pieces of data, then overriding a pilot's hands-on judgment can unleash some colorful terms that the Federal Communications Commission believes really should not be broadcast over the air. But that's the TC/TD's job, and they have performed it quite well on the B-2 program.

★ ★ ★

COL. RICK COUCH:

During B-2 flight tests that I was on, there were numerous times that the TC told us to knock off a maneuver. Twice, he told us to terminate the mission and return to base because an AMAD was acting up. The TCs also provided valuable real-time guidance during ground testing, too.

For flight or ground tests, they first had to take all the diverse requirements for a test and come up with a logical, well-sequenced game plan. That usually required melding together several detailed test plans and selecting the right series of test points to get the most data possible out of a particular event or maneuver.

The TC/TDs did a superb job of orchestrating all these activities and allowing us to wring the most out of every minute of test time.

Another interesting thing . . . . These guys developed such an ability to sense what was happening—just from all the diverse inputs they were getting—that, at times, their situational awareness was better than the pilots'. In other words, they had a better handle on what was REALLY happening to the airplane than the guys flying it had! That educated awareness was a big factor in the overall safety of the program.

★ ★ ★

ENGINEERING

Obviously, a major element in the design, manufacturing, checkout, development, testing, and fielding of a new aircraft is the engineer. He/she is part of a community charged with taking a wispy concept out of thin air and translating it into hardware that can fly through the sky for thousands of hours over its lifetime, performing whatever task is demanded of it.

Even experienced aerospace insiders still marvel at the skill of a good engineer. He or she is both thinker and doer, at once. The engineer must envision what this complex creature of an airplane must do, how it must do it, what it will look like, then apply his own brand of ingenuity to make it appear.

At every step of the B-2's evolvement, engineers played a key role. For example, during prefirst-flight checkout on AV-1, the same engineers who designed a system also monitored the ground tests, determining what was right and what was wrong with their system. If something did not work correctly, they had to decide what needed to be changed, either in their system or in another system that affected theirs.

Watching the logical deduction process of these experts—representing all design disciplines, from avionics to hydraulics to engines—as they performed real-time analysis in the middle of a test gave one a great appreciation for the incredible contribution these unheralded professionals make to the aerospace industry and their country.

SECURITY MANAGER

One of the most feared, yet respected, people in the B-2 Combined Test Force was the security manager. He also had one of the toughest jobs in the place. This person was charged with both the big picture and the nitty-gritty: implementing basic security guidance dictated by the B-2 System Program Office, while also handling the day-to-day security operations of the CTF.

If anyone broke a security rule, be it large or small, he or his staff had to deal with it. Typically, security infractions were more perceived than real, but they still required a thorough review or investigation to be conducted. These were always done quickly and fairly.

The stereotype security person in an organization dealing with highly classified information is a textbook paranoid. He absolutely believes there is a terrorist behind every bush and that a horde of Communists will be climbing over the perimeter fence any moment now. Although it's understandable, given their responsibilities, security personnel are basically suspicious folks who would much rather say, "No, you can't do that," than take the more risky approach and say, "Yes . . . looks OK to me."

* * *

COL. RICK COUCH:
This typical security approach caused some real battles between the security chief and yours truly. Balancing my strong feelings about getting a job done against what is a security guy's normal reactions was a tough job at times. But the security manager handled these bouts very diplomatically and usually helped make me look like Solomon. I appreciated that.

Dealing with changing security rules as the B-2 program became more public wasn't easy, either. After rollout, hardly a day passed but what our [CTF] people read something new about the B-2 in the newspaper or a magazine. Generally, the guidance we received about what we could and couldn't say came through about a day later.

Yet, the security manager and his team strived continuously to get the best information they possibly could and pass it along to our employees so they would know how to respond.

Imagine what it was like to go home one evening and have a neighbor ask what you thought about an article in the paper that morning. If all you could ever say was, "No comment," you started feeling pretty stupid, like everybody knew a good bit of what you knew, but you couldn't even acknowledge it. For quite awhile, that's all we could do.

However, as soon as the security people were told how the rules had changed, they put out the information to everybody as fast as possible. This was done professionally and effectively. And I will be forever grateful for the style in which it was handled.

* * *

IFDAPS TEAM

As discussed earlier, buying hardware and software for the Integrated Flight Data Acquisition and Processing System (IFDAPS) was no simple task. Still, it was almost trivial compared to making the complex system work properly.

IFDAPS was totally separate from the aircraft's instrumentation system, but the two had to play together. Hundreds of sensors on the aircraft sent electrical signals to a central unit that matched them with the telemetry system, which continuously beamed millions of data bits to the ground station at Edwards.

One of IFDAPS' chores was to turn that data stream of ones and zeros into "engineering units" that could be understood by humans. This required a tremendous number of manipulations and number crunching, just to turn a series of digital signals into a message on a computer or TV screen that simply said, "3,998 p.s.i.," for example. Needless to say, the overall process of doing this was very complex.

About the time a group at Palmdale was installing an instrumentation system in the first B-2, another group at Edwards started the tedious process of making IFDAPS and the onboard instrumentation "talk to each other." The IFDAPS group was handicapped by three factors:

One, the telemetry system was being handled by the instrumentation group at Palmdale, and it was running behind schedule about then. The Palmdale group was in the process of loading data calibrations into the TM/instrumentation system at the same time the Edwards group needed to set up its processing system using the same calibration figures.

Two, the aircraft data system was operating only a very limited amount of time, further frustrating engineers trying to checkout IFDAPS to ensure it would handle those data properly.

Third, engineers who would constitute the end users of IFDAPS' outputs were characteristically particular about format, parameters, and units of measure. It's hard to satisfy an engineer who likes things his or her way, and getting a roomful of them to be satisfied with a particular format or presentation scheme was next to impossible.

In spite of these hurdles, the IFDAPS team was determined that its system would be ready for ground engine runs, taxi tests and the first flight. Squeezed by circumstances often beyond their control, IFDAPS engineers worked long hours for weeks at a time, loading, fixing and reloading software, then running new checks of the system. It seemed these dedicated troops were always at their stations.

* * *

COL. RICK COUCH:
　Somewhere in this process, I attended a meeting with one of the IFDAPS engineers. I swear, this young kid looked like death warmed over. More than a bit concerned about his health, I asked what was wrong with him. He said he had not been home for five days and that he had been living on about four hours of sleep. He would crash for awhile on a cot in an empty room somewhere in the Test Support Facility, then get up, and go back to work. Now, this engineer had a wife at home. What do you suppose she was thinking about all this?!
　It turned out that we had a whole group of IFDAPS folks who had been quietly working for days on end without a break. We finally had to throw some of those guys out of the TSF, just so they would finally go get some rest.

* * *

The IFDAPS system was ready when it was needed and it worked like it was supposed to. It has been, and shall continue to be, a vital element of the B-2 test program. The sacrifices and superhuman efforts that ensured the IFDAPS worked, especially for first flight, probably will not be required again on this program. But the people who made sure it was available when it was needed have to be counted among the program's superstars.

INDEPENDENT FLIGHT TEST REVIEW TEAM

During the frantic days leading up to taxi tests and first flight, the Combined Test Force was asked to host a team of flight test experts from outside the B-2 program. This team was charged with watching over the entire test operation and providing an independent safety assessment.

It was the brainchild of the two-star general that headed the Air Force Flight Test Center at Edwards, and was a new factor that typically had not been a part of past programs. The general also was a test pilot and was aware of the mounting pressures endured by any test team as the all-important first flight approached. He knew that people tended to become focused on getting their new aircraft into the air, almost at any cost, and that attitude was fertile ground for problems.

When the concept was first introduced, most senior CTF personnel scratched their heads and asked "Why?" It seemed like a definite case of overkill. After all, the operation was swamped with safety concerns and plenty of people to check and double-check every aspect of the planned taxi and first flight tests. Why add one more layer of safety checkers?

In retrospect, the same CTF chiefs agreed the independent review team was "a Godsend." First, the team made sure that, even with CNN and most of the world's prominent media watching every move, the B-2 test organization remained focused on the job at hand. Second, the team's independent assessments gave the CTF additional leverage in getting problems fixed.

Typically, there is a difference of opinion between the flight testers and managers and engineers—whomever they might be—about the need to modify or correct an item; testers might see the item as a possible safety concern and changing it would simply be good judgment; managers charged with getting the aircraft into the air as soon as possible might see the same item as a trivial concern with all the earmarks of nit-picking and a mere impediment to larger issues; engineers might see the item as a big job to fix and hardly worth dealing with under the pressures of the moment.

The independent review team—having no axe to grind and being above all the pressures of the program—was able to determine, probably in a more rational manner than those inside the B-2 program, whether or not the item in question warranted action before taxi and flight testing. Program insiders, including Col. Couch, said they were convinced that this team contributed significantly to the overall success of activities surrounding the B-2's first flight.

MAIN MANUFACTURING TEAM

The people who actually built the first B-2 deserve special recognition because it was their skills that transformed the confusing bits of an erector set into a sleek aircraft. They were the leaders, the first ones to actually convert lines to wings, electronic or paper numbers to hardware.

Along the way, this team ran into a never-ending stream of things that did not fit together, regardless how well the engineering was performed and how many times it was checked. At the put-it-together level, concepts and "think-it-will" arguments bump smack into the laws of physics. And the manufacturing team was usually the first to discover when one of the laws had been violated.

These people worked many long hours and endured countless frustrations. Yet they persevered under tremendous pressure, knowing that, only if they completed their jobs right could the first B-2 ever get airborne.

An important segment of the B-2 manufacturing superstars were, physically, some of the smallest people on the manufacturing floor—the fuel tank team. This group had one of the most trying, thankless, but quite important, jobs in the factory.

These men and women routinely donned special cotton jump suits and cotton booties that slipped over their own shoes, then crawled inside the bomber's cavernous fuel tanks. While the tanks will hold thousands of gallons of fuel, they have a narrow top-to-bottom distance and scores of compartments, requiring workers to move around on their hands and knees. In some places, one can only wriggle from one area to another by lying flat and crawling.

Workers normally spent their eight-hour shifts, every day for month after month, inside the tanks. They located and sealed every crack, rivet, and joint that could be a potential leak point. The job was tedious beyond imagination, yet vital.

Fuel leaks are serious business on any aircraft because fumes trapped in an area could cause an explosion and loss of control.

* * *

COL. RICK COUCH:

To get an idea of what it's like to work in those tanks, imagine putting on a special suit and booties, then crawling around in your dark closet. Of course, you have to leave all the clothes in that closet and turn the whole thing on its side. Then, you spend all day looking for cracks where light leaks in and plugging them with chewing gum.

As if that wasn't enough of a chore, these people had to repeat the whole exercise. Somebody was worried that the sealant being used was not adhering properly to the tank structure, so the tank team went back in and resealed every area.

But, the team's diligence and efforts paid off. So far, AV-1's tanks have not leaked. Since fuel leaks were such a big problem on the B-1, this was a major step for the B-2. Thanks to these "tank superstars," it looks like the B-2 may not have major fuel leak problems.

* * *

Insiders who worked on the B-2 program undoubtedly can point to hundreds of other individuals who deserve recognition as superstars, and they are correct. There were superhuman accomplishments and efforts in the Pentagon; in the Systems Program Office at Wright Patterson AFB, Ohio; at Northrop's Pico Rivera plant in Los Angeles; at White Sands, New Mexico; at Boeing's Seattle facilities, and at LTV facilities in the Dallas/Ft. Worth area. Equally outstanding individual efforts were unquestionably turned in by the thousands of other B-2 subcontractors and their civil servant counterparts throughout the Air Force.

Hopefully, managers and supervisors throughout the B-2 network will take a moment to recognize these superstars in some meaningful way. Ultimately, the pilots who fly the bomber, and the mechanics who maintain it in service, will thank every person who brought the B-2 into being. To them, everybody was a superstar in his or her own way.

14

Outlook and
reflections

AS THE B-2 BOMBER PROGRAM MOVES THROUGH its remaining test phases and years of production, probably the one thing that will remain unchanged about it is relentless controversy. Congress, the administration and the American public will continue to debate the need, cost, and viability of this aircraft. Arguments will be heated and emotional, but, hopefully, will also be rational. The United States can afford nothing less.

This is a heady, fluid time in the world's history. Traditional Cold War barriers and tenets are crumbling, simultaneously exciting us while causing a basic uneasiness and uncertainty about where we are headed. Are traditional, well-defined adversaries now our buddies? Is the day awaited by humankind for centuries, when men will truly beat their swords into plowshares and work side-by-side in peace, just around the corner? Or do we shake with one hand while hanging onto our club with the other, to be sure nobody blindsides us?

Just when some thought they had all the answers neatly in hand—at least in their own minds—a brutal dictator in Iraq upset the jigsaw puzzle by invading Kuwait, thumbing his nose at the rest of the civilized world.

GOOD TIMING

Whatever the reasons, his timing could not have been better for the B-2 program. The influential chairman of the House Armed Services Committee had gone on record as advocating termination of the bomber program after 15 aircraft had been built. And the Senate was voting on the program's fate the same morning that Sadaam Hussein sent his troops into Kuwait City, stunning the world with his blatant disregard for international order. It was enough to shake up a majority of senators, and the body voted in favor of building two more production B-2s in fiscal year 1991.

Still, they and their colleagues in the House wonder aloud whether the B-2 is needed or not, whether this country can afford it, and will it work or not. Would this sinister, gray-black symbol of American nuclear power be any significant deterrent to Third World dictators who choose to devour their smaller neighbors? In out-of-the-way conflicts, will the mere presence of this bomber discourage large, aggressive countries from jumping into the fray and upsetting already delicate situations? Whether it will or not, can the U.S. even afford such a weapon in the post-Cold War world of today?

These are the questions, in various forms, that U.S. leaders must ponder as part of the B-2 debate. History tells us in no uncertain terms that peace is directly related to strength. In the past, that strength has been equated to military might. Today, we are learning that a nation's strength also encompasses vast economic issues. And, some say, military strength has been gained at the expense of economic health over the last decade or so—the equation is unbalanced and must be reordered.

The need for a manned, penetrating bomber such as the B-2 must be firmly established as the cornerstone of a well-defined government defense policy, or it will never survive the annual budget battles. The Air Force feels it has done this, but powerful congressmen do not always buy the service chiefs' reasoning. Elected officials—often with their own hidden agendas—are demanding stronger justification and proof of need for the aircraft before they make a long-term commitment to the stealth bomber program.

How the question of need will be resolved is anybody's guess right now, but its importance is crucial. The B-2's fate should definitely not be trivialized in favor of more expedient, insatiable pork-barrel agendas. If it is, Congress might be mortgaging this nation's future far more seriously than it can begin to imagine today, and will force the next generation of Americans to live with its shortsighted folly, perhaps at tremendous cost.

Although nobody seems to have a clear crystal ball that will show what will happen to the B-2, program officials have their own ideas, based on living with the program for years. Couch and Hinds, even though they were at the working level of the program, did rub elbows with service chiefs, senators and representatives shortly after their first flight, and have formed their own opinions:

★ ★ ★

COL. RICK COUCH:

The B-2 probably will continue through its flight test program, regardless of how the debate over the viability of its mission or need goes. It seems that an aircraft which can evade conventional methods of detection will have a place in the nation's airpower arsenal, no matter where the next battlefield is. Therefore, we need to develop the capabilities now inherent in the B-2.

We also need to develop countermeasures that can be used against stealth airplanes like this, because we may face the same capabilities someday. The development of both sides of this equation will cost money and take time. It seems that this development could still continue, even while the nation debates the future of U.S. strategic deterrence in a new world order.

★ ★ ★

* * *

BRUCE HINDS:

The biggest factor in the debate today obviously is [B-2] cost . . . that's driving everything now. The toughest battle for the program seems to be in keeping the fiscally conservative congressmen that are on key commit- tees, especially in the House, on the B-2's side. Right now, [with the bud- get situation as tight as it is,] the tendency is to vote against anything that spends money as long as not enough money is coming in . . . regardless of the need for a product or how good it is. This not only applies to the B-2 program, but for a lot of other programs that are hurting now.

* * *

Billion-dollar costs for a new bomber are hard for any congressman to swallow as the country faces huge deficits. B-2 program managers know that and they are striving to cut costs wherever they can. Still, any number of very costly inefficiencies are simply built into the government/military acquisition process and individuals at the program or contractor level are powerless to cor- rect them, at least in the short term. Meanwhile, costs continue to mount, and Congress—the very people who instituted many of these inefficiencies in the first place—continues to scream about the exorbitant price of the B-2.

The whole defense procurement situation is a Gordian knot of mind- boggling proportions. In its commendable efforts to eliminate waste, fraud, and abuse of the military acquisition process, our elected officials and their watchdog agencies have unwittingly forced very costly procedures onto high- ticket programs like the B-2. Today, there are any number of questionable reporting requirements dumped on the B-2 organization that provide no added value to the weapon system, yet cost a small fortune to prepare and oversee.

Typically, Congress passes legislation mandating that hundreds of reports be prepared and submitted at various stages of a program. Then, the Govern- ment Accounting Office sends its officials out to check on program progress, scrutinizing thousands of areas and preparing even more reports for Congress. All this takes time and staff—in the Air Force and at the contractors' loca- tions—to accommodate, costing millions over the life of a program, yet adds nothing to the final product.

At the testing level, the government's contracts require Northrop and its subcontractors to hire hundreds of people to perform functions that are only peripherally related to building or evaluating an aircraft: cost accounting, secu- rity, configuration management tracking, software configuration manage- ment, and the like. These obviously have a place in the overall testing scheme, but they tend to be overdone in some cases, and they really contribute little to getting a viable aircraft into the field, according to contractor officials.

Still, the Air Force needs many of these functions—such as detailed cost accounting and configuration management—and it pays contractors to do these jobs, so they do them. It must be acknowledged, though, that they drive costs up. In some cases, Congress or the Pentagon or the Air Force has dictated that these functions must be performed, striving to control costs and abuses while maintaining visibility into the depths of high-dollar programs.

A close analysis of the whole situation can only come to one conclusion: all this oversight drives costs up. Time and again, people at the working level shake their heads and say, "I can't believe the government forces us to spend $5 to save $1, then screams about the high cost of weapon systems. We'd save more by eliminating some of these requirements and accepting a trickle of loss."

Unfortunately, a very small minority of unscrupulous contractors, consultants or other people, by their past actions, are responsible for perpetrating these costly procedures on every weapon system procurement that came after them. And only when the taxpayer gets good and tired of paying for these wasteful watchdog procedures will Congress be forced to grab one string and start unwinding the Gordian knot they have helped create. Even better, maybe they'll grab their all-powerful pens and, in a single sweep, destroy the knot and eliminate much of the government-induced, atrocious waste in programs like the B-2. Contractors, the Air Force, and taxpayers alike, would love it and welcome the relief.

PUBLIC INTEREST

Public and media interest in the B-2 program will remain high, and help accomplish these reforms, simply through heightened awareness of what drives the cost of such weapon systems, then demanding changes. It seems that people all over the world have taken an unusual interest in this aircraft, and will continue to do so.

In the U.S., we are better educated and have a better understanding of defense issues, and their potential cost, than our leaders might believe. Reasons are not hard to find, at least for the B-2: The aircraft has a unique design and a deadly mission. The B-2's stealth capabilities directly affect the Air Force's ability to deter war, or, if necessary, win it if one starts. And, it costs a lot of taxpayer money to build.

These are attention-getting features, and a general understanding of them will influence the bomber's future tremendously, whether it is canceled outright, or it continues to be developed and delivered to the Air Force. If given the facts, through honest congressional debates and an accurate, unbiased media, the American people will decide whether the nation really needs and wants the bomber or not.

REFLECTIONS AND LESSONS LEARNED

The future of the B-2 and other complex, expensive weapon systems is entwined with the past. There were many old lessons heeded—and new ones learned—on this program, and they can apply equally well to other, even non-governmental efforts. Some of them are subtle; others simply make good sense but are not always easy to carry out. Fortunately, B-2 leaders seem to have paid attention to these lessons along the way, and are trying to pass them along to future programs.

The B-2 was very lucky, right from the outset. From its earliest days, it enjoyed a "resource-rich environment," as managers would later describe it. The promise of stealth technology, plus the political situation at the time, resulted in ample funding. If the program had been launched five years earlier or five years later than it was, there is reason to believe that many of the benefits it enjoyed would not have been available.

This comfortable situation was reflected throughout the B-2 organization, but was especially influential in the test unit. In the past, most of a program's money was dumped into the design, engineering, and production of a weapon system. Resources to thoroughly test that system, however, generally were in short supply—and that included time, as well as money. Every other function on the development schedule could slip, but flight and ground testing could not. The final delivery date rarely, if ever, could be moved. As a result, testing was squeezed between upstream schedule slips and the rock-hard delivery or *initial operational capability* (IOC) date of the using command.

Unfortunately, complete testing of the aircraft or weapon suffered. Planned tests were shortened and accelerated. Although they hate to admit it, managers in charge of testing an aircraft must agree that, at times, systems were sent to the field with a lot of unknown gremlins still hidden in them. There rarely was enough time or money to complete the development testing that had been carefully planned, so aircraft were fielded before they should have been.

The result, painful though it might be, was that airplanes and people were lost. Operational pilots and crews were unwittingly testing an unproven aircraft, uncovering deficiencies that, given the resources, test pilots and engineers would have found. Again, funding and time pressures arising from within the Pentagon, administration and Congress often were to blame, although seldom accepted in those quarters.

The B-2 test program leaders, however, were determined to avoid many of these mistakes. Their chosen weapon was smart planning. They spent inordinate amounts of time ferreting out lessons learned by other test programs, regardless of the aircraft or weapon system type. People were sent to other test units and to operational deployment sites. They asked questions of managers, pilots, mechanics, logistics personnel, and commanders, trying to assimilate as much data as possible.

The B-2 System Program Office spent hours studying what went right and not so right on the B-1 bomber program, and assembled a comprehensive database that was accessible to a wide variety of people. These data had a significant influence on several decisions made by the CTF leaders at Edwards. One of the most important was related to logistics testing. Other test program chiefs at the base, plus their operational counterparts in the field, emphasized the need for good, timely logistics testing.

If there is a single legacy about the B-2's test program, it will be that logistics testing was integrated and well coordinated with flight activities—but not without its growing pains. This approach was based upon an attempt to thoroughly understand all requirements related to logistics and flight testing, as well as maintenance and unfinished manufacturing work. The B-2 team used a system of test work orders (TWOs) as a vehicle for detailing all test, data acquisition, instrumentation, and data reduction requirements.

This worked fairly well for identifying ground and flight activities, but was complicated tremendously by a constant requirement to complete manufacturing jobs, normal maintenance tasks, and the special engineering ground tests needed to solve a particular problem. At this point, the best-laid plans often became hopelessly complicated.

A management task that fell out of the situation was deciding who was in the best position to integrate, plan, then coordinate all this work so it could be completed in an efficient manner. In the end, both the maintenance job control and project engineering groups worked out a feasible plan, then the maintenance unit actually performed the necessary tasks during ground phases.

For flight tests, a designated flight test engineer ran the show. He was responsible for taking everybody's inputs and developing a mission profile that would meet as many desires for data as possible. He then directed the flight from a ground-based control room, ensuring the plan was executed as closely as possible.

* * *

COL. RICK COUCH:

We learned some major lessons on this program. The first that became immediately apparent as we prepared for first flight was the futility of trying to perform manufacturing, system checkout, and ground testing all at the same time. This was very counterproductive. I realize it doesn't take a rocket scientist to figure this out, but the pressure we felt to get the aircraft airborne forced it to happen.

Obviously, the best way to accomplish everything leading up to a first flight is to finish building the airplane, then check it out, to be sure it's built correctly, then run necessary ground tests to prove all the systems function properly. But, when we got behind, there was a feeling that the more we could do concurrently, then the sooner we would be ready to fly.

Much of the work was mutually exclusive, and the concurrent approach, trying to do a bunch of things in parallel, led to conflicts. A lot of other unexpected factors made matters worse . . . late or incomplete engineering, late parts deliveries, engineering changes that had to be made to systems or components already built. . . . Pretty soon, the concurrent approach started to fall apart.

Management of this kind of conflicting activity is extremely difficult, but it must be done or everything grinds to a halt. Trying to keep as many activities as possible lined up and done sequentially may seem inefficient, but it's the best way to get through the entire cycle in the least time. It'll pay off as the earliest possible completion of the airplane and, subsequently, accelerate first flight.

* * *

The same advice can be applied to almost any time- and pressure-sensitive activity, whether it's building a highway, publishing a newspaper or running almost any business. The temptation to try to do everything in parallel is hard to resist, but experience shows the tactic usually does not work.

Leaders in the B-2 test organization also learned that safety reviews should be a continual process, covering every facet of a test program. A typical aircraft test program schedules a series of safety reviews at certain key stages to examine the basic airworthiness of the vehicle, and to verify each block or phase of testing has been well thought-out.

The B-2 test team performed the traditional reviews, but added safety assessments before and after each ground test event that led up to first flight. They found that this approach gave each member one final opportunity to air any safety-related issues that might have a possible impact on subsequent tests. Additionally, these reviews proved very useful to senior Air Force and contractor managers, giving them valuable insight into the test activities and their ramifications.

Senior test managers at Edwards, outside the B-2 organization, required the bomber test team to carefully consider the ground test capabilities and limitations of resources they planned to use at the Flight Test Center. This ultimately forced a closer look at the overall B-2 concept of operations at the base, and probably avoided some embarrassing situations. As a result, the CTF made sure the correct people were developing good procedures for ground and flight tests, then carrying them out under solid, well-defined safety guidelines.

To summarize this issue: Air Force and contractor managers and safety experts went to great lengths to emphasize the importance of safe testing procedures. They continually stressed that safety was directly related to the health of everybody involved in a test, and that the multimillion dollar aircraft they were dealing with was unique. Neither people nor aircraft could be replaced easily.

Another important lesson learned by the B-2 hierarchy was the value of thorough systems integration and simulation. This was the direct result of early-on decisions to invest heavily in the sophisticated ground test facilities and laboratories discussed in earlier chapters. Laboratory testing, in essence, allowed the entire aircraft to be tested as stand-alone systems, well before everything had to play together in the first B-2. Engineering designs were proven and glitches were identified early and corrected, well before they showed up on the aircraft.

This approach is becoming more important as aircraft become increasingly complex, especially with the proliferation of software-intensive systems. The process of integrating and testing systems in special laboratories is time consuming and expensive (a significant chunk of the billions spent on B-2 research and development went into the labs), but it pays off.

The B-2 program proved that statement. The No. 1 aircraft went from its first self-powered movement to first takeoff in only seven days. It was made possible through the extensive integration and systems checkout completed previously in the laboratories. As the test program continues, its pace will often be set by how quickly these labs respond to isolating and correcting problems discovered in flight.

Extensive planning, and the introduction of previously unheard-of test plans, was another key factor in the B-2's early testing success. Between the program's Critical Design Review and the start of serious ground testing, planning dominated the activities of CTF members.

Many of the new plans were attempts to reduce procedures, responsibilities and methods of operation to paper, then have the correct parties agree to a formal approach laid out there. Some plans had never been attempted by other Air Force CTFs, such as: Reports Plan; Detailed First-Flight Plan; CTF Concept of Operations; Manpower Billet Plan; and Flight Test Configuration Management Plan. Some of these were fairly straightforward to define and get approved. Others took more than two years to iron out and get all the players to agree.

But, as the old saw says, "The best laid plans . . ." often were difficult to execute when the time came. For any number of reasons, people decided to strike out on their own, making things up as they went, rather than follow a structured approach they had agreed to earlier. Of course, this caused tremendous confusion for all players, especially those committed to following the original plan.

Although examples of these deviations abounded, suffice it to say that keeping all parties on track, following agreed-to plans, constituted a major management chore. It would seem that, after all the work people put into laying out these plans, reviewing them, and signing their names in agreement, they would go to great lengths to make sure the plans were executed properly. Didn't seem to work that way, though.

The bottom line lesson here is self-evident, but we all seem to have to re-learn it now and then: Stick to the plan unless there is ample justification for modifying it. Once it's changed, then stick to the new plan.

* * *

COL. RICK COUCH:

Perhaps one of the most important things we learned on this program was that fixating on single events can be extremely counterproductive, especially if the event is only important in the short-term and doesn't relate directly to a long-term goal.

We tended to work ourselves to death trying to achieve any number of interim milestones, then were too worn out to start working towards the next one right away. We had to go through a recovery period before we could get on to the next important event.

The IFDAPS [Integrated Flight Data Acquisition and Processing System] checkout experience is a good example of this mistake. After each IFDAPS capabilities demonstration, our folks were so exhausted that it took days to get them functional again! These spurts of activity only wore everybody out and caused us to lose our focus between really critical milestones.

The pressures of getting up to first flight were big contributors to this phenomenon, but nobody wanted to be the one responsible for delaying that flight. Our schedules never had much slack in them, and it was mighty difficult to avoid fixating on small problems and losing sight of the long-range, really important goals.

In any endeavor, management needs to, as a minimum, select the most important long-term goals, then make sure everybody focuses on them, not the trivia in between, regardless of how essential it may seem at the time.

* * *

An interesting footnote to this "lessons learned" aspect of the B-2 program—especially after reviewing the testing approach—falls under the heading of *total quality management*, or TQM. This is a popular term in management circles today, and employees at all levels of government and aerospace companies are trying to find their place in the new TQM order sweeping this industry.

In reflecting on some of the approaches adopted by the B-2 organization, leaders decided that they really had not intended it that way, but TQM was pretty much what resulted. For example, the program assumed a strong customer orientation, focusing on what SAC really wanted and needed—both from a flight crew and maintenance point of view—and strived to build the aircraft accordingly.

The concept of "continuous improvement" also has been given a high priority in the program, perhaps to its detriment at times. The endless flow of engineering changes that plague the program frustrate manufacturing, and seem to slow the test program. People at the working levels wonder if they'll ever see the final configuration.

If the principles of TQM apply, the answer is "no" because there will always be something that can be improved. Aircraft now in Air Force service are updated throughout their lifetime, and there is no reason to believe the B-2 will be any different. That's the nature of high technology.

Finally, B-2 managers have strived—not always successfully, but generally so—to seek out individuals who know the most about some aspect of the aircraft or its ultimate mission. Then they listen to those experts, no matter what their rank or station in the organization, before making a decision that will affect the aircraft for years to come. That's another tenet of TQM: Everybody is an important part of the team and has something to contribute, as long as supervisors and managers care to ask them, then listen.

Perhaps this industry is growing up and relearning what managers maybe forgot in the throes of the Industrial Revolution: People are important. People are what airplanes—or any other product—are all about. Take care of the people doing the work, and the product will turn out just fine.

Index